4/16/98

UNTO

FULL

STATURE

MINISTRY OF LIFE PUBLISHERS

*"...Behold I lay in Zion for a foundation
a stone, a tried stone, a precious corner
stone, a SURE FOUNDATION:..."*

SF ISBN 0-936595-03-5

8 9 10 11--97 96 95 94 93

De Vern Fromke

Unto

Full

Stature

PUBLISHED BY

SURE FOUNDATION

2522 Colony Court

Indianapolis, Indiana 46280

4

CONTENTS

INTRODUCTION

By Wayne Butchart

MOVING UNTO FULL STATURE! What glorious anticipation that the Father might see the fulness of His Son in us and be satisfied. The reader will rejoice, as I have, in the author's emphasis that there is a much greater measure of spiritual stature attainable now than we have usually dared to imagine.

There is a noticeable awakening everywhere among believers that the central issue in Christianity has more to do with developing character and spiritual stature than in merely going some place in the "sweet by and by." To be occupied with "going some place"—namely heaven—leaves us so far short of God's high calling to full stature.

I am delighted to write this introduction for it affords me an opportunity to emphasize certain aspects I consider most vital, and it also allows me an opportunity to prepare the reader's mind so he will be fully alert to appreciate certain imperative issues as they are mentioned. Accordingly, may I call to your attention:

This FULL STATURE is no mere self-seeking effort in attainment. The author rightly insists that we only take our first real steps toward full stature as we become alive unto God and the honor, glory, pleasure and satisfaction He will realize through our lives. As he has done in his other writings, it might be expected that he would disclose the necessity of a God-centered instead of a man-centered approach. How wonderful to be centered in "what we can be unto God" instead of "what He can do for us."

This FULL STATURE is not merely some distant hope to be realized, but is a very present reality. One of the most evident marks of immaturity in our day is the tendency to relegate spiritual reality to the past or to the future. How significant then, that from the opening preview of this book, the author should insist upon projecting the reader into that glorious present tense of living in reality now. Once the reader is "caught" with the impact of this glorious participation in the life of the Spirit, he will never be satisfied to return to the barren pathways of living in past experiences or the dreamy hopes of the future. Be sure to catch the full impact as the author emphasizes that ours should be a continuous living relationship with Christ. It is true we have *received* His Life in our birth from above, but we are to be forever *receiving* more and more of His life.

This FULL STATURE is not something achieved apart from Christ. Quite rightly the central thesis of the book is that the Eternal Father, who delights in His only begotten Son, has determined to have a vast family of sons who reflect that same full stature the Father beholds in Him. We need only look at the Lord Jesus to understand the Father's highest conception of Full Stature. Christ is the sum-total. Yet to realize that the Father has such an expectation of full stature in us could leave us in despair and discouraged if we did not know that He has also provided the Holy Spirit as the utterly Adequate One who will accomplish this full stature in us *if we will but let Him.* How uniquely it is the Holy Spirit's work to reveal the Lord Jesus *to us* so as to form Christ *in us* in order to manifest Christ *through us.*

This FULL STATURE is both an individual and corporate matter. In his closing chapters the author faces our greatest problem squarely. Too many of God's children become so enamored with their own individual stature and (perhaps quite willingly) sidestep the necessary interdependence of the various members in bringing each other to full spiritual stature. Actually there is no such thing as individual full stature. How arresting is the thought that "our full stature is quite dependent upon the full stature of other members in the Body of Christ." No man liveth unto himself.

Finally, there are no facile answers here, because Mr. Fromke has not intended to give pat answers which are really none at all. Instead he has sought to stimulate the thinking, perhaps at times to even irritate one out of the staid rut of traditional thinking. This is no book for the superficial, but for those who are prepared to use their minds and hearts it may well give some fresh glimpse into the vast purpose and intention of the Father in bringing many sons unto the glory of full stature.

TO HELP YOU SIT
WITH THE AUTHOR

E VEN THE MOST CASUAL OB-
server of the present religious
scene has recognized certain spiritual movings. While this is the
hour of much spiritual hunger and turmoil, it is also a time of
unusual expectancy. It is almost as if a gentle wind blowing
through the mulberry trees were speaking in silent undertone.
Surely you have heard it—that whispering by the Spirit through
yearning hearts as though to announce: another fulness of time
has come. Prepare! Prepare! Prepare!

One cannot escape the testimony of increasing numbers who
are tasting the fresh breath of life in the Spirit. Everywhere there
are little groups from every background who are entering into the
fellowship of the living way. They are discovering the glorious
secret of a life-union with the Lord. Whereas once they reckoned
upon past experiences, now they know the joy of daily living by
His Life. What a difference this has wrought in their outlook and
ministry.

We rejoice that a great majority in the fundamental churches
are earnestly beseeching God for a spiritual awakening (after
their own style and conception) but it is also true that there is
already discernible a measure of floodtide. Evidence of this is
twofold: floodtide always produces the shallows while it is the
deeps that straighten out the river-course. Many have been preoccupied with little shallow whirlpools and muddy eddys along
the way. While they have groaned against the shallow tendency
of many who seek to use God for personal advantage, they have
virtually missed that hidden flowing channel which is moving in
depth with mighty power to straighten out the course of spiritual
things.

In this writing we have not primarily concerned ourselves with all the little side pools wherein men have sought to build up something for themselves. Rather we have sensed an unexplainable groaning within to share our heart with those who are just now entering the deeps—the flowing of life in the Spirit. Many are enjoying a whole new kind of life and outlook. They are being carried along in the deeps, sometimes unaware of the pitfalls and dangers. They only know that this spring the grass has become greener, the flowers more fragrant—life seems more zestful and meaningful. It has seemed almost as though they were passing out of time into the eternal NOW.

Who can explain all this means? Certainly I cannot. Yet perhaps there are some bits we can piece together as we summon the testimonials and groanings of many of God's children who have already been along this way. We shall let them speak for themselves, and trust that the Holy Spirit will impart His conclusions to you.

I can anticipate that other readers will feel we have only raised more questions than we have satisfactorily answered. This also has been a deliberate intention. In many instances we do not have the "pat theological answer." Nor are we interested in passing out staid, articulate phrases which can be passed on in parrot-like fashion. We have felt that any time we can even alert the reader to the problem or present the question so as to awaken his mind and spirit, then the Holy Spirit can lead that hungry heart to His own conclusion.

We ought to learn to use books as thought-starters. Is it not God's way that the Holy Spirit so direct us that we can arrive at a much sharper and higher conclusion more fitting to our individual need than an author could ever have given? Once a seed of truth has triggered our mind into action we should cooperate with the Holy Spirit as He continues to infuse light in leading us along. He will usually make a most practical application to fit our specific need, and that in a most unique manner. The reader who has been thus disciplined and led in his thinking will become a seer rather than a scholar. "The scholar sees and the seer sees through; and this is indeed a great difference. The seer lives by infused light from above, the scholar is apt to walk in his own light."

Again I cannot help but anticipate another response from those who are exceedingly systematic and thorough in their mentality. While we have sought for an outward pattern and design of continuity in the various chapters and sections of this book, there is a marked inner incompleteness. We have not sought to cover in any thorough manner such areas as the mind, the will, the emotions or the physical. We have only considered certain most obvious weaknesses in these areas which have seemed to make us vulnerable in our moving toward full stature.

In recent months we have been awakened anew to the danger of writing merely for mental apprehension. To illustrate this danger may I use the words of Watchman Nee who explains why the things of the Spirit will ever come as "broken fragments."

"Some years back I was very ill, and the doctors said I could only live a few months. In the face of this I felt burdened to write down in book form what the Lord had shown me on the subject of 'The Spiritual Man' and thus to share with others the light I had been given. I did so and it was published, and the edition is now exhausted. It will not be reprinted. It was not that what I wrote was wrong, for as I read it now I can endorse it all.   It was a very clear and complete setting forth of the truth. But just there lies its weakness. It is *too* good, and it is the illusion of perfectness about it that troubles me. The headings, the orderliness, the systematic way in which the subject is worked out, the logic of the argument—all are too perfect to be spiritual. They lend themselves too easily to a *merely mental apprehension*. When a man has read the book he ought not to have any questions left; they ought all to be answered!

"But God, I have discovered, does not do things that way, and much less does He let *us* do them. We human beings are not to produce 'perfect' books. The danger of such perfection is that a man can understand without the help of the Holy Spirit. But if God gives us books they will ever be *broken fragments,* not always clear or consistent or logical, lacking conclusions, and yet coming to us in life and ministering life to us. We cannot dissect divine facts and outline and systematize them. It is only the immature Christian who demands always to have intellectually satisfying conclusions. The Word of God itself has this fundamental character, that it speaks always and essentially to our spirit and and to our life." (From: WHAT SHALL THIS MAN DO)

Again, I can anticipate that certain readers will feel this *full stature* which we have pictured as possible, is far too much to expect or hope for in this life. Many have so long settled down in contentment with "just getting to heaven" for their own enjoyment and blessing, it seems hard for them to imagine that one might reach any measure of spiritual maturity which could bring delight and pleasure to God. In their carefulness to avoid the extreme of *perfectionism* many have turned away to become absorbed in an equally disgusting *carnalism* so manifest in our day.

Perhaps, as no other, these two things—our proneness to carnalism and our fear of perfectionism—militate in our mind to hinder our moving unto FULL STATURE. While *carnalism* reacts against the false position of those who claim too much, yet it seems almost to exalt human failures and shortcomings. *Perfectionism* in its reaction to low and careless standards has merely produced an empty standard of holiness with an equally empty ring in its testimony.

What is God's answer? It is neither carnalism or perfectionism. We must discover our union in death and resurrection with Christ. Then in Him all things become new. He becomes our new source and dwelling place.

Finally, may I anticipate that God will have some seed beds prepared for these words. And in His own way He will sovereignly direct this message into those open hearts in just the right timing. Indeed, may the same Spirit who has thrilled our own heart, again breath upon these most fragile words to quicken some fragment into life and meaning. What an amazing spiritual operation: to expect that mere words, so empty, so lifeless, should become spiritual food and direction for helping some hearts in MOVING UNTO FULL STATURE.

IT IS IMPERATIVE . . . . .

. . . that we understand God's conception of full stature. But we can only understand His conception as we move into His viewpoint. There—in His viewpoint—we shall be able to grasp the "hope of (in) His calling" us unto full stature and the "glory of His inheritance" in those saints who reach full stature.

It would seem that both Apostles – Paul and John—lived in God's viewpoint and shared His yearning father-heart desire in seeking to move us through childhood into young manhood and unto fatherhood. With this posture of a spiritual father we hear John exhorting:

"I write unto you little children . . . "
"I write unto you young men . . . "
"I write unto you fathers . . . " (1 John 2:12-14)

John saw believers on these three different levels of maturity, and knew that the eternal Father could be satisfied only as they were brought into the stature of spiritual fatherhood—sharers with Him in His life, nature, purpose and vision. But he also saw that

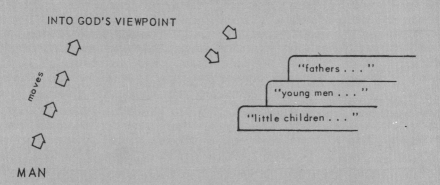

WHAT FULL STATURE MEANS TO THE FATHER

INTO GOD'S VIEWPOINT

moves

"fathers . . . "
"young men . . . "
"little children . . . "

MAN

mere passing of time, gaining mere knowledge, or more experiences were no guarantee of spiritual development. Above all,
there must come a change in attitudes, needs and conceptions.

So John writes explaining that "little children" are mostly
conscious that "God is our Father" and "our sins are forgiven
for His name's sake." In this first level of growth it is quite
natural to rejoice in what we have received and can expect to
receive from a loving Father. No one is alarmed when "little
children" rejoice in what their Savior has wrought for them in
giving personal forgiveness and in providing a relationship with
the Father. Yet there is reason for concern when, after twenty or
thirty years, they remain "little children" who live only to be
ministered unto and who are mostly alive to the blessing, benefits and gifts they can receive. While as little children they
may possess knowledge about redemption—even about their identification with Christ in His death and resurrection, yet they have
only interpreted God's working as it related to them, to their
welfare, their victory and blessing. In attitude, purpose and conception they are yet blessing centered, salvation centered,—
seeking to move God in orbit around their little center. How far
short they are of the Father's standard of full stature!

Next, John writes of those who have matured into young manhood. Two things are overshadowing in this level of growth: "Ye
have overcome the wicked one" and "ye are strong, and the word
of God abideth in you." This is a marked advance. No longer
babes who need milk, they are now young men who require the
meat of the Word. Through experience they have moved from the
defense to the offense; instead of running *from,* they are now
overcoming the Wicked One. If many could just reach this level
they would feel they had arrived. Yet as young men it is so easy
to become occupied with *doing* than with *being.* Those in this
level are apt to be centered in activity for the Lord as though
our *instrumental* calling were more important than our *expressive*
calling.

Last, John describes those who have become spiritual fathers.
In this highest level of stature we are suddenly awakened to
something quite wonderful. As "little children" we recognized
Him as our Father in a begetting-relationship; as "young men"
we honored Him as our Father—in a governing-relationship; but
now as "fathers" we are one with Him in His fatherhood—through
an intimate identification we have an expressive-relationship. It

would seem there is a transference of His father-heart yearning to our heart. We come to share a union with His Spirit, purpose, desire, vision and dedication.

No wonder John writes twice (vs. 13 and 14) that as fathers they have come to "know Him that is from the beginning." Surely there is more in this statement than we have usually caught. Is not John trying to unveil that our oneness with His father-heart means we have been seated with Him "before the beginning" when He originated all His plans and purposes? How revealing to sit with Him in that beginning when His father-nature yearned for a vast family of sons just like the Only Begotten Son. Suddenly we are gripped by the fact that His fatherhood is the determining factor in all things. Since He is before, above and beyond all else THE FATHER, then we are also called as fathers to be participators in the GRAND THEME of the universe.

OUR CONCEPTION OF GOD DETERMINES OUR DEDICATION

So as we proceed in this writing it will become most evident that the fullest and highest conception of who God chiefly is, determines our calling and dedication. We well remember as "little children " just born into His family, what our conception was. It is usually expected that our first acquaintance and introduction to God is in the role of Saviorhood. With this overshadowing conception our calling and dedication was to reach heaven and get others there. As we then saw our full stature it meant trusting Him to deliver and prepare us for that glorious place called Heaven.

However, God is always crowding us to a fuller understanding of Himself. It was true that in conversion His lordship seemed quite real, yet it took some real spiritual development before we could appreciate His fuller authority and lordship over the life. Thus, as "young men" we are confronted with bringing every facet of our life under His authority and government. So we come into a much fuller conception of who God is: the most Holy, Sovereign, Ruler, Architect and Creator of all things. Yet in this conception we have merely seen Him in the scope of His wonderful *activity,* and accordingly we become engrossed in *what we can do for Him.*

In the second level of stature we find a higher dedication and calling. As "young men" we are not merely interested in getting folk to heaven, but of bringing heaven's authority and reign over them here and now. It would be expected, since our primary conception of God is as One who is *doing,* that we be occupied with *doing.*

But this will never satisfy God, for He must press us beyond the plane of mere activity to see who He chiefly is in His being before He started any world activity. Thus we behold Him as the Eternal Father. Those who have attempted the depersonalization of God would make Him out as some majestic spirit beyond personality. And many who have reacted against the Devil's counterfeit conception of Fatherhood are almost afraid to call Him THE FATHER. But truth demands that we see Him in this exalted role: ABOVE ALL ELSE, THE FATHER. What astounds our finite mind is that God has done nothing to become THE FATHER, for the Lord Jesus has always been the Eternal Son. So it is not His *doing,* but His *being* that overshadows all else.

It becomes much more meaningful now, why the Apostle Paul in his writings never starts *with* the foundation of the world, but instead takes us back into the Father-heart to see that desire, purpose and intention which He cherished in Himself *before* the foundation of the world. Paul writes that the Eternal Father chose us before the foundation of the world (Eph. 1:3-4). He is calling us unto full stature which means being "holy and without blame before Him in love." It is to this glorious calling that we were "marked out," that is, predestined in Christ Jesus.

Thus we recognize how our highest and fullest conception of God, as THE FATHER, determines our dedication, calling and conception of full stature. As spiritual fathers we are called to be *expressive* of Him. We are not merely instruments in His hand—

OUR CONCEPTION OF HIM . . . determines . . . our calling

THE FATHER

The Sovereign

The Savior

As "fathers" we awaken to our calling to be like Him.

As "young men" . . . we are most alive to what we can do for Him.

As "little children" . . . we are mostly alive to what we can receive from Him.

working for Him, but we are allowing Him to live and manifest Himself through us. As we continue in His viewpoint we shall appreciate the unfolding of full stature.

ACKNOWLEDGEMENTS

We gratefully acknowledge the following quotations:

Page 16 No. 1 — R. K. Strachan from tract: MATURE DISCIPLESHIP
Page 34 No. 2 — T. A. Sparks, book: STEWARDSHIP OF THE MYSTERY
Page 39 No. 3 — W. Nee, from book: WHAT SHALL THIS MAN DO?
Page 49 No. 4 — T. A. Sparks, booklet: CHRIST IN HEAVEN AND WITHIN
Page 59 No. 5 — A. W. Tozer, editorial: THE ALLIANCE WITNESS
Page 61 No. 6 — A. W. Tozer, editorial: THE ALLIANCE WITNESS
Page 83 No. 7 — Dr. M. Fakkema, from PHILOSOPHY OF EDUCATION
Page 101 No. 8 — E. S. Jones, from book: CHRISTIAN MATURITY
Page 105 No. 9 — G. C. Berkouwer, in CHRISTIANITY TODAY
Page 108 No. 10 — A. W. Tozer, from book: THE ROOT OF THE RIGHTEOUS
Page 117 No. 11 — O. Chambers, from book: PHILOSOPHY OF SIN
Page 121 No. 12 — E. S. Jones, from book: ABUNDANT LIVING
Page 128 No. 13 — E. S. Jones, from book: ABUNDANT LIVING
Page 142 No. 14 — James Allen, from book: AS A MAN THINKETH
Page 143 No. 15 — A. W. Tozer, editorial: THE ALLIANCE WITNESS
Page 150 No. 16 — A. W. Tozer, editorial: THE ALLIANCE WITNESS
Page 165 No. 17 — A. W. Tozer, from book: ROOT OF THE RIGHTEOUS
Page 167 No. 18 — Thomas Merton, book: SEEDS OF CONTEMPLATION
Page 167 No. 19 — A. W. Tozer, editorial: THE ALLIANCE WITNESS
Page 169 No. 20 — E. S. Jones, book: CHRISTIAN MATURITY
Page 171 No. 21 — A. W. Tozer, book: BORN AFTER MIDNIGHT
Page 184 No. 22 — Bill Cady, adapted from article in:THE ULTIMATES
Page 187 No. 23 — T. A. Sparks, from paper: WITNESS AND TESTIMONY
Page 191 No. 24 — Authors book: THE ULTIMATE INTENTION
Page 192 No. 25 — T. A. Sparks, paper: WITNESS AND TESTIMONY
Page 193 No. 26 — C. A. Jones, adapted from unpublished manuscript
Page 200 No. 27 — T. A. Sparks, paper: WITNESS AND TESTIMONY
Page 214 No. 28 — N. Grubb, book: THE LIBERATING SECRET
Page 216 No. 29 — V. R. Edman in ETERNITY Magazine, March 64
Page 222 No. 30 — Witness Lee, book: THE KINGDOM AND THE CHURCH

THE FIRST QUESTION WE MUST SETTLE:

In analyzing the problems of missionaries and Christian workers, a discerning missionary executive writes: "It is a lack of maturity that is chiefly responsible for the young missionaries who return defeated and disillusioned from the mission field. And behind much of the frustration which plagues us on the field are these same traits against which we must carry on unceasing, exhausting fight.

"Under fire or pressure, the immature individual cracks up; he can't take it, and unconsciously seeks to run away. Where no special emergency or pressure is brought to bear upon him, he manifests his immaturity by a general lack of self-discipline in life—in work, personal habits, social relationships, spiritual culture, witnessing, etc.

"You say, but isn't maturity a matter of growth and won't that come in due time—as a result of experience on the field? Yes, to some extent it is a matter of growth. But there is a foundation that has to be laid long before one ever gets to the mission field, and it's because so many of us did not lay down this foundation properly that we have such a hard fight now—and some of us have given up It frightens one to see so many child adults today in full-time Christian work. (Child adults beget child adults spiritually as well as physically.) That is why I cannot think of anything more important in preparation than this LAYING DOWN OF FOUNDATIONS FOR MATURITY."

THE ONLY FOUNDATION UPON
WHICH TO BUILD FULL STATURE

THINK WE ALL should be amazed could we actually know how many who have entered Christian service have never experienced a vital relationship with the Lord Jesus. But even among those who have, there is an alarming misconception regarding His Lordship and rightful authority over the life.

Perhaps the misconception begins at this point. In this present generation there has been so much emphasis placed on the *crisis act* of believing the finished work of Christ that many have either neglected or misunderstood the *continuous work* of the Spirit. Many have believed, but God intends for us to be a believing believer every day. Many have received His Life, but know little of daily receiving His Life by the flow of the Spirit. Many have, in a crisis act, acknowledged Him as Lord, but care little for the involvements in a *daily* acknowledging Him and living under His full authority. Thus we see there is the finished work of Christ which we appropriate in a crisis-act; but there is also the continuous working of the Holy Spirit which is a daily-participation.

Now the whole issue boils down to this: How much is to be expected in a crisis act and how much is to be left to the process of growth? There are those who put so much emphasis on any crisis experience as to leave little room for the process of growth. Yet others relegate so much to growth that the initial crisis in a life seems almost insignificant. What is God's intention?

To understand we must go back "before the beginning" where in our Eternal Father's heart we see how He purposed to share Himself with a vast family. Thus it was not man's sin or defection that determined this purpose of sharing. Oh no! It was in the Father's original planning, long before man was ever created or before he sinned, that He determined to share Himself through His only Begotten Son.

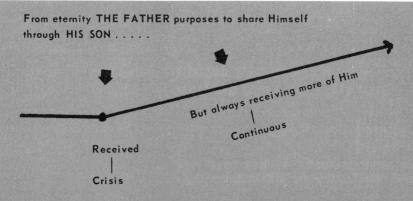

From eternity THE FATHER purposes to share Himself through HIS SON . . . . .

But always receiving more of Him | Continuous

Received | Crisis

Then what happened when man did turn to his own way? God's plan has not changed one bit! He will still share Himself through His Son, only now He has provided redemption through the Cross as the important gateway (X to Y). It is just as this point man has such limited perspective. When God lifts fallen man out of his lost predicament (X), it is by a crisis act: man believes, receives and acknowledges a new Lord in his life. But having believed and received this divine Life, God then intends for man to move along the high-way (Y-Z) of believing and receiving. Alas, too many have been content to stop at (Y). They have been most interested in the crisis-act in which *they* believed and received — for in this act *they* seemed to benefit the most. But they have had little heart for moving along on the high-way of believing and receiving which would allow them to daily live by the Life of Christ — the resource for fulfilling the Father's original intention.

Thus we have pictured both the finished and the continuous work. In God's sight He reckons the finished work of Christ a finality and wants us to reckon the same. But there is also that which He designs as the continuous work of the Spirit which makes possible a daily receiving or sharing of God. Both of these are absolutely necessary in their proper order and right balance. Until one is clear in the finished and the continuous work — there is no adequate foundation upon which to build spiritual stature.

It must be recognized that some would seek to enter the highway of continuous believing and receiving *before* they have appropriated the finished work. To do such is to ignore man's awful defection into sin and rebellion (W-X-Y). For all of Adam's sinful

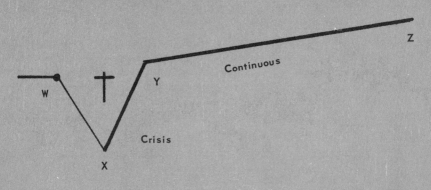

SINCE THE FALL His Eternal Purpose remains the same. However, the Cross of redemption is now incorporated into the plan of sharing . . .

family there must be a crisis of regeneration when we first "believe unto righteousness" or "receive Him" as divine Life. And having believed and received we are then ready to enter the high-way of "living by faith," i.e. a believing believer. "The just shall live by faith." Following the crisis there is then the continuous participation.

It is just here we see the glaring weakness in many fundamental circles. Too many emphasize the past-tense crisis act and almost ignore the privilege of the continuous present participation. They rejoice in the finished work, but know or seemingly care little about the continuous operation of Life within them by the Holy Spirit. It is one thing to have received "Life in the Son," but it is surely an equal privilege to enjoy this vital participation in Life every day by His Spirit.

As with the missionaries and workers considered in the opening, perhaps there is a reader who inwardly longs for this daily sharing. You are weary of the defeat and frustration in trying to "live the Life." You are dissatisfied with only a past-reckoning and long for a present-reality. You know you have believed and received, but there has been no believing and receiving daily. There is no escape! Before any of this writing will produce any lasting benefit there must be a daily flowing and receiving by our union with Him.

Why not now, without reservation, determine that the first crisis of Lordship you experienced long ago will now become a daily acknowledging His Lordship. Having made this deliberate, glad-heart recognition of His authority, then just as deliberately honor the Holy Spirit in His continuous sharing of Life, Light and Love into your being.

With this FOUNDATION settled: resting in the *finished work* of Christ but also enjoying the *continuous work* by the Holy Spirit, we are now ready to consider the other levels in moving UNTO FULL STATURE.

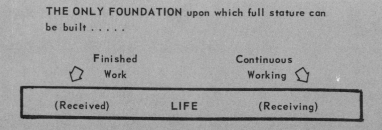

THE ONLY FOUNDATION upon which full stature can be built . . . . .

Finished   Continuous
Work   Working

(Received)   LIFE   (Receiving)

Moving . . .

UNTO FULL STATURE

in

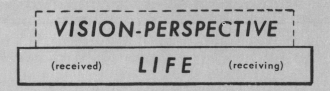

We now have a proper foundation upon which to build. Let us consider how vision-perspective is the first imperative level if there is to be any real moving unto full stature. In this section we shall discuss some of these questions:

IN CHAPTER ONE: Would the Lord Jesus have visited this earth even if Adam had never sinned? *yes*

IN CHAPTER TWO: It seems so few understand God's ways of unfolding vision-perspective. What are His ways?

IN CHAPTER THREE: If we only appreciate that part of God's working which relates to us, how narrow is our framework of vision. What has caused certain men to live beyond their day and the usual framework of vision?

IN CHAPTER FOUR: There is only one way to understand or appreciate the pressures and problems of our daily life and ministry. What is it?

A PASTOR ASKS:

Something quite unique and wonderful has happened to a fellow-pastor with whom I have been praying each week. He testifies God has brought him into HIS ultimate viewpoint where one begins to see all things in divine perspective. It surely seems something has utterly revolutionized his life and ministry; I long for the same kind of vision and reality in mine. But he insists this comes by a revelation. Now—in the most simple words please tell me what this ultimate viewpoint is, and how I can also come into its reality.

WHAT IS THIS
ULTIMATE VIEWPOINT?

I N BEGINNING let me provoke your thinking with this question: Did Jesus Christ visit this earth only because Adam and all his posterity have sinned, or was it in the original plan and Eternal Purpose of the Father that His Son should visit earth, become incarnate, and thereby make possible a vital union with man? In other words, was it according to the Father's Eternal Purpose for His Son to visit earth even if Adam had never sinned?

Too long we have been so encumbered with the sin-problem and the time-perspective we have become nearsighted and allowed a redemptive consciousness to overshadow. Indeed it is important that we should see both the incarnation and the redemption phases in their proper relation to the Eternal Purpose. To do this we must move out of the time-perspective into the eternal-perspective where we can view every part of God's

program as it is related to the whole background. Let me illustrate:

One day a friend who is an expert in developing unique camera
shots handed me a picture which showed only a small tree. He
asked, "How tall do you suppose that tree is?" Somehow he had
blocked out all the background, and since there was nothing with
which to relate the tree or compare it, I could only make a wild
guess. To my untrained eyes the tree looked like a small seedling, perhaps four or five feet tall.

"Now you will see the absolute importance of background!
Here is the whole picture!" He handed me another snapshot with
all the background in view. I was amazed! Suddenly that little
tree had grown up. With a full landscape of woods and houses
it became apparent that the "seedling" was at least thirty-five
or forty feet tall. I could hardly believe that background could
make such a difference.

Then I realized this was exactly what the Lord had been
trying to show me for months. Without the background of the
Father's eternal purpose, how could I know the true meaning
of any part? To see Jesus the Son in a time-perspective alone
would be as misleading as to see the tree with no background.
And as surely as that little tree grew from a four-foot seedling to
a forty-foot pine, so the Jesus we all know — when moved beyond
the horizons of time—towers above everything; the all-glorious,
eternal Son, THE CENTER and SUMMATION of all things.

It comes as quite a shock to many a present-day evangelical
when he discovers how he has had such a limited view of the
lovely Son whom he has so desired to exalt and magnify. It is
because he has lacked the perspective and background which
comes only as we start with the Eternal Father "before the
beginning" when He purposed to share Himself, yes, to even
express Himself throughout the universe in a vast family of
human-divine sons. Let us consider how the apostle Paul gives
us this eternal vantage point from which we may keep all the
parts related to the background of the Father's purpose. In the
opening verses of his letter to the Ephesians several things
are clear:

(1) Paul starts with the eternal Father—not the Fall of man.
(2) He indicates that God's purposing was *"before* the foun-
    dation of the world."
(3) He emphasizes that God's purpose is to be realized

through, and is to *center* in the Son.

(4) All this we see is determined in God's Father-heart, *not because of the Fall,* but before the world was made.

From this perspective let us now consider these verses: "According as he (the Father) hath chosen us IN HIM (the Son) before the foundation of the world" (1:4). "...Blessed us with all spiritual blessing...IN CHRIST" (1:3). "Having predestinated us unto the adoption of children BY JESUS CHRIST to Himself..." (1:5). "...He hath made us accepted IN THE BELOVED" (1:6).

Let us repeat that these are the things that the Father had settled in His heart *before the foundation of the world* (v. 4). Paul later points out that because man did sin and needs redemption, this provision was also available in Christ, the Son: "In whom (the Son) we have redemption through his blood, the forgiveness of sins, according to the riches of his grace" (v. 7).

Then finally the Apostle brings us to see the goal toward which God the Father is working: "That in the dispensation of the fulness of times he might gather together in one all things in Christ, both which are in heaven, and which are on earth; even IN HIM..." (1:10). "According to the eternal purpose which he purposed in Christ Jesus our Lord" (3:11).

By focusing attention on these verses which outline the *eternal* purpose, we lift the Son right out of the usual time-perspective that He may be seen more clearly from the Father's eternal perspective. This will help us to understand how the two ends of our line of purpose (A and Z) are grafted into eternity. We should come to understand more clearly how the Father determined that His Son should become incarnate as *the means* of

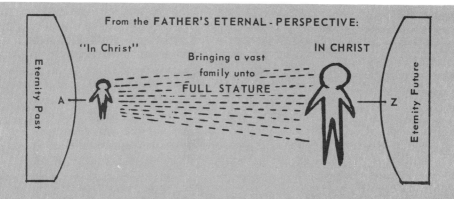

From the FATHER'S ETERNAL - PERSPECTIVE:

"In Christ"   Bringing a vast   IN CHRIST
                   family unto
                   FULL STATURE

Eternity Past   A   Z   Eternity Future

bringing a vast family of sons into the glorious measure of FULL
STATURE. This we shall see later as the placing (or adoption)
of children in full sonship rights.

Things look different when we are, in Paul's words, "seated
with him in heavenly places," viewing the whole picture from
the veranda of the universe. As we see what God sees, we grasp
the divine perspective—from eternity to eternity. We understand
how One who is, above all else, the eternal Father, would yearn
for a vast family of sons conformed to the image of the eternal
Son in whom He has found such delight. We understand how our
Father before the beginning of time planned to share Himself,
His life, and even to express Himself throughout the universe
during ages to come.

It is only as we move out of the time-perspective into this
eternal-perspective that we can view every part of God's program
as it is perfectly related to the whole. It is only as we consider
the Father's goal in His eternal Son that we can have clear
vision of His goal for us, His sons, through Christ.

INCARNATION AND REDEMPTION RIGHTLY
RELATED TO ETERNAL PURPOSE

What blessed fellowship with the only Begotten in eternity
past brought the Father to desire many sons conformed to His
image! With what anticipation He must have planned that the
Eternal Son would one day become the incarnate Son, robed in
flesh that He might share Himself in a vital way with the human
family yet to be created.

What we are saying may come as a new thought to many, but
it is imperative that we see the *eternal* purpose of God in the
incarnation. For the Father, it seems, planned to visit this planet
by the incarnation of His Son – not because man sinned, but –
even if Adam had never turned to his own way. Rather than to
interpret the incarnation as an emergency measure because of
man's defection, we point out that *it was purposed in eternity.*
Sin and the Fall did not alter God's eternal plan, but only necessitated that redemption should be incorporated. While we know
that Jesus Christ came to earth to die on the Cross for man's
redemption, His coming included a more far-reaching purpose—
the realization of the Father's original, ultimate intention: to
share Himself through a vital union with man – a blending of the
human and divine.

The more clearly we see the imperative necessity of this eternal perspective, the more significant becomes the reason for the apostle Paul's starting place – "before the foundation of the world" – in the Father-heart of God. We shall also more fully appreciate how the Father originally purposed for everything to be accomplished *through* and to *center in* His Son. This Son was to have become our very life even if man had never sinned. Foreknowledge easily foreknew man's waywardness. God was prepared for the emergency of Adam's fall, but this in no way determined or altered that eternal purpose that all things should find their summation in Christ.

Here then is the essential reason for man's low conception of that full stature God intends for him. The tragedy of this "redemptive consciousness" is that it makes sin and redemption seem to be a necessity, and redemption the primary purpose of God. Because the horizon reaches only to man in his fallen condition, the picture shows the incarnation of Christ only in the light of God's redemptive plan. Because our horizons are too narrow, everything in God's planning seems to take its color and meaning from the Fall instead of from God's eternal purpose in Christ. This is another manifestation of the perverse, man-centered perspective which is blighting men to immaturity.

It is always our concern in coming to this larger perspective, that no one will come to minimize or overlook the importance of redemption in God's recovery program. The fact is, only as we see redemption rightly related to all God's plan can we appreciate it as we ought. As it is seen against the background of the eternal purpose how much more important and imperative it becomes as the initial step in realizing the Father's ultimate intention. Could this be what Paul was conveying to Timothy when he wrote that the Father "...hath saved us and called us with an holy calling, not according to our works, but according to his own purpose and grace, which was given us IN CHRIST JESUS BEFORE THE WORLD BEGAN, but is now made manifest by the appearing of our Saviour Jesus Christ..." (2 Tim. 1:9-10).

As we have pictured in the diagram, God's redemptive work in grace is the line upward (X to Y). It is lifting man from his fallen condition. We see the importance of the Cross as the gateway to that original holy calling "which was given us IN CHRIST JESUS BEFORE THE WORLD BEGAN." So now the calling is twofold: according to grace and according to His eternal purpose.

The first issues out of our fallen condition in time, but the second issues out of His original father-heart desire for a family before the ages began. When we have comprehended this, we shall also be able to keep . . .

DELIVERANCE RIGHTLY RELATED TO DEVELOPMENT

How did the eternal Father begin to effect His eternal purpose? Having first created this earth as His theater of operation, He created Adam and placed him in a lovely garden. Now let us ask, was Adam *all* that God intended? That is, did he, as created, stand in full stature? The way we answer this question will reveal how much we understand of the Father's larger perspective and ultimate intention.

There are those who believe that Adam, as he came from the creative hand of God, was all God intended he should ever be — the zenith of full stature. Accordingly, after Adam's fall, they contend, man's greatest need is restoration of that stature which Adam once had in the Garden. In this context of reasoning, it seems to them, God's present program is (insofar as possible) the restoration of all things to Adamic and Edenic perfection.

How come-short is this perspective! Not until we come to see from God's perspective can we realize how really narrow is this view as compared to the eternal purpose and program of the Father. For while Adam did receive the divine image by God's creative hand, there was much more in God's purpose for Adam's race. The plan included more than a creative touch could accomplish, for it required a *vital union* with the Source of Life, and man's cooperation. While Adam was created perfect, even as

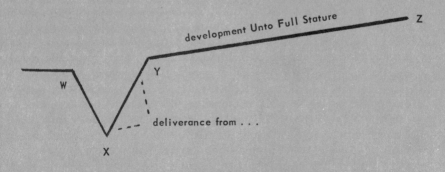

an innocent babe is perfect, yet he was wholly untried and undeveloped in his moral nature. Further, we must distinguish between what Adam *was* by creation, and what he *was to become* by union and cooperation with God: By natural endowment he had created life and *was* to be a container which could receive the divine life of God when he would choose it. Thus, in the master design, Adam *was to become* a son in full stature through inner spiritual development. Like a flower bud moving to full blossom, so was God's design for Adam's development; and it in no way necessitated sin or the Fall as means for accomplishment.

However, as Adam stood at the open gateway there were two trees — representing two ways — before him. He could choose God's way or his own way. There was opportunity for development along two mutually exclusive lines. If he chose to go his own way, by eating of the tree of knowledge, it would mean the development of his soul-powers independent of God. To choose God's highway would mean cooperation with God — a *living union* through eating of the tree of life. Either choice would bring a development in stature, either soulish or spiritual.

Since Adam and his posterity have tasted of the tree of knowledge, this fruit has ministered to the expansion and development of the soulish powers. The soul with its independent power of free choice has taken the place of the spirit which was intended to be the animating power of man. Before there can be any true spiritual development unto full stature, there must be a radical deliverance from this wrong development of the soulish powers.

Here again, we find the divine perspective makes a difference. In his desperate need for deliverance, man is prone to forget that

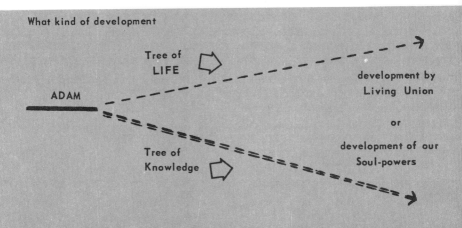

What kind of development

Tree of LIFE

ADAM

development by Living Union

or

Tree of Knowledge

development of our Soul-powers

deliverance is only the doorway to spiritual development. The history of Israel and the Church has demonstrated how many were more interested in *deliverance from* (X to Y) than in *development unto* (Y to Z). Just to get out of bondage! Just to be free from slavery! Just to make it to heaven! This overshadowing deliverance consciousness has warped and blighted the average church and its members unto lethargy. Because their goal has been escape from sin and its penalty, they have never seen or heard of God's calling to the full stature. Nor need we expect for much change in any life until this controlling philosophy has received a death-blow and we have learned how to keep . . .

ESCAPE RIGHTLY RELATED TO FULFILLMENT

Did you ever consider why there is so much emphasis on escapism — on running from obstacles instead of facing up to the circumstances which might "work for the furtherance of the gospel"?

One afternoon I slipped into a prayer meeting just in time to hear a lady praying, "Lord, I want you to use me any way you see best." But it was hardly five minutes later that she poured out to me a volume of troubles — she was being misunderstood by her husband and son, and was about to be persecuted out of the church for her insistence on a separated life. To sum it up, she kept begging me to pray (to put it simply) that God would grant her an easier way.

The undertone of a life speaks much louder than any words men say! The undertone reveals that at heart men are still controlled by a philosophy of escape. They have never moved through the Cross to become "dead indeed unto" their old selfish center that they might become "alive UNTO GOD."

Listen for the undertone in the apostle Paul's writing. Not once do you find any self-pity or one bit of escapism. Nor do you hear him pleading with the churches to pray in his behalf that his way might be easier. Instead he is gripped by one concept — how all things that happen to him might work "for the furtherance of the gospel" (Phil. 1:12).

As we have pictured (below) God's original intention for Adam — and for every man — was that he should embrace *the way of fulfillment.* Yet those who live only in the narrow perspective of *escaping* by Christ's Cross can hardly understand Paul's kind of dedication, calling and purpose.

We must remember it is true that our conquering Saviour *has* made a way of escape, that all of Adam's fallen family may be set free from sin, self, the world, the devil and death. Too long the family of Adam has been in bondage to these five monarchs, but now this tyranny has been broken. While it is indeed wonderful to see that He died and rose for our escape, it was for much more than that. Too many stop with *a way of escape* who should see that the Cross really leads to *a way of fulfillment.*

Nor should anyone assume that after having reckoned on the Cross as the means of escape, one is thereby through with the Cross. No. It is as we reach God's *highway of fulfillment* that the Cross which was once merely outward, becomes an inward principle at work in our lives. The Cross as we first saw it — outwardly — pictured *God poured out.* Now the Cross as it works inwardly in us means *we are poured out.* It is our giving our lives for the fulfillment of God's purpose. The more fully this Cross is inwardly embraced as a way of life, the more fully will we move along the *way of fulfillment.*

So it seems man stands at another gateway (Y). The very issues of dedication which Adam dodged (at W) are once again present. What are the issues at this gateway? Will man attempt to settle down inside the gate because he is interested only in *a way of escape,* or will he become truly alive unto God in embracing the *way of divine fulfillment?*

Christians who live in the narrow perspective of redemption are prone to emphasize only deliverance and escape. The servant of God who sees the Cross and redemption primarily as a way of escape will not endure as a good soldier. Paul knew how

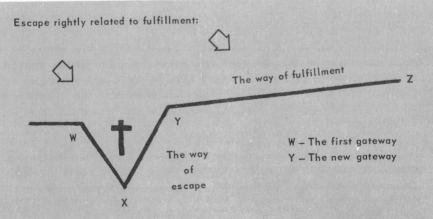

Escape rightly related to fulfillment:

The way of fulfillment

Z

Y

W

The way of escape

X

W — The first gateway
Y — The new gateway

imperative this right perspective was for young Timothy. He wrote encouraging him to expect opposition and obstacles in the way of development and fulfillment.

"Accept, as I do, all the hardships that faithfulness to the Gospel entails in the strength that God gives you. For He has rescued us (but shall we live only for escape) from all that is really evil and called us (and here is our joy in fulfillment) to a life of holiness—not because of any of our achievement but for HIS OWN PURPOSE" (J.B. Phillips, 2 Tim. 1:8. Parenthesis mine).

Notice further, how characteristic of Paul that he goes back to the eternal viewpoint. He does not start with man and his fallen condition, but with the Father in His original purpose — *before time began:*

"Before time began He planned to give us in Christ the grace to achieve this purpose, but it is only since our Saviour Jesus Christ has been revealed that the method has become apparent" (J.B.P. 2 Tim. 1:9).

Still another hindrance in our moving *unto full stature* will be overcome as we live in the divine perspective. It is the ability to keep . . .

EMERGENCY RIGHTLY RELATED TO ULTIMACY

Ever since the Fall everything is in a desperate state of emergency. We cannot expect things to return to the normalcy of the Garden as long as sin and Satan are present in the world. So we must see how the emergency created by the Fall is to find its proper relatedness to the long-range purpose of God. Otherwise we will find ourselves so occupied with the feverish urgency of doing only what seems immediately necessary we will miss the more important purpose of life.

Imagine what would be thought of one who handled emergencies like the man whose tire had a slow leak. He felt he could spare no time to change it, so for several days he stopped at a station every four hours for more air. His perspective was faulty. And how many people work for God with this same emergency consciousness. (like trying to cut off outward sins)

To illustrate, let us consider Lot and his wife in flight from Sodom on that day when God sent judgment. Here was an emergency. It was an escape for life. Of course we are not told what occupied the mind of Lot's wife which caused her to look back and suddenly turn to a pillar of salt, but it seems evident that she was more interested in escape in this awful emergency than in fulfilling anything ultimate and eternal for God.

Now here is one more thing which reveals not only Lot's wife — but us. Almost immediately one asks, "What about Lot's wife? Was she saved?" Does it not prove since she was delivered from Sodom, even though because of disobedience she was turned to a pillar of salt, that she is saved and will be in heaven?"

How revealing the question. Why are folk more concerned for a woman's escape than for God's desire and purpose in her life? It is quite natural for those who are man-centered to see only one kind of "lostness," the lostness which relates to man and his safety.

But there is another fact which is usually overlooked. It is possible to be saved from destruction and yet *be lost to the ultimate intention of God*. How can anyone rejoice that Lot's wife merely escaped from Sodom, in the light of the awful fact that she utterly missed God's fulfillment through her life?

We can be sure there will be no real moving *UNTO FULL STATURE* until we have learned how to properly relate any emergency to the ultimate. It has been our purpose only to introduce the problem here, and to consider it more fully in a later chapter. So let us say now, it is good for man to live with the sense of urgency; but he should learn to distinguish between the urgency of crisis and the urgency of opportunity. As we have seen in the example of Lot's wife, there is a feverish frenzy which sees only crisis and looks back, but there is the urgency of opportunity which looks ahead to the new opportunity of fulfilling God's ultimate.

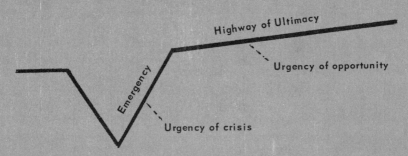

Emergency rightly related to ultimacy

Highway of Ultimacy

Urgency of opportunity

Emergency

Urgency of crisis

HOW DOES THIS REVELATION COME?

Any true work of God with us is not when we consecrate ourselves to Him, but when we *see*. Consecration should *result from* spiritual vision, it can never take its place. This is where God's work begins. Our work may begin at any time; God's work through us can spring only from divinely given vision-perspective. Watchman Nee has written:

"Without that vision, our service for God follows the impulse of our own ideas but not in accord with God's plan. When we come to Paul, we see that for him this revelation was twofold. 'It pleased God...to reveal His Son in me': that was inner revelation, subjective, if you like the term (Gal. 1:15,16). 'I was not disobedient unto the heavenly vision': that was outer vision, objective, concrete, practical (Acts 26:19). The inner and the outer together make perfect completeness, whereas either is insufficient without the other.

"And this is the need of the Church, of the people of God, today. Inward revelation must go along with outward vision: not only knowing the Lord within, but knowing also God's eternal purpose; not stopping at the foundation, but understanding too how to build upon it. God is not satisfied with our just doing odds and ends of work; that is what servants do. We are His friends, and His friends should know His plans."

How does the revelation of God's purpose come? One has answered this question like this: "As long as I wanted to use God for my own purposes, I could only see everything as related to me. Then a crisis in my health came and the outward cross I had known became an inward cross—with Him I passed from death unto life where 'ALL THINGS BECOME NEW.' Then I saw how I belonged to Him for His own purpose. What a change! Once my inner being was corrected, my inner eyes could see what He sees. And I realized how true it is 'the pure in heart shall see....'"

A TEACHER COMMENTS:

It seems to me that any real moving unto full stature in life and ministry requires one to accept the unfolding or progressiveness of revelation. To support this conviction I offer these words of T.A.S.:

"... it is hard to dispute that there are evidences of progress in Paul's understanding and knowledge of Christ, and it is clear that progress and expansion and development in his knowledge of Christ led to adjustment. Do not misunderstand. They did not lead to a repudiation of anything that Paul had stated, nor to a contradiction of any truth that had come through him, but they led to adjustment. As his knowledge of Christ grew and expanded Paul saw that he had to adjust himself to it.

"Take an illustration. Paul's letters to the Thessalonians were his first letters. In those letters there is no doubt whatever that Paul expected the Lord to return in his lifetime. Mark his words: '... we that are alive, that are left unto the coming of the Lord....' In his letter to the Philippians, Paul has moved from that position, and also in his letters to Timothy that expectation is no longer with him: '... I am already being offered, and the time of my departure is come. I have fought the good fight, I have finished the course....' He had anticipated Nero's verdict. He knew now that it was not by way of the rapture that he himself was to go to glory. Are we to say that these two things contradict one another? Not at all! In going on with the Lord, Paul came into fuller revelation about the Lord's coming, and of his personal relationship thereto, but this did not set aside or change any fact of doctrine which had been expressed earlier in his letters to the Thessalonians. All that had been set forth there was fully inspired, given by the Holy Spirit, but it was still capable of development in the heart of the Apostle himself, and as he saw the fuller meaning of the things that had come to him earlier in his life, so he found that in practical matters he had to adjust himself." *(Continued)*

"No fresh revelation, nor advance in understanding, ever placed him in the position of having to repudiate anything that had been given him by revelation in earlier days. It is a matter of recognizing that these differences are not contradictions but the result of progressive, supplemental revelation, enlarging apprehension, clearer conception through going on with the Lord. Surely these are evidences that progress in Paul's understanding and knowledge led to adjustments." [2]

GOD'S UNIQUE METHOD
IN UNFOLDING
VISION-PERSPECTIVE

WE MUST OBSERVE God's method in giving vision. Even though God shares His complete intention for a life, it is rarely understood until much time has elapsed. Divine vision when first given is much like a flower-bud which must blossom before it can be fully appreciated. In observing this let us consider three examples: Joseph, Abraham and Paul. In an early period divine vision was given to each, yet not understood until it unfolded like a flower. In these three we shall see what God intends for each of His children as they grow to full stature. With them, as with us, there must be the pathway of patient adjustment, faith-comprehension and finally vision-enlargement. What we think we *see* at the beginning is only a dim reality compared with what we shall see and understand at the end.

Nevertheless, this "seeing" is what keeps us from fainting and enables us to press toward the divine fulfillment. It was in a dream that the young lad Joseph was given a bird's-eye view of his future. First he saw his brethren as sheaves doing obeisance to his sheaf. Again he saw his entire family represented by the sun, the moon and the eleven stars doing obeisance to him. What did all this mean to Joseph? Surely it meant very little until afterward when God, through suffering and adjustment, finally brought him to the throne of Egypt where he could comprehend things in the divine perspective. Then he could announce to his brethren, "God meant it for good."

How much did God's first words mean to Abram when He called him out of his father's house "unto a land thát I will shew thee"? Could he possibly imagine what God meant when He announced—like a miniature flower bud—this fourfold vision: that Abram should one day be a great nation, have a great name, be blessed and be a blessing. Surely at this beginning hour these words were, for Abram, but a small bud compared to what he was to understand of the heavenly vision toward the end of his life.

But what is more wonderful is for us, who now sit in a still more favored viewpoint, to look first in the account of Genesis and see that which God starts with as a miniature in Abraham's family unfold into grand magnitude in the book of Revelation. We see how our Heavenly Father will one day have a twofold family in heaven and on earth. Even as Abraham was to have a family which would number as the stars of the sky and the sands of the seashore, so shall our Heavenly Father have a glorious twofold family. Who could possibly grasp this apart from the tedious path of patient adjustment, faith-comprehension and vision-enlargement?

Then we come to our pattern-man, and we remember the words in bud form given by the Lord to Paul that day on the Damascus road. Twenty-seven years later those words still seem to be most precious to Paul as he recounts to King Agrippa how God appeared unto him for this purpose: "... to make thee a witness both of these things which thou hast seen, and of those things in the which I will appear unto thee"(Acts 26:16). "Whereupon ... I was not disobedient unto the heavenly vision" (Acts 26:19).

How much more meaningful these words must have seemed now as he explained the power of this heavenly vision which had so constrained him through the years. No wonder Agrippa was moved and "almost persuaded." Men of vision always move people and leave them without excuse.

The question is this: Can we expect God to share with each of us—as he did with Paul, and even with Joseph and Abram—that bud of vision which in due time will blossom into divine fulfillment? I believe if we expected and wanted the divine pattern we would see such a vision and fulfillment. There is so much substandard vision that when God seems to make this initial vision real to any life many assume it is abnormal instead of according to the normal Christian life.

Now let us see the process by which God may use years of *patient adjustment* in bringing one from the initial to the enlarged vision and its fulfillment. How often we have heard someone tell what God has unveiled to them of their life, work and ministry, and have sincerely wondered about their adaptations and interpretations of it. What they first saw was just a bud. What God has since unfolded through difficult adjustment and suffering has allowed them to comprehend in a whole new way what He really meant. Such experiences reveal how prone we are to become centered in the means as though they were the end. We must be slow to interpret these first glimpses of God's purpose.

With Paul it was not experiences, nor gifts nor revelations; not organizations, nor even the Body of Christ itself which became his center of attention. All of these—needful in their place —were but means to that greater end. These would all unfold into still greater purpose requiring new adjustment and comprehension as T. A. Sparks so wisely puts it:

"The means employed by God at one time may—and very likely will—pass or be changed. In the sovereign ordering of God one particular phase, method, or means will pass out, though greatly used and blessed so far. This does not involve a *change* of vision (unless it is ours and not God's) but an enlargement of vision. With God all that He uses and blesses, however wonderfully, is only relative and not final or ultimate. Therefore we must not cling to what has been and regard that as the form for all time. So often this has been a most disastrous attitude of mind, and has resulted in God having to go on with His full purpose in other directions and by other means, and leave that fixed thing behind to serve a much lesser purpose than He wanted with it. Eventually it has spiritually died, although perhaps carried on by human effort and organization. It just lives on its past and tradition."

One need only look around to see many movements, organizations and works which indeed started with a man or a group who had spiritual insight from God. In the refreshing hours of beginning, God's approval and initiative were so manifest. In its first apprehension the work seemed to have great significance. However the real implications of any movement of God are not always recognized at the beginning. If we go on with Him we shall find that much that is done here is of time and must be left behind. God is so working that the spiritual and the heavenly are pressing for a larger place in us. This work is spontaneous—something that just happens. We wake up to realize that we have moved into a new realm or spiritual dimension; nothing of the old can any longer meet the need. It is not only something *more* that is demanded, but something different. This very real crisis in the life will only be safely passed if there is vision of God's ultimate objective. The entire religious world around one may seem to be tumbling to pieces, but it is God's way to bring us to that new level which is fuller and more final.

The great pity is that so many *will* cling to the old framework or partial vision. They have no capacity for spiritual ADJUSTMENT. God presents His unfolding *heavenly* pattern in greater fullness and in His light we *see* and become adjustable.

With each new adjustment there is a new faith-comprehension. Oh, to be more adjustable that we might appreciate divine vision. God is working with a foreknowledge of a future day which is imminent and this fuller vision alone will be *the* answer. He must lead each one to embrace it even though now it seems "revolutionary" and too idealistic for this hour. Many retire to the cautious way of quiet safety, and reject the new order which God is bringing in because they are afraid of the divine order. Yet there is surely coming a day when their *programs* will flounder, and all sorts of expediencies will then be resorted to with the hope of saving them. Because they *would not see* there was no *faith-comprehension.*

There is a deep groaning and shaking going on within the hearts of those who are afraid to go on in the things they have dimly seen; and those who are afraid *not* to go on—even though what they have seen seems presently impossible. If we dare to be counted with this later group we shall not be caught off guard nor found warring against eventualities, contingencies and emergencies. As we move *on in His light we begin to see* how all things, whether good or evil, are not ends in themselves.

Let us consider the proper significance of the words so often quoted: " . . . all things work together for good. . . . " We so rarely see things in their proper setting; therefore stop short of their full importance. We just say, "all things work together for good" and stop there. The context has two aspects: (1) lives wholly

under the Holy Spirit's government are in view, and (2) His
purpose is governing. Without these two things operating, *all
things do not work together for good*—do not serve that glorious
end.

Who could understand Joseph being sold by his brethren, or
unjustly committed to prison by false accusation, or so un-
graciously forgotten by his benefactor when he was in prison?
What patience and adjustment God was working in preparing this
young man for the throne of Egypt! *Now* we *see* and understand.
But it is because purpose governs all, and the *purpose* is the
substance of God-given seeing. What is so needed is a *seeing*—
a vision—of God's final purpose in greater fullness; a seeing of
the whole not just the parts. The purpose comprehends all the
parts and no phase or part is an end in itself. One wheel of a
machine has no adequate meaning in itself. There lacks a real
adjustableness if we are not led on to see how all the other parts
are in view. Only after passing through many experiences, crises
or levels shall we *see:* we must not be too obsessed or taken up
with the phase that momentarily engrosses us. If we linger too
long, the whole becomes bound up with (related to) that phase
for *us,* and we see no more.

Look around you and behold some choice servant of God who
has become *so preoccupied* with one theme or emphasis in his
ministry. It was wonderful at the beginning, but now after twenty-
five years it is still his one emphasis. Everything has become
related to that, and is in danger of becoming warped. It may be
grace or the dispensations, prophecy or even body-truth, missions
or the need of the Holy Spirit. Any one theme however important
must not continue as the overshadowing theme or it cannot be
properly related to that which is truly supreme, and ultimate.

With both Abram and Paul we see how God's way is through
continuous adjustment to bring the life into *vision-enlargement.*
When Abram was separated from Lot he *saw* the land which God
had promised; when separated from earthly possessions he *saw*
the Lord Himself as his reward; when finally separated from
Isaac he *saw* what he had not appreciated before: how he was
indeed more than an earthly father (Abram) but also the "father
of a multitude"—even as the visible shadow of the heavenly
Father Himself. It was by the pathway of continuous adjustment
that Abraham moved into increasing comprehension of God's
purpose and his relation to it.

THIS QUESTION OFTEN COMES:

Since this divine vision-perspective is so imperative in moving unto full stature, what about the Old Testament saints? How much could they – or did they – see and understand? Today it seems we are so much more privileged, even as Watchman Nee has said: "Vision of God's purpose today brings into view all the people of God, but it is also *for* all the people of God. That was not always so. What the Old Testament saints saw, great as it was, concerned only an earthly people, however typical they might be of the heavenly Church. And only chosen men such as Joseph and Moses were entrusted with that vision. (And we are not really sure how much they understood.) It was not common property, but was only given to the few. Today, however, it is different. *Heavenly vision now is for the whole church.* Though it is true that Paul and others in the New Testament period were chosen of God in a special way, His purpose is not that the vision should be confined to the ones and the twos, but that *all* should see (Eph. 1:18). This is the special character of this age." [3]

So as Paul understood it, his own part in this ministry to the Gentiles during the dispensation of grace was governed by this single object, namely, *"to make all men see"* (verse 9).

MEN WHO LIVED
BEYOND THEIR DAY

IN EACH GENERATION God always has had those men whose framework of vision reached beyond the general consciousness to see God's larger purpose. They lived and breathed with a divine destiny consciousness imparted by God. Such men always moved beyond the narrow vision of their own day.

Today as individuals we also face these questions: How far do we see? How comprehensive is our consciousness? What compel-

ling vision has laid hold of us? What are we ultimately living
for? Perhaps no one is more alert to the narrow vision of the
general religious crowd than the servant of God who *has seen*
and feels impelled to expand and enlarge the framework of others.
To illustrate this, let us consider the importance of Israel's
leaders in her history.

We shall start with Israel as a captive people in Egypt. During
more than four hundred years as strangers in a strange land, the
family of Jacob increased into a multitude of people. At first
they enjoyed privileges in Egypt, but after Joseph's time they
came to suffering and severe oppression. Yet most tragic of all
is that during these long years in Egypt, Israel lost all sense of
divine destiny and purpose. The vision-perspective which passed
from Abraham to Isaac and to Jacob had long since faded. Now
in their hour of affliction they cried for just one thing: to be
relieved from the galling yoke. How conveniently this served
God's plan. He had waited for this hour in order to bring Israel
out of Egypt and into the promised land where He would in due
time accomplish His full intention through them. We say—this
was what God planned, yet we must first face the question:
What was Israel's primary consciousness?

On the blackboard see FRAMEWORK A (center). Above all
else, Israel was sick of slavery. Perhaps nothing mattered more
than *getting out* of Egypt and being free from her taskmasters.
The overshadowing consciousness of the average Israelite was
simply *getting out* and enjoying freedom. As Israel cried out to
God for His deliverance from bondage it was largely for her own
sake. Yet as God saw it, deliverance was merely the initial step
in realizing His fuller purpose. Of course we know that God had
an immediate concern to show compassion on His people in their
dire need, but He had much more in view. Thus it was to His
emancipator, Moses, that God gave that fuller measure of vision.

When Moses went to Pharoah with God's demand for Israel's
deliverance, it was on the ground that they were His people and
they were to leave Egypt to worship and serve Him (Exodus
5:1-3; 8:8, 20). Yet when God approached Israel about their
redemption from Egyptian bondage it was on the ground of His
covenant relations with their founding fathers. He wanted to
deliver them, to enter into covenant with them, and to restore
them to the land of their fathers (Exodus 2:24).

We know the story! They listened to God's words, but were

primarily conscious of only one thing: getting out of Egypt, and what it would mean to them. This was the extent of their framework of vision. (Alas, for many today who want to be saved from their slavery, this also is their only concern—what salvation will mean to them.) Once Israel was free from Egypt they wandered forty years because they had no heart to "go up and take the land." Their small, selfish vision could only result in one thing —weakness and unbelief.

SEE FRAMEWORK B. The new generation who had grown up in the wilderness had one concern: *getting into the land of promise*. The entire adult generation which had left Egypt died in the wilderness, except for two men, Joshua and Caleb. These men had God's insight and lived beyond their day. Once again we are faced with the same problem. For the average Israelite, crossing Jordan meant little more than *personal gain*—that of enjoying the land flowing with milk and honey. They saw the land as it related to them and their welfare instead of God's larger purpose.

Yet it was Joshua who sought to enlarge the vision of the people saying: "Don't stop here but possess the land." Joshua

HOW LARGE IS YOUR FRAMEWORK OF VISION?

could say this because God promised him that "Every place that
the sole of your foot shall tread upon, that have I given you, as
I said unto Moses" (Joshua 1:3).

Again we know the sad story! Israel saw the land as her own,
not in relation to God. Repeatedly in the prophets we read how
God desired to gather fruit from His vineyard, Israel, but she
was interested in getting the fruit for herself. (See Isa. 5:7;
Hosea 10:1 and Psalm 80.) It was not what she could be unto
God, but what God's gifts and blessing could mean to her.

So she had little heart for driving out the nations round about
her; she made treaties with them and soon reaped the judgment
which God had warned as the sure result of being yoked with the
ungodly. The very nations she should have taken captive rose
up to take Israel captive. Either she would get rid of the thorn
or the thorn would forever prick at her side. Why could she not
accept the vision of Joshua and possess the land for God?
Because she was, like previous generations—centered in using
and relating everything to herself and not to God's larger purpose.

SEE FRAMEWORK C. It was only in that dark hour of Israel's
bondage to the nations of Canaan that she could be awakened
to see the need for possessing all the land. So God in His own
sovereign timing raised up King David to unify the tribes into a
nation; and finally King Solomon was used to bring the kingdom
into the greatest glory any nation had ever known. In God's design Israel was to be a visible example of the blessedness of a
people who would honor and sanctify the Lord God in their
midst. Thus Israel became a glorious kingdom who built the
house of prayer for all nations.

Again the same old problem still haunts this new generation—
Israel seemed more interested in using and possessing for her
own glory and advantage. Instead of becoming a priesthood
people to all the nations of the world, it was not long before
Israel misused the temple for herself and refused even to allow
the Gentiles to enter their own court. She saw the temple as
hers and failed to see how it had been dedicated as a house of
prayer for all nations (Isa. 56:7).

Yes, she had possessed the land and built the temple—*but
only for herself.* She settled down to be the *object* of His blessing
instead of becoming the *channel* of His blessing. Instead of
obeying the sabbath rest for the land, she abused it and God

finally enforced a seventy year rest while she was away in captivity. This captivity came because the people had lost their vision and their kingdom was divided. Except for a small remnant who returned, the people were scattered throughout the world. Israel has now been set aside, yet not cast away forever. Even in His chastisement God has a larger purpose as we shall see.

All of this would teach us one important lesson. We must remember that each enlarging framework is not *because* of man, but actually *in spite of man*. It is a unique pattern in all God's working. Even though man seems always to fail, yet God steps in and through sovereign intervention brings Israel closer and closer to His divine intention.

SEE FRAMEWORK D. What has caused the world-wide dispersion of Israel which we see today? It was because of the narrowness of her vision. Even after the remnant was restored to the land and God in the fullness of time finally offered to her the long-awaited Messiah, she refused Him. She wanted a king for her own personal advantage. She wanted a king who would deliver her from the bondage of Rome and restore her to the glory she had known under David—but she did not want THE KING whom God would use to bless the whole world. It was once again the same old selfish vision. Because she could not fit this Christ into her narrow framework of personal blessing, she nailed Him to a cross. She only did what others have been doing (in principle) for generations: *sought to use God for herself*. But we can rejoice that once again God enlarged the framework to include a more glorious day yet to come.

In Exodus 19 we read how, after she left Egypt, God had revealed His unique purpose for Israel as a peculiar people. He called her into a fellowship and glorious destiny with Himself. She answered glibly—"yes," but hardly understood that this meant she was to be God's prophet, priest and king in the earth. As prophet she was to speak for Him and share His word with all the world; as priest she was to be a spiritual mediator between God and all peoples; as royal king she was to enjoy the exercise of governmental authority for God over all the earth. What an unique and glorious high calling! We know only too well how she failed to realize God's purpose because her narrow vision turned her to seek *self-blessing* and *glory*.

Now in spite of repeated failure, we see God sovereignly working to bring about His ultimate intention for Israel. What

He has promised in Deuteronomy 30:3-5, He will yet accomplish:
"...then the Lord thy God will turn thy captivity, and have
compassion upon thee, and will return and gather thee from all
nations...and will bring thee into the land...and multiply
thee...."

But we must go beyond Israel's calling as a nation, back to
Abraham as the founding father if we would see that ultimate
framework of vision. Many who have allowed the coming glorious
kingdom to overshadow have failed to see God's larger perspective: that the Eternal Father will have a vast family.

THE FORWARD LOOK GOVERNED BY
THE BACKWARD GLANCE

Throughout the enlarging framework of vision we have been
looking at various goals of different generations and their
leaders. Now let us see how each framework is grounded in the
promise God has made to His *key man*. God always has His
chosen vessel who represents a specific purpose. If we can see
it, there is a sense in which every chosen vessel must stand on
the shoulders of his predecessors. This is like standing in the
stream of divine purpose and vision. Since there can only be
one stream—there must be a recognition of the place and importance of each previous founder. David and Solomon fulfilled
their place, but they were really standing upon the shoulders of
Joshua and Caleb. Joshua and Caleb stood in line with Moses.
Moses in the stream of purpose reckoned back to Jacob and
finally it all had its source in Abraham who gives us the largest
framework for he represents God's unique shadow of Himself:
the earthly father and his family picture the Heavenly Father
and His vast family.

LIVING BEYOND OUR DAY

Does God limit a man simply because of the hour in which he
lives? Surely the heavens are open to whoever wills to see. Yet
it is true that no one can "crash the gates," for such insight
is not *grasped*, but *given* to those with pure motive. Can we not
say that whoever would grow to full stature in seeing with God,
must surely be atuned to God's representatives through the
ages? One who does not sense the stream of Moses' vision cannot live beyond nor reach back before Moses to understand God's
earlier framework. Here is the glory of coming to *full stature*. It

identifies us with all God's people as *one,* and makes for that spiritual unity He has ultimately designed. (Perhaps Hebrews 11:39-40; 12:1 would be a confirmation to this.)

It was not long ago that one little phrase came home to me with new force; it was something I had never seen before. Those who live in this divine stream of purpose and authority will always hear the Lord repeat: *"as I said unto"*... David, *unto* Moses, *unto* Joshua, *unto* Jacob, *unto* Isaac and *unto* Abraham. There is no standing *alone* when we stand in *this stream*—in the full vision perspective of God's ultimate. Yet those who live unto themselves can only live in the immediate time-stream; for what they see is only related to them and their immediate welfare. While those who have moved into the eternal-stream live unto God's working and glory. It is living where the time factor vanishes and spiritual reality has become the one outstanding characteristic.

Finally, in the enlarging framework we have seen how many have lived with Israel and her one concern—getting out of bondage; or with Moses and the need for moving into Canaan; or with Jacob and Joshua and the need for possessing the land; or in that largest framework with Abraham and the need for realizing a vast family. Is it not strange that each generation seemed able to take but one step into fuller consciousness of purpose? Because of this, God must intervene so as to bring them to His higher level of purpose.

It is important now that we learn from Israel's failures. Today we must understand what it means to live in the stream of "as I said *unto,*" for it is essential to reaching any measure of full stature.

We shall need to see how God has given to the Church the Holy Spirit as the means by which not only leaders but all of us can be "in touch" with this divine stream. This is His primary work today. To bring us together, He has given apostles, prophets, evangelists, pastors, teachers who must all recognize their place in the divine stream and live with vision-perspective. Any private kingdoms or personal ambitions will be swept away when an individual moves into this divine stream. Since this is our calling and privilege, let no one fall short.

THIS PROBLEM:

Recently the director of a home missionary board confided: "There are so many Christian workers tossing around from one place to another. The moment they run into pressure, difficult personalities, unexpected providence, they begin to seek another place of service. Of course I recognize that many organizations may be working along unscriptural lines and this may justify many — who come to a fuller vision — in moving about. But I wonder if there is not a deeper problem: While many may be earnestly praying for God's direction, they have already set up a pattern of escape in their lives. In continually seeking an easy way they are actually avoiding God's method of crowding them into that place where He can unfold His will more fully. Then they will recognize most every difficult place as God's open door — for them."

Surely the pathway into THIS NEW VIEWPOINT where "all things become new" is through a very real union in His death, burial and resurrection.

LIVING IN THE DIVINE
VISION - PERSPECTIVE

W E HAVE BEEN SAYING that God's child must be turned from every false center. Until this happens, he will be constantly moving from one place of service to another. What he apparently does not realize is that the great need is in his *inner life* — not in finding a more favorable place of service which fits his own vision. Indeed he needs a most radical inner adjustment which comes when one discovers his union in death, burial, resurrection and ascension with Christ. Just as surely as the Cross has wrought an inner change, so it will mean a new position of seeing as God sees.

Alas, for too many modern-day believers, this identification with Christ seems yet to be but a deeper-life doctrine, or just another interpretation of the victorious life. When understanding of truth is only objective it is inoperative. Such a believer has not yet moved into reality. He does not have the divine vision-perspective where "all things become new."

Among other things, at least these four will become operative-reality as we live in this new vision-perspective. To help you remember we will use the first letters of the alphabet. Enlarged vision will bring *adjustment*, *balance*, *cohesion* and *dynamic*.

I. GOD-CENTERED VISION EFFECTS A RADICAL *ADJUSTMENT*

Whenever men hear of God's purpose, they usually glow with anticipation; and as they meet you at the church door they will remark: "Yes, I'm so glad God has a purpose for me." "God's purpose for *me*" is the measure of their vision, and it requires a radical adjustment at the Cross ere they will move from a self-center to become God-centered.

① Really any enlarged vision must first be *the seeing of God's purpose for Himself*—what He supremely desires, eternally purposes, and ultimately intends – not for man, or Israel or the Church – but FOR HIMSELF. To become truly occupied with Him and what He purposes—all the while to leave ourselves completely out of the picture – that is to become alive to HIS ETERNAL PURPOSE and begin reckoning from a NEW CENTER. This is the first adjustment.

Then vision will bring still another adjustment. Whereas once ② the life was controlled by the philosophy of escape, it will now be fulfillment. Once it was escaping the pressures and trials, escaping life's dreary road and somehow making it through to heaven. In fact it was escaping for your very life, as though to keep it for yourself. Instead the heart is now atuned to Him, the life is placed at His disposal for the fulfillment of all He purposes. The consuming passion is to use trouble as a servant; to glory in tribulation, as it fulfills God's working of stature in the life; to rejoice even though He has not called us to an easy way but to a fruitful way. Thus we are no longer escaping, but fulfilling His purpose for placing us here. Yes, once this outlook has changed our philosophy, we no longer pray for deliverance, but rather rejoice in the inward development He is working.

This adjustment in us will help us to adjust others. But helping those who are smug and content, or blind and unteachable, requires an adjustment in our own methods of working. On every hand we see people going to pieces. We know just what they need. The Bible says, "Where there is no vision, the people perish"–"disintegrate," "fall apart" or "go to pieces." Whether our translation is correct or not, it is quite true in fact. Disintegration and falling apart is manifestly clear in the despair of lives all about us. But the fact that we see what is needed — for we have been enlightened by the larger vision–does not mean that friends and relatives will receive or understand our diagnosis. In fact unless divine salve is applied by the Holy Spirit they will not see. They will reject our point of view as being unrealistic and too spiritual – or mystical.

(3) At this point we ourselves will probably find need for a deeper adjustment. It is one thing to see what is God's eternal purpose for Himself, but still another thing to see the methods He will use in realizing that purpose. We usually fail right here because our vision needs further enlargement. When we are adjusted to His methods of working we shall be adjusted in our own methods of helping others.

So, it is not enough to know *what* God is after; it is equally important to know *how* God will get there! Many people have glimpsed quite accurately God's end, but they have gone astray and failed in helping Him to realize that end, because they have sought to reach it by false means. So we must not only see what God purposes, but the principles which govern that purpose. That is, we must clearly understand how God ordains to reach His purpose. These principles which govern God's procedure in realizing His ends have not been sought out or generally recognized.

(4) *Here then, is the point of greatest adjustment in vision.* Vision means that we see *how* and *why* things are contrary to God's mind. This is very important! There are many people today who realize that things are not right – that God's end is not being reached – but they cannot put their finger on the cause. The prophets who were seers – men who had vision by revelation of God – were able not only to declare what God required, but were also able to correct and adjust other men as to the way to achieve God's purpose, and to set forth the laws of God's realization.

II. ENLARGED VISION GIVES *BALANCE*

Two years ago we printed an article in our journal which caught much attention. Many found it a clear picture of an important aspect of truth. We told of a friend who made a motto which read: "KEEP LOOKING DOWN." When folk commented upon the difference from the customary "KEEP LOOKING UP," he reminded them that the big difference is where one sits. If one is down here, then of course he must look up to see Christ in His heavenly position. But if one has truly recognized that he is positioned with Christ in heaven, then he can LOOK DOWN — his vision will be from the Lord's point of view — "... the Lord looked down from heaven upon the children of men ..." (Psalm 14:2).

Now what is both amazing and amusing is how quickly some folk will emphasize one aspect of truth to the exclusion of the other. It would be quite typical for some to build a following and new movement around the motto: "KEEP LOOKING DOWN." To them it has become the "all-important" center from which we all must view, and to be God-centered is to always use the phrase "KEEP LOOKING DOWN." In warning against such T. A. Sparks has written: [4]

"It is tremendously important that we should keep a proper balance of truth. A very great deal of our trouble is because of there being an unbalanced emphasis upon some aspect of truth. It is good to know the truth, and it is good to rejoice in it, but it is just possible that even truth may get us into trouble. There are many perils lying in the direction of truth, even spiritual truth; and there are not a few of the Lord's people who have fallen into those perils.

"It is not that they suffer from want of light, but they are suffering very much because they have not got their light properly adjusted and balanced. Thus it becomes very necessary for us to get things in their right perspective and proportion. The history of many instrumentalities which have been raised up and used by the Lord is eventually the sad story of a loss of power and effectiveness because of striking an unbalanced emphasis, of putting some side of truth in a place out of proportion to that which is complementary to it.

"What do we mean by complementary truths? It is important to see both: that Christ is in heaven and also that Christ is within the believer. The Scripture pictures us as both down here and up there. These two things are, as it were, twins, running together, and to overemphasize or overdevelop one means to throw the whole order out and to bring about serious limitation and weakness." Truth out of true perspective is far less effective than it would otherwise be.

We can be sure that enlarged vision will always mean the balancing of truths. In one of his last editorials the late Dr. Tozer warned that man is usually trying to fly with one wing and then wondering why he goes round and round.

So it is in spiritual things. There is one thing true, but there is always something to go with it to keep it in its right measure and to cause it to fulfill its purpose and to serve its end most effectively. When we see the truth of God's sovereignty, we must also see human responsibility. When we see the divine will we must also see the place for man's will. When we tend to emphasize only the individual, we shall miss the beauty of the corporate. When we tend to overemphasize the rational, we soon become cold and calculating and cease to see the need for the wonder and awe of the mystical, which can hardly be examined or explained. Many other truths appear in "sets" both of which are necessary if we are to stay on course, just as both wings are needed if a bird is to fly.

It is very possible for the adversary to use God's own work in an attempt to defeat His purpose. He seeks to turn truth around. This fact is made very clear in the Scriptures, and we may observe it in experience and in history. This line of action is more successful for the adversary than perhaps any other, because it raises prejudice against God's work and God's truth. By securing an over-emphasis or an unbalanced apprehension of divine truth, he closes the door to the acceptance of what is of God.

III. VISION – THE *COHESION* OF LIFE

Enlarged vision is not only sure to bring balance, but it will bring a proper cohesion to life. Where there is no vision, the people disintegrate – go to pieces – cohesiveness breaks down. Consider any group of people who have been welded together by a common cause or objective. The very moment they fail to agree in their purpose, or in the means and methods of fulfilling their purpose, they will cease walking together. There must be oneness in vision if there is to be any real value in their association or any strength in their testimony.

Surely the divine foundation of the Church as a whole is a revelation, a vision – a "having seen the Lord." The Church started with this and took its rise from a seeing of the Lord, high and lifted up, exalted at the right hand of the Majesty on high. The Church went forth on the basis of that vision as a cohesive testimony, as a corporate vessel, and what is true of the Church must be true of the relationship of all believers. You and I can never hold together by agreements. We can never hold together by certain rules and regulations, or by a creed. It can only be as we are one in vision, one in revelation of Him. If this vision is necessary to hold us together as individuals and to keep us from falling apart in ourselves, it is equally necessary to keep us together as the Lord's people – and that is going to be one of the tests of these days.

There can be no doubt that we are soon to face some desperate times. We can hardly imagine (nor would we predict) just what might come to produce the "shaking." Consider the scattering now taking place amongst God's people. On every hand there are little groups forming and seeking to become a New Testament expression of Christ. Some are merely seeking escape. Others are really after fulfillment of God's purpose. The old line of corporate expression and fellowship along creedal or denominational lines is breaking fast.

Now, is this outward breaking apart going to be the end, or is there going to be with all that a spiritual cohesion triumphing over apparent division? Is there a larger spiritual vision which can truly unite these smaller group expressions to become one glorious expression? What cohesive element will manifest a living testimony to the religious world?

As the "shaking" progresses, it will be seen that all the work of the enemy, all the division and confusion, all the breaking up and outward disintegration can have no effect upon those who have really seen God's purpose and His methods. There still remains, in the unseen before God in heaven – and here on earth as a testimony – that oneness and cohesiveness of God's people which Satan cannot destroy. Those who have begun to live in the divine vision know its cohesive power.

IV. VISION IS ALSO THE DYNAMIC

He who has "seen" with God knows how vision becomes the very dynamic of life, the thing which keeps us going, which is the strength of our hearts. Take Jeremiah, for example. From his own point of view, Jeremiah had to face a hopeless situation.

To him his ministry seemed an utter failure right to the end. Yet we today have the sequel. We see how others have come to value his work generations later. But in Jeremiah's own lifetime it appeared that his ministry was a failure. He sometimes had strong things to say to the Lord. At one time he told the Lord that He had deceived him and led him into a trap by putting him into a prophetic ministry, because this ministry was such an utter failure. This seemed true only because of the prophet's own narrow time-viewpoint.

Another time Jeremiah cried, Oh, that I might get away from everything — out of all this — into some place apart from men! We all know something of this feeling from time to time. Oh, to get away from everything and everybody—even this great thing which, at other times, we realize to be the greatest thing that God could put us into. We want to get out and away. Why? Because of the apparent hopelessness of the situation, the slowness of spiritual growth, or the utter absence of spiritual growth in others (as it seems to us). So we see Jeremiah, sometimes looking through his own eyes and complaining because of the darkness and failure; but then again we find him looking with God as from the enlarged vision.

Nevertheless, through all those vicissitudes, those changes, those differing moods, Jeremiah was a man with fire in his bones, and though he determined he would not go on, he could not refrain. That *fire in his bones* was caused by the vision which God had given, and through all, it held Jeremiah. This vision

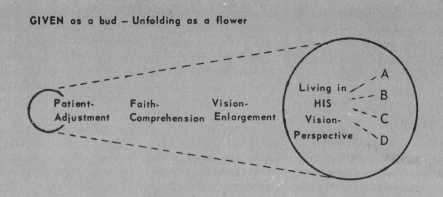

GIVEN as a bud — Unfolding as a flower

Patient-Adjustment   Faith-Comprehension   Vision-Enlargement   Living in HIS Vision-Perspective   A B C D

was the dynamic that held him while in the dungeon, it held him in the pit, it held him in persecution, it held him through despair. Although he might one day go right down into the depths of darkness and hopelessness of spirit, he could not stay there. It was an experience; but he came out and the fire was still there, still burning in his bones. The vision was there to the end.

Beloved, that is how the knowledge of God's purpose has to dwell in us. It has to be something that is stronger than the situation surrounding us, deeper than our own feelings and emotions or emotional experience. It has to be something that is more than what we are in our moods, a mightier thing than all that to which we are subject in our soul life. It has to be able to bring us up out of our spiritual pits and mire, and keep us going. Vision is the only adequate dynamic in days like these, and this will be proven more and more.

As we approach the end of this world system, with everything going to pieces around us, strivings among the nations become more desperate, and disturbing reports come from every quarter of the globe, we must be able to say, "I have seen God's purpose; I know what God has in view and what He is working toward." This is the only secret for facing the tests.

Does the divine vision dwell in your heart? Now, there could be no more utter test and challenge for us than this. It will not be of any purpose if that thing has not entered into us in such a way that, when everything outside is in a hopeless state, this vision keeps us going and is capable of bringing us up out of our own hours of deepest despair; for I do not hesitate to say that even prophets can go down into deep despair for a season. But, because they are prophets, because they are seers with God, because they have vision, they come back again – and it is that fire in their bones that brings them back. *Have you a fire in your bones,* a fire born of that eye-opening work of the Holy Spirit, that vision of God's purpose?

It is true we are not all called to be prophets. The Body of Christ has more than "eyes." There is a *specific seeing* which belongs only to the prophet. But we are saying there is a *general seeing* which all can and must experience. This general vision is the balance, the cohesion and the dynamic of our lives. Thank God for the strength of such a thing. Now let us go on to see how this enlarged "seeing" will affect every other facet of our being as we move toward full stature.

Moving . . .

UNTO FULL STATURE

in

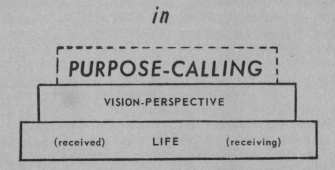

Those who have grasped the imperative necessity of living in the divine vision-perspective will also appreciate how purpose and calling must be the next important level if there is to be any real moving unto full stature. As we shall see, to live in His Viewpoint is to understand His Eternal Purpose and our glorious High Calling in it. In this section we shall consider:

IN CHAPTER FIVE: When men live without meaning, purpose or direction it is because they are missing one thing!

IN CHAPTER SIX: If we do not know our calling, how can we hope to fulfill God's highest expectation?

IN CHAPTER SEVEN: What was the secret which explains Paul's devotion and dedication to God?

IN CHAPTER EIGHT: Does everyone have the same glorious high calling?

IN CHAPTER NINE: In our two-fold calling we are to be something "for" Him, and something "unto" Him. What?

WE MUST MAKE THIS DISTINCTION:

A pastor asks: "I am perplexed! I plead and pour out my heart to this congregation! Why — why do they manifest such indifference toward really fulfilling God's purpose and calling?"

In hearing him, one has answered: "It is true that in every breast there is a *sense of destiny* — in some it is more intense than in others; but this is very different from the *sense of divine destiny consciousness*. The first is naturally built into every man, while the latter comes only by divine awakening and impartation. It is much more than being 'born again,' more than an experience of sanctification or filling of the Spirit. Many who can testify to such experiences still seem to lack this special awakening which tunes the heart's strings with the Eternal Strings of God's own heart; thus making one spoiled for anything that is not wholly aligned with His Eternal Purpose."

As we shall point out in this chapter, we are sure there will be no real moving *unto full stature* until God has sensitized our inner compass to help us wholly follow His purpose and calling. Indeed here is an imperative need:

AN AWAKENED SENSE
OF DIVINE DESTINY

WHAT IS MORE TRAGIC than to see individuals who are placed here by God to fulfill some unique and glorious destiny, still wandering aimlessly with no awakened *sense of divine purpose or calling*? Thousands who sit in church pews week after week have somehow missed that one basic ingredient which alone can give meaning, direction, purpose and dedication to life: *the sense of divine destiny.*

Man was designed as the masterpiece of creation, and as one of his greatest gifts from God, he was given a built-in mechanism which works much like a compass. This inner compass is an inner sense or consciousness placed in every man by God that

He might forever have some means to tug upon the man of His creation no matter how indifferent or unresponsive he might become toward God.

To better understand just how this inner compass works, suppose we visit a plant where mariner's compasses are being manufactured. The needles of the compasses would point in every direction if they were not magnetized. In this process of being magnetized each needle receives a peculiar power. From that moment on it points only to the north and is constant and true forever. The compass needle can now be depended upon; it is predictable. It no longer points toward every object on the horizon. All of the heavenly bodies try to attract it; the sun may dazzle it; meteors may beckon it; stars may twinkle at it as though trying to win its affection. But the magnetized needle remains true to its objective. With a finger that never errs in sunshine or in storm, it points constantly toward its star.

Consider what God did in that first morning of creation when He magnetized every needle (Adam's and every *man in Adam*)— magnetized them with the eternal purpose they were created to serve. Yet we know, all too well, how the Enemy slipped into the Garden and the needle was deflected toward other purposes. Now the needle, even though it still has its original pull, seems mostly unpredictable. For the most part it seems almost to have lost its sense of destiny and direction. Like an erratic compass it seems pulled by whatever is closest to it. Yet in those precarious hours when one is left all alone, in those fleeting seconds when life seems almost to ebb away—the needle somehow flicks back to its "true north" as though to remind each one just how far he has missed or just how little he has fulfilled the divine purpose for which he was once magnetized by God.

It is indeed a crisis hour when God awakens man and he by his own choice wholly gives himself for a new spiritual magnetizing and synchronizing to fulfill God's eternal purpose. Suddenly life takes on new meaning. He realizes that the most important thing about anything is its purpose and it is with purpose we must always begin. Understanding purpose gives full meaning to everything.

Look around you in the room where you sit. Consider every object that comes before your eye: the chairs, the table, the lamp, the rug. What is the most significant thing about each of these? It is not the size, the color, the nature or the quality—

though these may seem to be important. The primary thing about any of these is its *purpose*. If a chair will not hold one up as he sits on it, the size, the color or the quality really do not matter. If the table does not fulfill its purpose as a table, everything else about that table which seems important becomes unimportant. Its design, style, finish or condition has little significance if it will not hold a lamp, books or the family dinner.

Just think then what happens when one's life is magnetized by ultimate direction and eternal purpose? When our long-term objectives are accurately focused and fully supported by our physical industry and spiritual powers, then size, quality, condition—nothing of lesser importance can pull our needle. When one's life is really dedicated to its mission, then distractions lose their power. No moon that shines with borrowed light, or meteors that dazzle but never guide, can turn the needle of one's purpose from God's ultimate "north." It is perfectly astounding how undreamed of mental and spiritual faculties rush to our assistance when once we have committed our whole soul to one unwavering aim.

Life may be long or filled with breadth, but it becomes monotonous if it is meaningless and unmagnetized; it is not monotonous however if it is truly gripped by divine purpose. We must see then how these following three things are so important in our moving toward full stature of purpose. We must discover:

why *goals are imperative*
why *some goals have no drawing power*
how *to keep all immediate goals in line*
with THE ULTIMATE GOAL.

Now by way of contrast, think of human personality as we so often see it around us, lacking in definite focus and in the supporting energy of accomplishment. When some little problem develops, magnetism loses its charge and permits the compass needle to jump around and divert to another attraction. If any one of a thousand little upsets come along this needle deserts its star to follow whatever new interest is knocking at its door. Thus when there is no focused goal or gripping over-all purpose, people generally concentrate on motion. Instead of working toward an ideal they keep changing the ideal and call it "progress." They do not know where they are going, but they are certainly "on their way."

They are so much like a sculptor who after hacking and cutting away at a block of marble all day was asked: "What are you making?"

He said, "I really don't know. I have not seen the plan!" No wonder he was bored, frustrated and the day was filled with emptiness.

Many people live ten, twenty, thirty and fifty years without an overmastering purpose. No wonder they find their existence humdrum and tiresome. If they were farmers, they would probably plant wheat one week, root it up and plant barley the next; then dig up the barley and plant watermelon; then dig up the watermelon another week and plant oats. Fall comes around and they have no harvest. If they repeated this process year after year, wouldn't they be considered insane? Yet it is this very meaninglessness of life that produces our present neurosis even in the lives of believers who are governed by an *escape philosophy* instead of being dedicated to a *life of divine fulfillment*.

All around us mass boredom is leading to revolution. A boy is given a BB gun. If the father gives him a target—a bull's eye on the side of a barn, or even an old tin can—the boy is happy to use his gun as it ought to be used. Yet if no target is given, or if it is ignored, the lad soon begins shooting at anything — particularly school windows. The revolutionary spirit in the world today is not confined to underprivileged nations seeking independence, to the colored folk demanding their rights, or to juvenile delinquents without direction or purpose. It is running like a deep undercurrent through all the churches—fundamental and otherwise. This revolutionary spirit is born of purposeless and meaningless existence. Lawlessness lays hold of those who are not properly occupied.

I like this homely bit of proof: "A university kept dogs for experimental purposes in two separate cages. In one cage were dogs without fleas; in the other cage were dogs with fleas, waiting to be dipped and defleaded. The professor noted the latter dogs had something to keep them busy. The other dogs howled and barked and in general created many problems of canine delinquency. The scientists concluded that animals are made to expend purposeful energy. The restlessness of the flealess dogs was a kind of regulatory mechanism for keeping the organism fit. In the higher realm, man's powers are directed to the expenditure of energy for an over-all purpose. If he lacks purpose, giddiness, restlessness and consequent boredom are the price he has to pay. The most bored people in life are not the underprivileged but the overprivileged. The moral is not to have fleas, annoyances or problems. The moral is to have something to live for, not for just today and tomorrow, *but always*. Man is so constituted that he must not only have goals, but goals that are imperative and worthy of his being as man.

What then, is the reason some goals have no drawing power? What we are in our inner being determines what we live for and are responsive to. Until our appetite is changed our desires and goals will not change. It is not new goals, but a new nature that we need. In explaining the "low state of affairs" among even "the evangelical wing of the church" the late A.W. Tozer cried out against changing our religious menus when we should be changing our appetites. He explained the obvious boredom in church like this:

"... boredom comes when a man must try to hear with relish what for want of relish he hardly hears at all.... By this definition there is certainly much boredom in religion these days. The business man on a Sunday morning whose mind is on golf can scarcely disguise his lack of interest in the sermon he is compelled to hear. The housewife who is unacquainted with the learned theological or philosophical jargon of the speaker; the young couple who feel a tingle of love for each other but who neither love nor know the One about whom the choir is singing— these cannot escape the low-grade mental pain we call boredom while they struggle to keep their attention focused upon the service. All these are too courteous to admit to others that they are bored and possibly too timid to admit it even to themselves, but I believe that a bit of candid confession would do us all good." [5]

But why all this emptiness and artificiality? It is simply that we have tried to change our minds without having a change of heart or nature. The New Testament standard of conversion demands regeneration—and this we have largely missed in our man-centered appeal for decisions. It is true the religious vocabulary is used, but one essential has been by-passed. God cannot change the heart and nature where there has been no governmental change—*no turning from our own lordship to His lordship*. With a true change of government comes a change of purpose and appetite. Instead of seeking to use God for one's *own purpose* this means giving one's being to Him for *His purpose*. In this crisis of giving ourselves unto Him, God begins the impartation of His own divine nature, and our responses change accordingly.

As long as man still desires *things*, he cannot be satisfied with *just God.* Was it not so with Abram? God had first offered to give him Canaan land, to make of him a great nation, to bless him and make his name great. How responsive was Abram to all this? He forsook his homeland and in due time left his father. But it was not until Abram had deliberately refused to take the spoil of battle that God could move in to announce to him: Abram, "I am thy exceeding great reward" (Gen. 15:1).

Here is our lesson. Until God changed Abram's inner desires and helped him to say, "I will not take any thing lest thou shouldest say I have made Abram rich"; what would it have meant to him to offer Himself as an exceeding great reward? God's way then is to change our inner being—to make us partakers of the divine nature so we will have an appetite for spiritual things. God does not change goals to fit our appetite, but works upon our inner being that we might truly come to have a hunger for God for Himself.

Until that inner change has been wrought, all religious life is completely exteriorized. Those who have no longing for God Himself, become preoccupied with things and events—nor can they understand or appreciate the songwriter's depth of meaning in the following lines:

> "My goal is God, Himself, not joy or peace,
> Not even blessing, but Himself my God."

It appears then, there are two reasons some goals seem to have no drawing power: what we *are* determines what we enjoy. God's goal can have no real appeal to us until we are in harmony with His nature and being. Our perverted nature must be exchanged for His divine nature before we can find His goal fully satisfying. Furthermore, man is designed in his inner being for that which is ultimate. Any lesser goal will only partially and temporarily satisfy. Man is made for an increasing measure of satisfaction. The inner gnawing will continue until he is fully prepared for that which is ultimate.

A LATE PROPHET HAS WRITTEN:

"It is a law of the human soul that people tend to become like that which they admire most intensely. Deep and long continued admiration can alter the whole texture of the mind and heart and turn the devotee into something quite other than he was before.

"For this reason it is critically important that we Christians should have right models. It is not enough to say that our model should be Christ. While that is true, it is also true that Christ is known mostly through the lives of His professed followers, and the more prominent and vocal these followers are the more powerful will be their influence upon the rank and file of Christians. If the models are imperfect the whole standard of Christian living must suffer as a result.

"A sacred obligation lies upon each of us to be Christlike. This generation of Christians must have models it can safely admire. That is not the primary reason for seeking to be holy, but it is a powerful one. Many beginners are taking us for their examples. Later they will become detached from us and will learn to fix their eyes directly upon the Lord Himself; in the meantime, for better or for worse we are their idea of what Christ is like. This is a wonderful and a frightening fact that we must face and deal with as we may." (A.W.T.) [6]

KNOWING GOD'S
HIGHEST EXPECTATION

IT IS HARDLY necessary to emphasize that one cannot reach his destination until he knows where he is going; similarly one cannot expect any sense of satisfaction in fulfilling his divine calling if he does not clearly understand what it is. Let us settle one thing right off: we can know – clearly know – our call-

<u>ing.</u> <u>God expects us to know.</u>

First we know that God has already dedicated every created thing in His universe to fulfill some distinct purpose. We look around us at the three lower kingdoms, the mineral, vegetable and animal and ask what was God's purpose in creating these? Perhaps the most simple answer is to describe all inanimate creation as a glove in which God will place His hand to reveal and express Himself. All is designed as a means by which He may fill the whole universe – give it shape and meaning; purpose and warmth – give it everything! What a glove is to a hand, so creation is to the Creator.

Now if this is the glorious calling for these lower kingdoms, just what is God's high calling for man? It is true that these lower kingdoms must necessarily respond to Him, for whom they are made. But when we come to the higher kingdom of man, God has a much higher intention for him. By granting man the moral faculties of mind, will and emotions man can voluntarily cooperate in this glorious calling. For this reason man is lifted far above the rest of creation, and through him there can be a more glorious expression of *who* and *what* God really is. It is this very fact that makes it quite inadequate to speak of man as a mere glove; he is a living personality who is called to extol, to magnify, to express the glorious attributes and qualities of the Divine Personality.

While it is true that things without personality hardly seem adequate figures of speech in expressing personality, yet even in His Word, God has often used a metaphor to illustrate some special characteristic in a very rich way. Man is pictured as a sheep in the fold, as a branch in the vine, as a living stone in the building. So throughout this writing we have sought to show how man in full stature is like a building with its foundation and many levels. Since the Apostle Paul often pictured man as a temple or building (Eph. 2:21,22; 1 Cor. 6:19,20) surely we are on safe ground. As we move along in this unfolding of full stature, we shall see how God is working and how man is cooperating to produce this glorious building – individually and corporately.

Now let us see how exactly God has shown us His highest expectation in full stature. We have been given not only THE PATTERN, but many patterns as the revelation of God.

In considering the diagram, imagine we are looking through a long tunnel, back–back into the very heart of God. What do we see? It is by the light of the Spirit that we may look at the

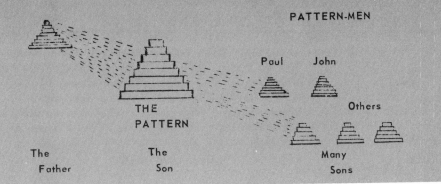

Paul   John

THE
PATTERN

Others

The   The   Many
Father   Son   Sons

Eternal Son, but even more: He becomes the window through which we behold the Eternal Father.

With what delight we behold the Son – but even more to see Christ in many sons who are being conformed to His image! We can better understand Who is calling us. He, the Initiator of our glorious calling, has called us to be like Himself: "Be ye holy (complete, whole, full) even as I am holy."

In the Lord Jesus we have the visible representation of what the Father expects. For no one has seen THE FATHER except as He has been revealed in THE SON. Thus we hear the Father announcing that if anyone would have THE PATTERN for measuring stature, they must measure by THE SON. Before the beginning, the Father planned and purposed that in Him dwells the fullness of the Godhead bodily – to Him belongs the pre-eminence and the centrality. This is the brilliant light which broke in upon Martin Luther when he was seeking to know more of the Father. In his biography of him, D'Aubigne explains how Luther would have "wished to penetrate into the secret counsels of God, to unveil His mysteries, to see the invisible and comprehend the incomprehensible." Then we are told that Stupitz checked him. He insisted that Luther should not "presume to fathom the hidden God, but confine himself to what He had manifested to us in Jesus Christ. In Him, God has said, you will find what I am and what I require. Nowhere else, neither in heaven nor in earth will you discover it."

So it is to THE SON and His *centrality* that our attention is fixed, showing us the Father's highest expectation in moving us unto full stature. In THE LORD JESUS we see all we need to know or understand about FULL STATURE. Yet we must be sure that we have really *seen* Him as the Holy Spirit would unveil Him to us.

Now acknowledging the Lord Jesus as THE PATTERN of *full stature* is sure to enjoy unanimous agreement. Throughout God's Word there are so many places we are told to be "like Him" or "as Him" that we need simply make the statement. He is indeed THE PATTERN – God's highest expression and expectation in full stature. Yet the very fact of using Him as THE PATTERN will serve as a block in some minds. The insistence that He was God manifest in the flesh causes many to falsely imagine that He assumed powers or advantages which are not available to others. For this reason, He is THE PATTERN in only an idealistic sense for the vast majority in Christendom – so they reason, and thus they find excuse for their below-par living. Plead as we might; argue as we will; He is nevertheless considered as Someone too high for humanity to seriously accept as THE PATTERN for measuring what they should become or for measuring how far short they might fall.

Perhaps for this very reason God has so often emphasized that He has given Paul as A PATTERN. We are left without any hiding place, for in Paul we have been given a real demonstration of what can be realized in any man who will allow God. In Paul we see the *adequacy* of the Holy Spirit to bring us to that glorious full stature God intends.

Even at the risk of being misunderstood, I would like to suggest that, while Paul knew he was not THE PATTERN, yet he was sure God had given him as A PATTERN of what He intended to do in others. For this reason he dared to say:

"Brethren, together follow my example and observe those who live after THE PATTERN WE HAVE SET YOU" (Phil. 3:17).

He seemed to discern with divine insight that God was intending to make a glorious demonstration through him, so he writes to Timothy: "... for this cause I obtained mercy, that in me first Jesus Christ might show forth all longsuffering, FOR A PATTERN to them which should hereafter believe..." (1 Tim. 1:16).

Here is a man who indeed was flesh and blood – even as we. He leaves us without excuse. Who can deny that he experienced those very real temptations and pressures which also plague our very tracks? In this hour when it is common to urge others to "keep your eyes upon the Lord–only" (and perhaps in the present low level of vision and stature this is good advice), does it not seem a unique thing for Paul to declare he is A PATTERN and encourage others to follow in his tracks?

"Those things, which ye have both learned, and received, and heard, and seen in me, do: and the God of peace be with you" (Phil. 4:9).

How this boldness reveals us and magnifies the confidence of the Apostle. I must admit that for years I have – along with most everyone else – exhorted folk to "keep their eyes upon Christ as the only worthy example and pattern." Yet I have come to a new understanding of what Paul meant and the lesson it can be to us. Paul is not glorying in what he is in himself. It was not that Paul was perfect or that he had even reached that ultimate measure of full stature. No, it was only that he could be the glorious expression of the Lord. He knew that the Holy Spirit had revealed the Lord Jesus *to him,* but even more, had formed Christ *within him* to such an extent that now He could manifest Himself *through him.* This is the secret of such boldness! What glory this would mean for God! That the Holy Spirit was fully *adequate* to reveal Christ through any vessel wholly yielded to Him. So (in the diagram) we have pictured two things: how we must see Christ reflected in others, and how we must also reveal Christ to others.

BUT WE ARE ALSO TO BE PATTERNS

When the mother reprimanded her little son for something he had done, how quickly he replied: "But Daddy does it!" No wonder the father wilted.

Have you ever considered how differently you act or react when you know others are gazing intently upon you—especially when you have become the apple of their eye or the example they will follow! It is no wonder so many are wanting to turn eyes away from themselves and their short stature.

The issue is really this: Either we shall be content to fit into the "common image" and relax in the anonymity it allows— thus avoid becoming any special example—or we shall accept God's call to be His man, daring to be AN EXAMPLE knowing full well that such a position does not need to invite other's attention, for it automatically attracts attention. How the average congregation dislikes anyone who dares to be a *full twelve inch ruler* so as to uncover their mere eight inch stature. Every gun is trained upon that individual who dares to deliberately be A PATTERN FOR GOD.

But this is exactly what Paul encouraged young Timothy to

become: "Let no man despise thy youth; but be thou AN EX-
AMPLE of the believers, in word, in conversation, in charity,
in spirit, in faith, in purity" (1 Tim. 4:12).

He further adds: "Meditate upon these things; give thyself
wholly to them; that THY PROFITING MAY APPEAR TO ALL "
(vs. 15). Others will surely observe as one grows in wisdom and
knowledge.

Again we have a similar word to Titus: "In all things shewing
thyself a PATTERN OF GOOD WORKS: in doctrine shewing un-
corruptness, gravity, sincerity, sound speech, that cannot be
condemned; that he that is of the contrary part may be ashamed,
having no evil thing to say of you" (Titus 2:7,8).

But Paul is also speaking to each of us! His exhortation
confronts us squarely. How much do we desire God to accomplish
full stature in us? Are we ready to embrace as did Paul the
divine purpose, pull and priority which will make this a living
reality within us?

We can see why Paul is God's pattern-man. As *A MAN OF
PURPOSE* he says: "[For my determined purpose is] that I may
know Him—that I may progressively become more deeply and inti-
mately acquainted with Him, perceiving and recognizing and
understanding [the wonders of His person] more clearly" (Phil.
3:10 A.N.T.).

In Paul we see *A MAN WITH DIVINE PULL*. "Not that I have
now attained [this ideal] or am already made perfect [of full
stature] but I press to lay hold of (grasp) and make my own, that
for which Christ Jesus ... has laid hold of me *and* made me His
own" (Phil. 3:12 A.N.T.). He who has seen with Paul will know
this divine pull — allowing God to realize through him His glorious purpose.

In Paul we see *A MAN WITH SINGLE PRIORITY*. "... but
one thing I do—it is my aspiration: forgetting what lies behind
and straining forward to what lies ahead, I press on toward the
goal to win the [supreme and heavenly] prize to which God in
Christ Jesus is calling us upward" (Phil. 3:13,14 A.N.T.).

Finally we have the Apostle's yardstick for encouraging
everyone to FULL STATURE: "So let those of us who are
spiritually mature and full-grown (i.e. of full stature) have this
mind and hold these convictions, and if in any respect you have
a different attitude of mind, God will make this clear to you
also." So speaks the one whom God has set as our pattern man:
"Brethren, together follow my example and observe those who

live AFTER THE PATTERN WE HAVE SET FOR YOU" (Phil. 3:17).

It is God's desire that as we look at Paul and others who are patterns—we see our lovely Lord, and in seeing the Lord Jesus we see the Father. We have looked through the long tunnel back—way back to see THE FATHER—the *ultimate pattern* of what we are called to be like; we have looked through THE SON who is given as the *Central Pattern,* but we have seen Him in the Apostle Paul and others who are intended as visible patterns revealing Christ. What a glorious demonstration of the *adequacy* of the Holy Spirit to accomplish this in everyone.

So it is not in Paul or in any man that we can glory, but rather in the God who can so apprehend a man for Himself that He can fully transform and conform that human vessel into a real measure of FULL STATURE — thus expressing Himself before mankind.

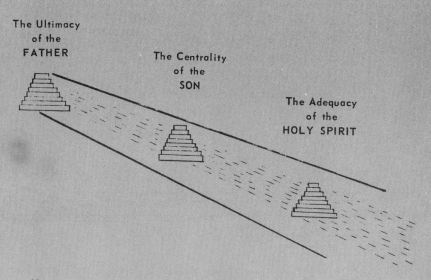

The Ultimacy
of the
FATHER

The Centrality
of the
SON

The Adequacy
of the
HOLY SPIRIT

If we have ever really "seen" what the Father purposes . . . . .
If we have ever really "seen" what the Son promises . . . . .
If we have ever really "seen" the uttermost adequacy of the Holy Spirit to provide . . . .
Then we shall also "see" how our calling UNTO FULL STATURE will surely become a glorious realization.

"Today the glaring weakness in Christian service is that many who know they are THE CALLED have become contented; they have stopped short of fulfilling their HIGH CALLING. Among other things there is this essential reason why so many have settled down in some byway and become unusable: They have been prone to look at the spiritual achievements of others and to compare them with their own meager efforts. To such I give this word of warning: *Beware of jealousy, beware of imitating, beware of comparing.* These three can become such cinders in the eye as to blind one from truly following that unique calling God has for his own life."

Of course it is safe to look at Paul. It would seem God intended not merely that Paul's conversion become a pattern, but also that the whole course of his ministry should be a demonstration of one who is gripped by divine purpose, pull and priority. It is our primary thesis in this book that no one can truly arrive at any real measure of FULL STATURE until he has recognized God's progressive calling.

IN PAUL WE SEE
THREE PHASES OF
THE PROGRESSIVE CALLING

ONE SUNDAY NIGHT as I returned from speaking I tuned in the radio just in time to hear the familiar voice of Dr. Charles Fuller say: "Now take your Bible and turn with me to the first verse in Romans." In the ten or more years since that night I have forgotten most of what he said except for this three-fold division of that first verse. Many times it has been helpful in directing others to see God's progressive calling for their life. Through Paul's own testimony, in this one verse, we learn that we are not only THE CALLED, but we are ever BEING CALLED.

> Paul, a bondman of Christ — the general calling,
> Called, to be an apostle — the special calling,
> Separated unto the gospel — the specific calling.

Just as Paul's divine calling passes through three main phases, so will ours. It will become clear how this is God's way to bring each life step by step into the unfolding purpose as we move toward our high calling.

1. *First, the general calling comes to everyone.* We are called to be bondmen—to be love slaves who have given up our own rights and gladly accepted a *new* Lord. Yet we wonder how many really understand. It is one thing to recognize that we are "the called according to His purpose"—which means we have been positionally taken out of the kingdom of darkness and have been planted into the Body of Christ (the ecclesia). It is yet another thing to understand and live in this calling. There are too many who glory that they are *the called*, yet who sense little of the present continuous "calling" which means a living *relationship*.

That day on the Damacus road, Paul became one of *the called*. In God's eternal reckoning this calling had already taken place. By special insight Paul was soon to refer to this fact-in-eternity saying, he was "Separated from his mother's womb." Thus he gave God's viewpoint. Yet in his own point of time-reckoning we hear Paul's response to that calling when finally he cries out, "Who art thou Lord?" and "Lord, what wilt thou

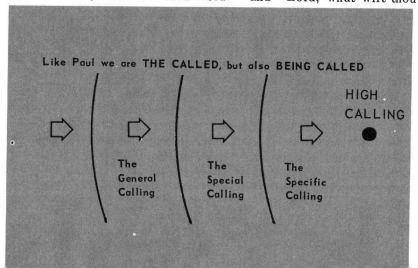

Like Paul we are THE CALLED, but also BEING CALLED

HIGH CALLING

The General Calling

The Special Calling

The Specific Calling

have me to do?"

Here we see something quite different about Paul's conversion —and why he becomes a pattern for us today. Through Paul's conversion we see that God's highest concern was man's presenting his whole being unto God for His purpose and pleasure. This was always typified in the whole burnt offering. From Adam to Moses, we see Abel, Noah, Job and Abraham presented the whole burnt offering which typified their utter dedication unto God. There was no mention of the sin offering until given by Moses to the children of Israel.

It would seem too many have been prone to emphasize the sin offering while they neglect the whole burnt offering. They desire forgiveness *from God* before they know a real relationship *with God*. We must keep this straight: Relationship as pictured in the whole burnt offering must precede fellowship—as pictured in the sin offering. It was to His people Israel, who were already in covenant relationship, that God provided through Moses the five offerings as a means not of relationship, but to insure more intimate fellowship.

For this reason it is important to see how Paul was—so to speak—born with dedication overshadowing. With him it was not forgiveness, fellowship, peace, joy, blessing or security he could get from God. Immediately he was asking, "What can I do, Lord, for You?" His was not merely a turning from sin, but a full-length turning *"unto God"* for His pleasure and glory. With Paul, conversion meant *giving himself* "as the whole burnt offering." How different is this from the usual level of modern-day conversions—where the emphasis is on the sin offering—picturing the forgiveness, pardon and cleansing which man *gets*. We must cease emphasizing fellowship before relationship.

We cannot help insisting that here is the basic essential in Paul's moving UNTO FULL STATURE and so will it be with us when we more fully understand this pattern-man. Here in Paul's crisis awakening, *dedication unto God* is the one distinctive feature God would have us notice. Too often we have missed God's normal intention for conversion because we have confused the offerings. Do we not see in Abel, Noah, Job and Abraham that God's first order was the whole burnt offering? It was because they had a deep inner sense of missing God's purpose and glory that they came to present themselves in utter dedication unto Him.

Today we are reaping a harvest of man-centered conversions (?) because we are more concerned for man than for God. Our modern emphasis demonstrates clearly whom we are most interested in—it is God serving man instead of man serving God.

In the light of this we can see how the conversion of both Abraham and Paul emphasizes *giving unto God* for the fulfillment of His purpose. Just here is the great difference between Paul and the usual convert today. Immediately Paul seems alive to what it means to be a bond-slave of the Lord Jesus. He is born awake to this *general calling*. Alas, this is not so with the vast majority of converts today. It is true they may emphasize service, yet they really think in terms of aligning God with their own secret ambitions of achieving great things for Him. They are more alive to successful service and zealous *working for God* than to devotion: which is *"dwelling with God* for His work."

Thus it is often many years before they are awakened to really see what it means to become a loving bondman and thus to really take the first steps in their *general calling*. Nor should we confuse the issue in assuming that this general calling is just for preachers, missionaries or full-time workers. The calling to be a bondman is God's (general) calling for everyone.

While many speak of being God's servants, they have usually missed what is meant in being "bondmen." In the Old Testament there were two classes of servants: the hired servant and the bondman. The bondman had no rights, had no recourse when wronged and received no remuneration for his labors; whereas the hired servant could enjoy all these rights. The Hebrew people were forbidden to become bond-slaves to each other; however they did take conquered peoples from other nations and make bondmen of them.

In the New Testament the picture seems to change. What amazing disclosure we have when Paul casts aside this prohibition and refers not only to his own relationship as a bondman, but Philippians chapter 2 presents the Lord Jesus as the great example of a Bondman. He explains how the Lord Jesus deliberately laid aside His rights in heaven, stooped to becoming a man. But even more, He "made Himself of no reputation and took upon Himself the form of a Bondman."

Is there any question as to how God might use us as bondmen? Here is the method often hidden from our view. We are not primarily called *to doing* but rather *to being*. It is when we will *be*

in His hands that we are made useable. We see this in both Paul
and the Lord Jesus. It was because our Lord was willing *to be* a
bondman that "He was made..." (Phil. 2:7). We see the same
pattern in Paul's testimony where he insists: "I have made
myself a bond servant..." (I Cor. 9:19 A.N.T.). Then a few
verses later we read how God "made him all things to all men."
This is God's way! It is not so much our working as His working
through us. When we choose *to be* then we *are made.* Oh that
God's children could understand this *being* instead of *doing.* To
be as broken bread in His hand, *to be made* food for the hungry,
water for the thirsty, light for the darkened. This is God working.
Once our eyes have been turned from all our *doing* we know what
it means *to be*—then we shall *be made* useable. Until this happens
we are merely involved with our *working for the Lord.* We have
almost missed that spiritual ministry which comes when *our
Lord does the working through us.*

   Second, how do we move into the special calling? Because
Paul had qualified and proved himself in the general calling as
a bondman, God could move him into the next phase: the *special
calling.* Many have assumed that Paul immediately rushed into
an active traveling ministry. Perhaps they have allowed their
imagination or wishful thinking to color, but it seems quite un-
likely that Paul reached out very far immediately after his conversion. First he developed his gift as a teacher and fulfilled
his ministry in the church at Antioch. A man wholly *under authority* would not rush out until he had been *sent.* Who could imagine
anyone moving forth without a word from God?
   Yet how many today have confused their calling with their
sending forth. *They* take the initiative instead of allowing God.
It would be good, yes, according to divine order, for every young
man to have a similar opportunity, as did Paul, in a New Testament church like that at Antioch. Then God, who alone knows
when a life and gift are prepared and developed for more exten-
sive ministry, will awaken the individual's inner awareness as
well as the local brethren, and in that hour of divine unfolding
will speak definitely by the Holy Ghost.
   This is the pattern we discover in the record found in Acts
13:2: "As they ministered to the Lord...the Holy Ghost said,
Separate me Barnabas and Saul for the work whereunto I have
called them." When God's order is followed and He is allowed
His sovereign place in the local church and in the individual's

life there is no premature "putting oneself into the ministry."

We do not know, but it seems likely that God had already been preparing the heart of Paul and Barnabas and this was simply a time of outward recognition by the brethren that they were now being set apart for a more special ministry. So they were *sent forth* with divine approval and direction as special messengers in founding and planting new churches.

Is the reader inwardly yearning for fuller stature in his own life and ministry? You know that God has some unique and special calling to fulfill through you? Does the "deep" within your breast keep calling out to the "deep" within God? Then here is the most crucial issue you must face: do not become anxious and rush out before you are sent. There is in almost every awakened believer this deep inner sense of "being called," yet there is the difficult winepress wherein we are learning to be bondmen. To seek to escape this inner preparation is to invite sure failure and fainting down the road. Could this be the reason John Mark was disqualified in the hour of severe testing? If Paul is truly our pattern-man we should recognize that he did not run until he was sent.

Again from the insight we have into Isaiah's life we know (from chapter one) that he sensed a divine calling to help Israel. Yet as God's called vessel, he did not run until (according to chapter six) he was duly prepared and sent.

It is quite natural for one to look at some chosen vessel who has truly known God's preparation, setting apart and sending forth and wish he could move into his own special calling. But he would like to escape the qualifying in the general phase. Perhaps this explains the thousands of frustrated Christian workers who have fainted along the way. Because of the modern misconception of God's pattern, many are thrust into pushing programs not wholly in tune with God's methods and are exhausting their self-energy until they give up with ulcers or broken health—finally languishing as disappointed shipwrecks.

What is the fatal mistake in this hour? Men see a very real need and they run to fill it. They hear emotional stories from men who have learned the art of moving others, although they themselves have not been moved to give all. They are not wrong in wanting to help the multitudes dying in darkened fields around the world. They simply have not realized that seeing a need does not constitute a sending forth.

God's way is for Isaiah to move in so close to God's aching heart that it will soon become one with His own throbbing heart. This only comes by living in His vision and dwelling with Him. And whoever will get that close to Him will surely hear the Lord saying, "Who will go for me?" Then from the union of vision and purpose, of passion and priority, will come the glad-heart response, "Lord, send me...." Thus in God's own time and way He will anoint another Isaiah and prepare another Paul and send them forth to His people. Such a one will surely know he has heard his Lord speak, not merely the challenging voice of a man. Nothing will stop him, neither shipwreck, suffering, persecution, hardship nor death.

So it is by God's initiative—yet man's qualifying—that one moves from the general to the special phase of his calling. Apart from God's special grace, who could withstand the rigorous pressure and privation that any special calling will entail? No one who has not first been proven as a bondman would continually face the sharp attack of the Enemy, nor long endure unless he has the seal of divine approval.

Thus Paul moves out in his apostolic calling. In God's intention Paul must become the sharp point of the phalanx, must face the bitter reproach and offense of the Cross in pioneering new fields. Once a local teacher he now becomes a teacher-at-large, not merely speaking forth words, but himself embodying the very message he declares. Many will enjoy the benefits of his ministry, yet seek to shun the One who has wrought the benefit in their life.

What travail of soul to be misunderstood not only by the very churches you have founded, but even by the associates you have nurtured. Who will long embrace this special ministry and not faint unless he has seen what God sees—been gripped by that larger purpose? Paul had *seen* and understood, so he could remind them: "...ye are full, now ye are rich, ye have reigned as kings without us; and I would to God ye did reign, that we also might reign with you" (I Cor. 4:8).

Paul knew someone must bear the brunt in battle. "For I think that God hath set forth us the apostles last, as it were appointed to death: for we are made a spectacle unto the world, and to angels, and to men. We are fools for Christ's sake, but ye are wise in Christ; we are weak, but ye are strong; ye are honourable, but we are despised. Even unto this present hour we both hunger, and thirst, and are naked, and are buffeted, and have no certain dwellingplace; And labour, working with our own hands: being reviled, we bless; being persecuted, we suffer it: Being defamed, we entreat: we are made as the filth of the world, and are the offscouring of all things unto this day" (I Cor. 4:9-13).

If this is what is involved in a special calling, who is interested? Without divine constrainment no one would long continue. But someone will insist, "This is only for apostles. What is now our calling?" Let us not be too sure, lest our own kind of special ministry will also include a peculiar kind of misunderstanding, reproach, loneliness and perhaps no certain dwelling place. Only he who has, without reservation, been overmastered by a divine destiny-consciousness will endure in this arena of hardship. But when he does, God can move him *into* and *on through* the special calling into the specific calling uniquely prepared for him alone.

Could we look back—many miles back—where the pathway is still crowded with "would-be experts" and "hope-to-be successfuls" we would see those who, with secret envy, cast their eyes toward the high calling. They behold those who have poured out their lives and reputations in fulfilling their special calling. How they long to reach that same measure of "useableness" but they cannot, for they will not honestly face what it costs to be a bondman. They cannot accept a life with no "rights."

Apart from gladly embracing such a life, there can be no inward preparation for their specific calling. Alas, the byways are filled with the disappointed who have only themselves to blame. They have become "disapproved" (not in salvation, but in their ministry) because they wanted only an outward cross and not an *inwrought* cross. Now let us move on to see how Paul reached that specific thing for which God had marked him out. Thus shall we understand Paul's high calling — and ours.

WE HAVE PONDERED at great length why God's servants so often settled down short of the high calling. Many will not embrace even the *general* calling as a bondslave; others will not move on to their *special* calling in exercising the spiritual gifts which become a life-ministry through them; but how very few go on to fulfill their *specific* calling which we shall now consider.

It would seem many can be illustrated by the three men who were shoveling dirt on the side of a road. A passerby asked what they were doing.

"I'm digging a ditch," the first said.

"I'm making a foundation," said the second.

The third laborer was of a different breed. "I'm building a cathedral," he answered. It is quite true that the servant who is merely digging a ditch for God is quite apt to become weary as a bondslave. Or if he has no further vision than making a foundation, he is apt to falter. It is the one who has *seen* with God that wondrous building for the eternal habitation of God who will be carried along by . . . .

THE GLORY OF
THE HIGH CALLING!

AM SURE ONLY GOD knows how and when to encourage and enlarge our vision that we might behold a little greater measure of the glory of our high calling. Will you indulge me a very personal incident? I recall such an hour more than ten years ago when, on a Sunday morning, I was privileged to sit in the congregation of a large college church in the Twin Cities.

As the pastor, whom I had not known, arose to share his message, he said, "This week I have been gripped by a book and in my own words I want to pass on what I've seen of the vision and heart throb of the Apostle Paul. I want us to see what it was that helped him to live in the stream of God's Eternal Purpose."

I thought surely this man is echoing my own heart. I wonder

what book that is? Then as he proceeded, I recognized the illustrations, the outline and certain precise words. Yes, I did know that book!

When the service was over and I greeted the pastor at the door, I thanked him for God's word to our hearts and the evident anointing in his ministry. But as I was about to leave, some close friends rushed up—"Oh pastor," they announced, "We want you to meet our friend." Then it happened!

He recognized my name. "Could you be the author of the book I referred to this morning?" My heart was so full I could only nod and assured him the morning service had been a most precious time in which God had encouraged my heart. We can hardly know just how God's truth can flow on and on from one life to another like a stream always building His spiritual house.

Now I have related this incident simply as a means of showing something God began in my heart and has been enlarging ever since. That morning as the pastor spoke I saw the glory of being a *spiritual father*. The stream of life which flows out from God's own being through our being is a never ending stream, as it will touch lives throughout the ages to come. I saw how Paul had the unspeakable joy of multiplying, imparting and extending his own spiritual life and vision to others who would likewise continue the stream. What greater joy could one know than being a spiritual father through whom our Heavenly Father could pass on reality from Himself to others?

If I was inwardly rejoicing in being able to share with this pastor—that he might share with his people—this was indeed but a foretaste of what God longed to realize in greater measure through every life. As I listened, it was most evident to me that this pastor was more vocal in expression and more adept in translating the meaning which I felt—but could not articulate so well. One thing I knew: Every man has his own unique calling to beget his own spirit, vision, intensity and dedication to others. Here was a pastor who was possessed; he was gripped and manifestly moving by divine inspiration to "beget himself in others."

While I had thought I was living and breathing the vision and spirit of the Apostle Paul, here was something much deeper — an insight into Paul's spiritual fatherhood. Indeed he was a love slave poured out, an apostle hazarding his life to found churches, but above all else he was a spiritual father who has been extending himself down through the centuries.

How often I had questioned, along with others, what is that HIGH CALLING which Paul presses for in Philippians 3:14: "I press toward the mark for the prize of the HIGH CALLING of God in Christ Jesus."? In one sense that high calling is very different for every life, but yet it is the same. It is far more than being a dedicated doctor, a missionary, a minister, a nurse or an apostle. These are but the special doorways which lead to the specific calling—when a doctor projects himself as a spiritual father, a minister begets himself in lives as a spiritual father, etc. It is in the measure that we have truly become a son in full stature "unto Him" that we shall share God's Father-heart and become a representative "for Him."

For millions Paul has continued to live. His vision, purpose, spirit, attitude and dedication are one with the divine stream of the Spirit flowing on to us. In his letters to the churches we see an amazing extension of himself into every believer and every church even down to this very hour. One need only allow the Holy Spirit to quicken Paul's writings and he immediately senses his groaning and travail, his yearning and prayers, his spirit and motive as he utterly gives himself in the care and nourishment of the churches then, and down to this hour. Surely we are confronted with this question: Can there possibly be any higher, grander or more glorious calling than TO BE A SPIRITUAL FATHER?

WHEN PAUL ENTERED HIS SPECIFIC CALLING

We have already considered how Paul proved himself in his general calling as a bondman and then in his special calling as a sent-messenger (apostle). Now we must see how his apostolic calling was the doorway to his highest calling. Without this qualifying and preparation he could not have been promoted to his specific calling – a spiritual father of the Church. From a traveling ministry he was to be shut up behind prison bars. What could God possibly have in this? Who could accept what seemed like banishment from active ministry, unless in it he sees God's hand to accomplish something greater for Himself?

Yet without this "shutting up, and away" there could be no fulfilling of that specific thing for which God had marked him out. He was "separated unto the gospel of God." But what was so distinctive about this gospel which God was to reveal through Paul? He explains it thus:

"Now to him that is of power to stablish you according to my

gospel, and the preaching of Jesus Christ, according to the revelation of the mystery..." (Rom. 16:25).

"For this reason, I, Paul the prisoner of Jesus Christ for the
sake of you, the Gentiles – for I suppose you have heard of the
dispensation of the grace of God that was given to me in your
regard; how that by revelation was made known unto me the
mystery...which in other ages was not made known..." (Eph.
3:1-5 Con. Tr.).

For many in that day, imprisonment must have seemed like
the finis to Paul's ministry. Only now, in the light of the inter-
vening years, can we properly appreciate how God has something
greater for Paul than perhaps even he could imagine. From his
prison cell flows the letters by which a spiritual father will
instruct and nourish the churches. What an extension of himself
– flowing on and on through every century into every church,
even down to this present age. *This is the glory of fulfilling our
high calling as a spiritual father.*

And there were others of the apostles whose ministry continues to us. Consider how Peter moves into his specific calling,
and as a spiritual father writes to the circumcision scattered
throughout the world. Or look at the Beloved John. Though
banished to the lonely Isle of Patmos, yet it was there that God
had separated him unto the glorious REVELATION which has
become the last book of our canon. Thus Paul, Peter and John
live on and extend themselves into *living* epistles in every
generation.

What we are saying is that as one enters that specific phase

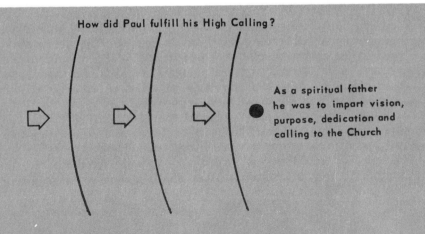

How did Paul fulfill his High Calling?

As a spiritual father
he was to impart vision,
purpose, dedication and
calling to the Church

to fulfill his *high calling*, he will above all be a spiritual father who extends himself into others. The more he senses that reproductive power, that pull and priority, the more he will, like Paul, reflect the Lord Jesus.

There is no other way to explain Paul's writing. Had he not been responsible for their (the Corinthians) begetting? Then surely he has a right to remind them: "...though ye have ten thousand instructors in Christ, yet have ye not many fathers; for in Christ Jesus I have begotten you through the gospel."

In his second letter to them he expresses his largeness of heart as a spiritual father: "I speak as unto my children." I am your father, you are my children; so you ought to be like your father. "...now for a recompense in like kind be ye enlarged." What he means is, since I have a big heart to you, if you are my true children then you will have a big heart back to me—you will respond in like kind.

Again we sense Paul's father-heart for his spiritual children as he writes to the Galatians. No spiritual father could beget a household of children then forget them. Even a bird does not hatch a nest of eggs and fly off, as some Christian workers are prone to do. Paul's father-heart seems ever watchful for their growth and writes: "My little children, of whom I travail in birth again, until Christ be formed in you."

We are sure Paul deeply sensed this strange and wonderful multiplying power which God imparts to anyone who enters into true fatherhood. It is so manifest as he encourages his friend, Philemon to act as a father toward his returning slave, Onesimus. Here is a true father pleading with another friend to *be* as *a father:* "I beseech thee for my son, Onesimus, whom I have begotten in my bonds."

If to fulfill fatherhood is the high calling, how truly Paul measures up to full stature. May I say it emphatically—the greatest need of the church in this hour is not more teachers, more evangelists, more pastors or more prophets as such, but that these men, above all else, bear the image of *spiritual fathers.* Oh God, give us men who are alive to their high calling.

Finally, what is the "prize of the high calling"? Can you think of anything more noble, more exalting, more satisfying than the joy resultant from a vast family completely expressing our Father God and His Son? Even so — we who are called to cooperate in this ultimate intention shall know the joy resulting from such a participation.

A PASTOR WRITES:

"At last I have found that *balancing truth* which was so long needed to end my frustration. For years I have been torn between *doing* and *being* in my ministry, but the message you shared that morning on our twofold calling as fathers and sons, has brought the rest and confidence which I have been looking for. It seemed for years I would move first toward one extreme and then another. I would launch into a round of activity with frenzied zeal as though God's work all depended upon me — almost as if God were on vacation and had left everything to me. This would last until the Holy Spirit whispered this simple rebuke: 'Salvation is of the Lord.'

"Then I would seem to react to the other extreme. Since all depended on God and nothing I could do would really change God's will, I found myself in a passivity and fatalism tending toward a sovereign determinism. Now God has shown me the place of balance: In Christ there is neither activism or passivism."

I am sure this is one thing which hinders so many from moving unto full stature. There is a prevailing attitude that really "no one can be expected to understand this inner tug-of-war between extremes in our being. Consequently this breeds a general confusion and then indifference."

UNDERSTANDING THE TWO SIDES OF OUR CALLING!

IT IS SAID that the Romans minted a coin which pictured an ox on both sides. On one side the ox stood by an altar with this inscription above: FOR SACRIFICE; and on the other side the ox was yoked to a plough with this inscription above: FOR SERVICE. What a reminder for Rome to give her citizens! That they had the unique privilege and calling to yield themselves *either for sacrifice or for service.*

Now in a similar manner our divine calling also has two sides.

It is important that we understand what we are called to be "for the Father" and what we are to be "unto the Father." It will require just a bit of explanation to help us appreciate this important distinction. On one side of our calling we are to be fathers "for Him"– down here on this earth. But on the other side we are to be sons "unto Him"– who wholly live unto His pleasure, glory and satisfaction.

In the diagram we have pictured the two sides and yet the perfect balance which is necessary in this twofold calling. First, however, let us see how this is unveiled in God's Word.

Surely there is much clearer light dawning in these last days to corroborate these two sides in man. It has been pointed out that many scholars are giving attention to the basic conceptions found in the book of Genesis. One of these conceptions which has attracted considerable interest is the double phrase of Genesis 1:26-27: "...in our image and after our likeness...." What does God intend to convey in this statement? I believe there is much more hidden here than we have usually recognized.

In the translation of F. Fenton we have a little fuller light on this verse as he translates it: "God then said, let us make men under our Shadow, as Our Representatives...." Does this, then, picture our twofold calling and purpose: (1) as sons to be as His shadows and (2) as fathers to be as His representatives?

We conclude that, as a representative for God on the earth, Adam was indeed to act as a father with kingly bearing. He was placed in the Garden to act in God's behalf, perpetuating himself as a father and subduing the whole earth: *"for God."* But in his relationship *"unto God"* Adam was to be a created son who

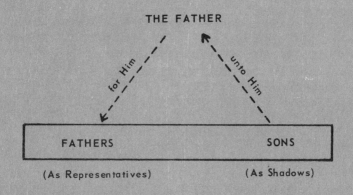

THE FATHER

for Him   unto Him

FATHERS	SONS

(As Representatives)   (As Shadows)

lived unto God. In this position of course a son is like a shadow,
like an image which points unto the Father.

We shall see how in his calling of representative father, man
becomes a leader, a master, a somebody, for he is like the great
Original Father in Heaven. But in the calling of sonship he is
more like the image or shadow of the Father, and his relationship places him in the position of servant, follower or "nobody."
Thus man is to be seen as both a father and a son. For man to
reach that full stature God intends there must be a proper recognition and balance of each aspect.

We have been greatly encouraged by the writings of Dr. Mark
Fakkema who has been led to present a truly God-centered approach to Christian philosophy by showing God's intended
balance between these two aspects in man. As we quote him,
you will recognize that Dr. Fakkema has used the words "original" and "IMAGE" to denote what we have here explained as
the father-aspect and the son-aspect. He writes:

"In creating man like unto Himself, God made him an original
— a "Somebody" who exercises dominion over creation and who
is personally capable of free choice. He also made man to be an
IMAGE—one who reveals God and by so doing he himself becomes a "nobody." As an *original* (a ' Somebody '), man is a
finite copy of the Sovereign Originator and Determinator of all.
As an IMAGE (a ' Nobody '), man is a self-effacing revealer of
God and His attributes."

"Man's 'original' and 'IMAGE' belong together and must be
so interpreted. We unify these two widely different aspects of
man by contending that man is an original-IMAGE of God....
Man was created to be a 'Somebody' who wills to be a 'Nobody'
that God may be all in all. This makes for a blessed union with
God." [7]

As we further consider man's twofold calling: being a father
for Him, and a son *unto Him* — we can see how Christendom has
become divided and two theological camps have arisen with each
emphasizing a different side. The Arminian camp has emphasized
man as a representative — as though he were primarily called to
take dominion, to independently do things for God, to represent
God as a "Somebody" on this earth; while the Calvinist camp
has emphasized man's utter dependence even as a mere shadow
who only shares in the glory as he lives unto God. This has
been simply the submission of a creature to his Sovereign Crea-

tor, not the relationship of a begotten son unto his Father.

There is only one way to understand the Arminian and Calvinist interpretations: that is to see each as the overemphasis of one side to the exclusion of the other. What we most need is a proper basis of harmony or synthesis. Both sides must have their proper place in right order and balance. In the diagram we have pictured the dangers which result from an overemphasis of either side. If man is called only to rule and have dominion as a representative for God, we shall soon have an extreme creature exaltation and arrogant humanism in the saddle. On the other hand, if man is to be considered only as a shadow or image who is helplessly dependent, then we soon have a mere robot and utter fatalism. Neither of these sides when overemphasized gives a true picture of fatherhood or sonship as God intended.

IN CHRIST WE HAVE THE BALANCE

We are sure that only One who walked this earth has ever fully manifested this balance of representing "for the Father" and living "unto the Father." It is in Christ that we have the hope and promise that we too shall be able to fulfill our high calling. We have had little difficulty seeing Him as the Son, but let us see how He also fulfills the other side as a Father representing "for the Father."

For years I could hardly understand Isaiah's prophecy of the Lord Jesus in that well-known portion which describes Him as "... the everlasting father, the Prince of Peace ..." (Isa. 9:6). It seemed such a confusion of persons in the Godhead to call the Son the "everlasting Father." Then when I read how F. Fenton translated this verse – showing that Christ was to be "Time's Father" – it all became clear:

> "The Wonderful Counsellor, call His name,
> Great Leader, Time's Father, the Prince of Peace!"

I could understand the difference between "Time's Father" and the Eternal Father. Isaiah is saying that the One, who from all eternity had been in the bosom of the Eternal Father, was now to walk the shores of time as a representative for the Father. Down here in time, Christ was not only to demonstrate His relationship as a Son unto the Father, but also as "Time's Father" to be a representative for the Father. Did He not say, "If you have seen me, you have seen the (Eternal) Father."?

Thus our Lord Jesus demonstrates this twofold calling as both a father and also a son.

How beautifully this twofold calling is demonstrated in the first man, Adam. When God placed him in the lovely garden, note the first words spoken to him which reveal this: "Be fruitful, multiply and subdue the earth." In other words God was saying, "Adam, I want you to fulfill the calling of fatherhood. Unto Me you are as a created son, but on the earth I want you to be an earthly father—a representative for me. Again we hear the same words spoken to Noah after the earth was purged by a flood: "Be fruitful, multiply and subdue the earth." Noah was also to continue in God's line of purpose as a father. And when Noah failed in his calling, we next see God sovereignly selecting another man to be his earthly representative. He named him Abram — which means exalted father. In due time this same Abram was promoted to be Abraham—which means a father of many nations.

Now was this calling for Adam, Noah and Abraham just a coincidence, or is there something distinctive God would say to us? Undoubtedly He intended for Abraham and his vast family to be as a reflection of the Eternal Father and that vast family He will some day enjoy. Surely the Eternal Father has designed that we might all be like Him. We do well to remember that "generation is not a push from below, but a gift from above; it is a reflection of the Eternal Generation in the Bosom of the Father, Who in the agelessness of eternity says, 'Thou art my Son. This day have I begotten Thee.' The roots of it are hidden

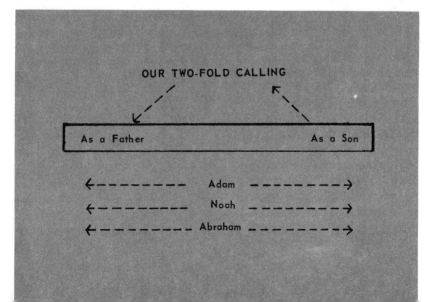

in Heaven, for in the great Hebraic tradition we read a line
wherein God speaks and says, 'Shall I·who give generations to
others, MYSELF BE BARREN?'" What else can we conclude!
Our most glorious calling is that we should be "unto Him" —
sons, and "for Him" on this earth — fathers.

Now another thing which needs careful attention. God has
only dealt directly with two men: Adam is the only created son,
and Christ is the only begotten son. In Adam we received created life from God; in Christ we receive divine Life from God. As
a created son, Adam could become a begotten Son — but only
through Christ. That "tree of life" in the Garden was an Old
Testament representation of Jesus Christ. There is the one essential difference between all the cultists and those in the main
stream of church truth! What pre-eminence do they give THE
ONLY BEGOTTEN SON and what is man's relationship to God?
For most cult groups Jesus is merely the first among many sons
who are *directly* begotten of the Father; however, we know that
Jesus Christ will always be the only directly begotten Son of
the Father. Any divine begetting or birth we have is "in Christ."
The Father only shares with us because of the relationship we
have "in Christ." While the translation of F. Fenton, in which
he refers to Christ as "Time's Father" is helpful, it is not the
only leg upon which we have built this twofold calling.

THE CONFLICT BETWEEN BEING AND DOING

In a conference a pastor who had awakened to his calling
confided: "It took quite a severe crisis to awaken me to God's
high calling. It was only when my young son was picked up by
the law that I saw how *my* religious *doing* was not God's method
of working. I had been so completely wrapped up in the mechanics and techniques of doing things for God that I had completely
overlooked God's way. Anything truly spiritual must be born, not
wrought of man, or of the will of the flesh, but of God. It became so evident; if I failed as a father, I completely failed in
my spiritual ministry — even though I might still maintain the
momentum of religious activity for a lifetime.

I realized that even as a pastor I was, above all, to be a
spiritual father to the people. They might be helped by my *doing,*
but they would be spiritually molded only by what I really was
in my inner *being.* I saw for people to be brought to birth, nour-
ished and conformed to the image of Christ, required more than

the mechanics of doing; it must be the Holy Spirit's working through me as a spiritual father. Let me close my testimony by saying: Since I started being a father for Him and enjoying that intimate fellowship which a son should express unto the Father, it has been glorious to see how God has been working through me."

What a glorious secret this is! When we truly learn to be a father "for Him" and know how to be a son "unto Him," then it is God who accomplishes His "doing" through us. It is hard for us to realize that it is not mere activity, so much as a proper relationship which God desires above all. Here then is the first law of God's working: As we learn *to be,* God is free *to do* through us. It is no mere play on words that our most effective *doing* is simply fulfilling our call in *being.* When they questioned Jesus, "What shall we do that we might work the works of God?" notice the answer He gave them. "...this is the work of God, that ye might believe on Him whom He hath sent." Then, it was not their *working,* but their *belief.* For belief is literally by-lief —by-life— the things you live by: then God does the working through you.

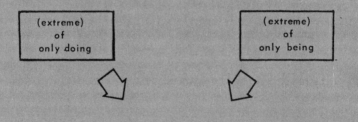

FINDING THE PROPER BALANCE IN CHRIST

| (extreme) of only doing | (extreme) of only being |

"IN CHRIST"...
We find our balance: we represent FOR Him and we live UNTO Him. When He can bring us into the balance we will both "be" and "do."

SECTION
THREE

Moving ...

UNTO FULL STATURE

in

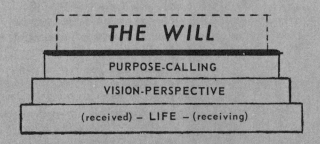

All that we have "seen" in vision-perspective and purpose-calling will be of little value to us until we understand the important function of our will. In this section we shall consider:

IN CHAPTER 10: Understanding God's purpose for our will; this is our real problem.

IN CHAPTER 11: What are the four steps in liberating the will?

IN CHAPTER 12: What is the master design in the universe?

HE GAVE THIS TESTIMONY:

"For years I was ashamed; I hated my immaturity and continual excusing myself and blaming others. Like Adam I kept insisting: 'The woman whom thou gavest to be with me, she gave me fruit of the tree, and I ate.' I blamed God for giving me the woman and blamed the woman for giving me the fruit; everybody else was to blame — but me.

I had convinced myself that I really didn't know what to do, but the confusion was simply that I would not do what I secretly knew I ought to do.

Then God showed me how I misunderstood the design and function of the mind and will. With my mind I was to honestly face the truth and admit my inability to cope with the problems. Then my will could serve as a door which opened to lay hold of His resources.

HERE WAS THE SECRET OF THE WILL: not that I will by my will-power to accomplish, but that my will is simply to open the door so as to receive His power and performance. 'For me to will is present...' and now Lord it is Your performing that does it."

UNDERSTANDING OUR
REAL PROBLEM

W HAT IS YOUR BIGGEST problem—*knowing* the will of God, or *doing* the will of God? In the past fifteen years I have asked this question dozens of times in meetings across the country. Some are quick to answer, and then wish they had not responded until later when they see just how revealing this question and their answer can be. So I have learned to caution them against any outward response—but rather just keep it to themselves.

There are some who insist, "If I really knew what God wanted, I would do it without a moments hesitation. Why I would pack up and leave for China tomorrow if I really *knew* that was God's will." Yet others insist, "my problem is not *knowing* but *doing* what I already know is God's will."

In Luke chapter six we have two incidents which reveal how the Pharisees thought they had a *head problem*—that is, one of knowing—but Jesus turns about to show them it was really a *heart* problem—one of doing.

Consider one more thing as we approach these incidents. Have you ever noticed how easy it is to allow the attitude of the heart to reach up and color the glasses of the mind? When you, for some reason, have an inner dislike for someone, it is so easy to misinterpret, or to put a wrong construction on what they do. An offended heart will latch on to an evil report of someone just like flypaper will attract a fly. And the proverbial phrase: love is blind, is just as true in the opposite sense. When you really love or appreciate someone, it is quite difficult to misunderstand, or misinterpret their actions. Love has a way of understanding, of covering over mistakes and failures, of being blind to anything but the good.

It was a sabbath day, and the Pharisees had observed how Jesus' disciples went through the fields, "plucked ears of corn and did eat." Long before this, something had "crossed-up" these religious Pharisees. They had become critical and were nursing an offended spirit. Now with colored glasses that desired only to accuse Jesus for allowing His disciples to break the sabbath traditions, they came announcing in effect—"we have a head problem. We need to *knou* why ye do ' that which is not lawful on the sabbath days?'"

In Jesus' response there is a good rule to remember: you can't give a satisfactory answer to an offended heart; it wants to accuse—not understand. Surely Jesus recognized their accusing spirit. Answers will never work where unveilings are needed. So Jesus proceeds to show them how theirs is not really a *head* problem, but a *heart* problem. They have allowed their wicked, rebellious heart to confuse their mind—and color their viewpoint.

He starts the unveiling by asking this question. "Have you not read what David did when he went into the sanctuary where none but the priests could go? He took of the shewbread for himself and his men."

How pointed was His question! They could not miss the deepest implications. Jesus was simply saying: "How is it that you sit in judgment on me and my disciples for plucking corn, yet you glory in King David and his men. In principle it is exactly the same."

It was like saying: "You have colored glasses. You do not misinterpret or even question what David had done because you have not been crossed-up by him. You sing the praises of David and have become blind to his actions. But because your inner spirit has been offended by me, you put a wrong construction on, or misinterpret almost everything I or my disciples do."

No more words were needed! There is something about the moral integrity of conscience that requires consistency. They well knew Jesus had unveiled that their real trouble was an offended heart which then affected their thinking. To make this plain, let us enlarge a little. Fenelon says, "pure religion resides in the will alone." By this he means that when the will, as the governing power in man's nature, is set right, all the rest of the nature must come into harmony. By the will I do not mean the wish of the man, or even his purpose, but rather the deliberate choice, the deciding power, the king—all that is in the man must yield obedience. Thus the mind will begin to lose its bias or colored glasses when the will is set for God.

When God is to take possession of us, it must be into this central will or personality that He enters. If, then, He is reigning there by the power of His Spirit, all the rest of our nature must come under His sway. As the will is, so is the man.

Finally in answering the Pharisees, all Jesus need remind them was that the One who had made and designed the sabbath in the beginning surely should know how to use it properly.

But is there some reader who still ponders why God did not strike David dead when he invaded this holy place reserved only for the Levites duly sanctified? The problem is simply this, that from our human viewpoint we can know only fragments. God must lift us into His own viewpoint if we would understand His fuller reasons. You recall that David is a type of the Lord Jesus. Which means that if Jesus is our Prophet, Priest and King then so was David, as a type, to fulfill that three-fold function. Since our Lord Jesus was a Priest after the higher order of Melchisedec, instead of the Aaronic order, He had the right to enter the holy place. For this same reason, God allowed His servant David, whom He considered after the Melchisedec order, this higher priesthood privilege. In man's limited viewpoint there are so many things we cannot understand. But it is usually because we look only upon the lower order and do not see the eternal order of things. God has reasons and purposes which can never be known by the natural mind. And He will only share these as our heart opens to Him even as the flower opens to the sun.

Could these jealous, green-eyed Pharisees understand the actions of Jesus? No, they could not, for they *would not.* It was not a matter of the Holy Spirit being unwilling to unveil truth to them. While their conscience condemned them for their inconsistency, only repentance could rid them of their mental block.

Immediately in verse six, we are introduced to another incident which has an identical setting. Again it is a sabbath day and the same accusing crowd is there to find fault. One wonders why they don't leave Him alone if they can't understand or appreciate His actions. The fact is this: no one can leave Him alone. He is ever disturbing and crowding men to make a governmental choice. He never leaves anyone neutral. Every word spoken and every encounter with Him forced men to a decision of one kind or another. So should our preaching not only enlighten the mind, but also expose the heart.

When Jesus saw they were once again ready to accuse Him for His actions on the sabbath, He takes the initiative. He does not wait for them, but precipitates an opportunity to once again reveal their *heart-trouble.*

He puts the poor fellow with the withered hand on the spot by asking him to rise up and stand forth in their midst. This was a crucial moment for the poor man. Would he stay snuggled in the crowd where his withered condition would not show so obviously? In doing this, he would remain identified with the accusing crowd. But if he dared to move out and separate himself, it was like taking sides with Jesus against His accusers. What an inward rending there must have been before a governmental choice could be made. It meant either obedience or disobedience.

There is another interesting thing about this first command to the poor man. Jesus always asks of us something we *can do if we will.* Was there anything wrong with the man's legs? Could he stand up and walk forward? Of course! Did he understand clearly what action to take? Without doubt! This is always what we can expect as a principle in God's dealings.

But if the mind would take its directions from a heart that begins to rebel, it will go through something like this: The enemy will be there to divert the attention and "throw a curve" —announcing—"you can't do what is asked." By confusing the issue, he will divert the mind from the immediate action to some distant impossibility.

Thus the attention is focused upon some *other issue*, and the confused mind overlooks the immediate issue which the individual *can do if he will!* But we see, without confusion or distraction from the real issue, the man obeyed. He could use his legs—and he did. It meant a real exposure of his withered condition and a deliberate taking sides with the Lord Jesus. The cardinal issue is: if you will *do* — you shall *understand.*

In every meeting there are those who hear our Lord insist— "rise up and stand forth," but the rebellious heart convinces the mind it will not be appropriate for a believer to allow some outward withered condition in his life to be exposed before the eyes of all the brethren. After all, it will ruin his testimony and weaken his influence among those he would like to help. What is forgotten is that others already sense that withered condition. We must understand that it is really an inward withered will which produces every outward withered condition.

Next, Jesus proceeds to unveil their hearts by asking this simple question: "Is it lawful to do good on the sabbath day—or evil?" Of course they could not answer. If they acknowledged that it was permissible for Him to do good on the sabbath, they would be allowing Him to heal the withered arm. But they would rather maintain their consistency of tradition and doctrine than see a poor man healed. And there are many today like them, whose hardness of heart equals the Pharisees' indifference.

While they stand completely silent and dumbfounded by their inability to answer Him, Jesus turns to the man with the withered arm. The Pharisees' hearts have been exposed, and the real captivity of their mind unveiled. But the poor man with the withered arm has also been exposed. By his obedience to the Lord, he has received an inward work of healing. In yielding to the Lord Jesus, there has come an infusion of His own life and strength within. The man had *done* what he *could do* and now would receive the power to complete the next request: "stretch forth thy hand."

The Lord now had an inner beachhead from which to work. And here is another rule we can always go by: once the inner government of our will is in perfect harmony with His will, He can move from this inner beachhead to fix up all the outward withered conditions in the life. Whether we have recognized it or not, God works from *inner* to *outward*. As long as man would seek to *use* Him for his own benefit, he is mostly concerned with the outward healing—that is, what God can do for him. What a difference when one is properly adjusted in the inner relationship and concerned only for what he can be unto God for Himself. Though we cannot see it working, the inner healing always prepares the way for the healing of all outward circumstances in the life. Was it not so with this poor man with the withered arm?

Perhaps the reader has imagined—my withered hands just cannot hand out that tract; my withered legs buckle under me when I would stand for a testimony or stand alone for some issue I know is right; my withered lips tremble so I cannot praise Him as I know I ought to. Perish the thought! It is first the withered will which controls all these outward withered members.

One could hardly imagine how these Pharisees could be "filled with madness" even to the point of wanting to destroy Him! Yet any heart that is resisting God is blinded by its own foolish ways and will not follow intelligent reason. Such a deceitful heart has reasons the mind knows nothing about. It cannot rejoice and bless God—even for things that are good.

We are back to our first question: What is our biggest problem —*knowing* or *doing* the will of God? Like these Pharisees, many

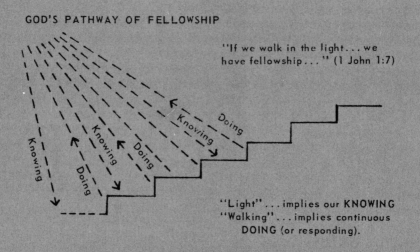

GOD'S PATHWAY OF FELLOWSHIP

"If we walk in the light...we have fellowship..." (1 John 1:7)

"Light"...implies our KNOWING
"Walking"...implies continuous DOING (or responding).

people have confused the issue until they do not *know*. But Jesus has put it quite tersely in these words: "If any man will do my will, he shall know of the doctrine...."

As we have pictured below, there is a pathway of constant *knowing* and *doing*. These two: knowing and doing, like the two wings of a bird, are both necessary for any progress. There must be a constant cooperation between the mind and the will. We see below how God takes the first initiative in giving man what he needs to know. Then man is responsible for the *choice* of his will and God does the *performing* (doing). By this response man is then lifted to the next step where once again God shares what is needed for the next level of life. Man must once again respond. We can depend on this as a sure principle: God only requires us to walk in the light we have, that is, to obey what we know to be truth now.

Yet this is where man gets stalled. Did you ever sit at a checkerboard for several minutes waiting for the other player to move and you finally ask him, "It's your move, isn't it?" only to hear him reply, "No, it is your move!"

I think this is what most folk do with God. After months and often years of "waiting for God to move" they suddenly discover that He has already made the last move. He has been waiting for their response to what He has already made known before they can be moved to the next step.

If they would only listen, He would remind them: "I've already shared what you need to know *now*. Just act on that." But too often the enemy has diverted their attention to some difficult issue ten years down the road when they could be joyfully using His resources for this immediate response.

When God is "working in us to will," we must set our faces like a flint to carry out this will, and must respond with an emphatic "I will" to every "thou shalt" of His. For God can only carry out His own will with us as we consent to it and *will* in harmony with Him. So the stairway of maturity is a continuous pathway of *knowing* and *doing*. Next let us consider the four steps by which we learn to *live in the will*.

BY FAR THE GREATER MAJORITY of folk are captive in their will. They are captive to people, to circumstances, to fears, to emotions, and to long patterns of indifference. As I was considering how to explain this captivity and liberation of the will, I came across this account of a successful businessman who was trying to help his unsuccessful friend, Charlie, get out of a slump.

In reporting the experiences, the businessman said that the interview had not progressed very far before he noticed that Charlie used one phrase over and over again. It was so repetitive as to give the impression of a phonograph needle stuck in the crack of a defective record: "You know, I have half-a-mind to investigate that idea," he said. "I have half-a-mind to do something about that."

The successful man explained that while he was urging Charlie to make some solid decisions and then to think and act more positively, Charlie repeated, "You know, I've got half-a-mind to do that." Finally his friend said, "Charlie, I know what's wrong with you; you're just a half-a-minder. Everything you think of doing, you have just half-a-mind to do. But it really isn't your mind—IT'S YOUR WILL."

Charlie is like multitudes of Christians who hear a Sunday sermon or read a book. They are inspired and enthused for the moment—even to the point of giving a mental confession: "I have half-a-mind to do something about that." But if there is no controlling conviction of the will, we can be sure the will has been taken captive and needs liberation.

FOUR STEPS IN LIBERATING THE WILL

LITTLE JOHNNY kept teasing his mother for "just another piece of cake," until finally she announced in desperation, "you've already had six pieces, but go ahead—just take one more and that is absolutely all."

As he reached for the cake, he looked at her with such in-
nocency announcing: "Mommy, you sure don't have much will-
power do you?" Five-year-old Johnny was, at least in the area
of his will, reflecting a good deal more persistence and will-
power than his weak mother. But they were both demonstrating
a very real immaturity. How?

The temptation will be strong, and very ancient—the most
ancient of temptations—to lay the blame on someone else for
their immature actions: "The woman whom thou gavest to be
with me, she gave me fruit of the tree, and I ate." Adam blamed
God for giving him the woman and he blamed the woman for
giving him the fruit; God and the woman, and not Adam, were to
blame. Such an attitude shows immaturity. To blame others and
our surroundings shows our immaturity.

Here is the first step toward maturity—to *accept the responsibility* for being what we are, and doing what we do. Let no
one deny that surroundings, people and places can and do influence us. But only that part of our environment to which we
respond influences us. We do the responding. The choice is
always ours. If you are a half-person with a half-output, then it
is because by a series of choices you have consented to be
that half-person.

This mother who kept yielding to her strong-willed son was
herself responsible for the kind of son she was allowing to
frustrate her. Would she blame him or herself? But the little
rascal was also responsible even as his unusual insight indicated. Mommy was lacking in her power to say no, and he was
quick to acknowledge her weakness—not his own.

But there are three more steps necessary to maturity of will.
The second is *to discover the place and effectiveness of the
will* as God designed and intended for the will to function. The
third is *to understand the importance of a full liberation* of the
will as it cooperates with the Holy Spirit. And the fourth is *to
learn how to live in the will*—that is, to continually reaffirm the
choices of the will which have already been made.

I am sure there is much more in these four steps than immediately catches our attention. May God begin to help them
unfold into fuller meaning.

Recently when a doctor confided that his wife's domineering
attitude in the home and church was aborting his practice and
frustrating his spiritual life, the Lord made these four steps a

reality to him and he acted accordingly. First, he, not his wife, was really responsible; second, he saw how God had given him a will which must be used effectively to stand with God as the head of his home; third, he saw not only that God wanted him to will HIS will, but to accept a liberation of his will from his feelings, and finally to take the abiding position of *living in the will*. It was for him like turning on the switch which allowed God to move in and perform. It happened like this:

The doctor claimed first, that the "Eve-spirit" which had so constantly risen up in his dear wife to "lord-it-over" him and others, should be put down and brought into captivity to the obedience of the Lord Jesus (not to himself). While indeed she had been guilty of ruling, *he* was responsible. It was like taking a position and then declaring the issue settled. Of course when circumstances arose which made the position he had taken seem a bit wobbly, he could reaffirm his position and choice which had already been made. Immediately he testified, "It seemed as though God was right there to perform what I could not."

It was as though Paul's words took on new meaning: "...for to will is present with me; but how to perform..." (Rom. 7:18). Now he knew it was only his part to *will*, but it was God's delight to do the *performing*. Yes, what a revelation it is to us to discover that God only wants us to exercise our volitional (willing) powers in complete accord with Him and then He will be free to perform. Again Paul points to this very issue of the will in 2 Corinthians 8:12. "For if there be first a willing mind, it is accepted...." Is not this the great discovery of Paul in Romans seven when he finally announces, "I thank God through

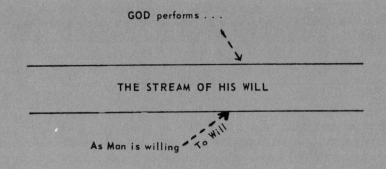

GOD performs . . .

THE STREAM OF HIS WILL

As Man is willing To Will

Jesus Christ our Lord..." (vs 24)? It is like saying: "I am but the *willer*, He is the *Performer*."

As we have pictured in the drawing, there will be no genuine moving toward maturity apart from honestly facing and accepting responsibility for conditions. To blame others is infantile; to face-up is the beginning–the first step. Second, there must be a real *seeing* as by divine illumination of the important place for the will in God's intention. A little five-year-old boy after seeing a puppet show expressed it: "I'm glad I'm not one of those pretending persons. They have to do what they are told." The lad was right. God could not be satisfied nor glorified merely by "pretending beings"–puppets who could not choose. He must have real persons, standing up and cooperating by the continuous act of their wills.

Someone has put it this way: "Here is a chessboard, and all the figures on the board, instead of being made of wood, are flesh and blood with wills of their own–true persons. The game for God would be simple if the figures would go where He desires them to go. But suppose, when God would make a move in the game against Evil, that the figures should balk and refuse to move, and instead should move on their own to other positions without reference to the player–God. How that would complicate the game–but it is exactly what often happens. That which has possibilities also has problems."

But this fact of freedom of will also has possibilities. Suppose those figures on the board should learn that moves on their own, and refusal to cooperate with the Player, always resulted in failure and mixup. Would not such natural retribution teach them to learn to cooperate with THE PLAYER? Then, consider how God and man play the game in cooperation and win! What a difference when the Player wins with real persons instead of only wooden pawns.

Now since the effects of the Fall are so deeply ingrained in the fabric of every man, it becomes necessary for the work of the Cross to liberate, to detach man's will so it can operate freely. All his fleshly tastes, inclinations, feelings and emotions rise up to entwine a will that should be free. God has made ample provision at the Cross that by our union in His death every vestige of self-will may be put down and the liberated will be free to wholly co-operate with God.

Finally, as we learn to enter the very *hub*–which is the center of His will—we can align our wills with His, can make His wisdom our own, and in the end can make the victory a joint victory. It was so with the doctor who took this inner position in the center of God's will, Regardless of all contrary circumstances or "lying vanities" he simply defended this position. In discovering, declaring and defending his position in Christ he was learning the joy and power of *living in the will.*

For some reader, perhaps this is like raising a red flag. To speak of *living in the will* serves to remind you of certain unhappy remembrances. It recalls to mind certain individuals who seemed possessed with living by a domineering will, who lacked both heart and head for understanding others. Herein is the danger of those who allow only a natural maturity without the fusion of the Holy Spirit with their spirit. There is nothing attractive, nor spiritual, about one who lives from a *tense will*— that is, one who has not entered into a *relaxed will* which joyfully cooperates with the Holy Spirit. The first, is our willing what we will, but the latter is a cooperation or complete fusion with God's will. It is our will, like a gear meshed into His will. Until this spiritual fusion has taken place there can be no *living by the will in His will.*

Here we are called to live GOD-CENTERED in that true dimension of the Spirit. In explaining the place of the will and how a theological fact may be held in the mind for a lifetime without its having any positive effect upon the moral character, the late Dr. Tozer pointedly asks this question: "At what point then, does a theological fact become for the one who holds it a life-giving truth? *At the point where obedience begins.* When faith gains the consent of the will to make an irrevocable committal to Christ as Lord, truth begins its saving, illuminating work; and not one moment before."

WE MUST BE CONVINCED . . .

". . . that both God and life *will* maturity. But they do more than passively will our maturity; they conspire in every possible way, short of breaking down our wills to make us mature. Life makes us discontented and unhappy in our immaturities. Suppose we could settle down happy and contented in being a half-person, then that would be a tragic situation. But we cannot. Divine discontent is a goal that impels us into higher, fuller life. Life won't let us settle down — to nothingness.

"And what kind of Father would God be if He did not disturb us toward maturity? No earthly parent could be content to have a child who refused to grow up. The parents' joy is in development, in growth, in going on toward maturity. God cannot be otherwise and still be God, our Father. So the disturbances we feel in our immaturities are not signs of His anger, but a manifestation of His love. He loves us too much to let us settle down in half-wayness.

"But if God should stop at the point of making us discontent, then He would stop this side of being God, our Father. To be our Father, He must provide literally everything for our maturity. And He has! He has put at our disposal all the resources for our being what we ought to be — everything except coercion. There He draws the line, for if He coerced us into maturity — then of course we wouldn't be mature. The will to be mature must be at the center of our maturity.

"If God and life and we ourselves *will* maturity, then there is nothing in heaven or earth that can stop us from being the mature persons we ought to be. We are destined to be mature, and that destiny is written in every cell of our bodies. We can slow down or block that destiny. The choice is always ours.

"Hope begins to spring up within my breast, for if I am destined to be mature then I can and do accept that destiny and make it my own." [8]

THE MASTER DESIGN
IN THE UNIVERSE

W HETHER WE BEGIN WITH THE
revelation given to us in His Word,
or whether we consider His design in the physical, celestial or
moral realms, we are pushed to the same conclusion: Everything
in the universe is made to work according to a master design.
God has designed for centers to work within centers, yet all are
to be properly related to Him, the Ultimate Center.

The heavens above declare His glorious design in the celestial realm. In recent years the Mount Palomar telescope has
pierced the vastness of space to reveal that our solar system,
with its nine planets revolving around the sun, is but an infin-
itesimal part of the vast system of the heavenlies. Scientists
tell us there are at least 240 million solar systems like ours.
These form an immense wheel called a galaxy. Each solar system
revolves around its center or sun, and all the solar systems in
the galaxy revolve around a common center. While this may
stagger our imagination, it is not all! There are at least forty
billion galaxies like ours revolving around an ultimate center—
the center of all centers.

Thus there are three typical centers in the celestial realm.
Our sun with its nine planets is the smallest. Next there is the
center of the galaxy. And then there is the whirling galaxies revolving around one ultimate center. Each of the 240 million solar
systems and the 40 billion galaxy centers has its particular re
latedness to the center of all centers.

In the diagram we have illustrated how God's design in the
outer universe demonstrates that everything is perfectly controlled as it is properly related to the Ultimate Center, which we
are sure is the very throne of God. From this throne *His will* is
to express itself throughout every realm. As our earth is related
to its center, the sun; and the sun to its center, the galaxy; and
the galaxy to its center, the *ultimate center*—everything func-
tions in a balanced perfection like a great mechanism of wheels
within wheels.

THE SAME DESIGN IN MINIATURE

In turning from the telescopic (magnitude of the outer universe) to the microscopic (miniature of the inner universe) we find the same design. Within every molecule there are entire universes of atoms moving around their center. And by probing even farther into the nature of matter, we find that in every atom hundreds of electrons (negative particles of electricity) are revolving at great speed around a positive center. So from the hidden universe within each atom to the majestic universes of the heavens, there is a sweep from miniature to magnitude which reveals this one basic law: Every center, from the most minute atom to the most gigantic wheel of galaxies, is directly related to the ultimate center. Every greater center, beginning with the Ultimate Center — God Himself — has a priority over every lesser center. Everything is made on the principle that it must exist *for the whole* (not for itself) if it is to function according to His ultimate intention.

This design also holds true in the physical structure of our bodies. Consider the cell, the smallest unit of life. We are told that all cells, when they begin their existence, are capable of *being the whole.* But they renounce this privilege and surrender themselves to be a *related portion* of the whole, in order to serve the whole (and fulfill their purpose in being). In this renunciation they can come to full realization of their existence. Each cell loses its life, so to speak, in order to find it. But when a cell refuses to serve the whole and tries *to be* instead of belonging to the whole, the result is CANCER!

A cancer, then, is a group of unsurrendered cells trying to be the whole, depriving other cells of their rights; a group of cells turned self-centered and selfish, wanting to be independent and unrelated. This is the characteristic of anything cancerous. And we shall see how every kind of cancer works against God's master design and therefore has the built-in seeds of death in it. In our body a cancer, if not arrested, eats its way to its own death and causes the death of the organism upon which it feeds.

THERE ARE VARIOUS KINDS OF CANCER

Now just as self-centeredness, selfishness, independence and unrelatedness in cells produces physical cancer, they cause spiritual disease and death when carried into the spiritual realm.

The sin of self-centeredness and spiritual independence really
began in the heavenlies when the "Anointed Cherub" turned in
pride to announce his five "I wills" against God. And we have
had this spiritual disease, spiritual "cancer," if you want to call
it that, spreading ever since. From the angelic hosts it spread to
Adam and Eve in the Garden, and thence throughout the whole
human family. Whenever men get out of God's design and seek to
be independent centers, unrelated to Him, moral or spiritual
"cancer" is the result.

Now a closer look at history coroborates this fact! How often
men have assumed wrong centers in their reckoning. You recall
there was a day when men believed that the earth was the center
of our solar system. They imagined that the sun and all other
planets revolved around the earth. What confusion this Ptolemaic
system of reckoning wrought. The calendar needed constant
revision; the seasons were coming either too late or too early.
Because men were off-centered in their reckoning, things were
eccentric.

Then Gallileo and Copernicus arose to challenge this wrong
centered reckoning. They insisted that the sun, not the earth,
was the true center of this solar system. But they were threat-
ened by the Roman authoritarianism of that day which often
burned at the stake those who dared to preach such heresy. Apart
from an open mind or illumination, the religious hierarchy of that
day could not see or would not accept any new conception. Is
this not God's graphic way of picturing how fallen men have
always sought to make everything (even God and His blessings)
to revolve around them for their own ends. Men who are cancerous
at heart will surely impose wrong-centered conceptions upon the
world.

Alas, today we face the same wrong-centeredness. Just as
men once assumed the earth to be the center, so religion has
assumed man to be the all-important center as though all things
existed for and revolved around him as the only center. WHAT A
BATTLE IS NOW RAGING! It is not between the modernists and
the fundamentalists, nor between the liberals and conservatives,
nor even between democracy and communism.

One can only see the battle array in spiritual realm. It is
between all those who have become a living revelation of true
God-centeredness and those who blindly insist upon following
Satan and Adam in attempting to be their own independent, un-

related center.

All over the world today there is an inward spiritual groaning for right relatedness to the stream of His will and authority. And what is happening? God has heard this cry. He is raising up those who see as Copernicus saw, and who will dare to challenge the authoritarian religious systems by insisting that man is only a *related center*, and not the ultimate center of all things. Perhaps there is someone now reading who has felt the inward tug to become a part of this present-day Copernicus company — someone who will dare to be the living expression of proper relatedness unto Him.

WE SEE THIS MASTER-DESIGN IN THE MORAL REALM

Not only is this majestic design manifest in the celestial and physical realms, but it is also the law of all moral beings. Only as we understand our calling "to belong" *to Him*, can we fulfill our calling "to be" *for Him*. We have already pictured this in our twofold calling. As sons unto Him — we are *to belong;* as fathers representing Him — we are *to be.* We must learn to keep both in their proper balance. If we seek *only to be,* the center is self. And if we seek *only to belong,* we become warped in a pseudo-God-centeredness which He has not designed.

G. C. Berkouwer has aptly explained: "God, in the Biblical view, does not enjoy greatness only as man becomes unimportant and small. It has been said: 'God is everything, man is nothing.' As opposed to human pride and pretense, such a statement has value. But it is not a Biblical sentiment. It is not true that man becomes nothing when God is all. Indeed, man truly comes into his own when God is most honored. Man comes into his own place, not into God's place. Man enters the service of God not into competition with God. When God is truly given His place at the center where He belongs, He in turn creates a place for man. When God is magnified, He does not negate man but makes him a real man once more. This is the great secret of *soli Deo gloria.*" [9]

THE DESIGN FOR SPIRITUAL RELATEDNESS

In writing to the Corinthians, Paul deals with this fundamental problem by explaining how men and things can be out of their intended spiritual relatedness. He says: "... For all things are yours ... And ye are Christ's and Christ is God's" (1 Cor. 3:21-23).

We have pictured God as the Master Gear with everything else perfectly meshed into Him. In this design for ultimate relatedness we can enjoy "the good, acceptable and perfect will of God." Anything else can only bring eccentricity and produce disharmony.

Paul explains how the Corinthians had spiritual cancer. According to their own tastes and preferences they were accepting certain men and rejecting the ministry of others. Some emphasized Paul, for they loved teaching and the intellectual diet. Another group gathered around Apollos, for no doubt his oratory and fluency of words stirred them to action. Still another group followed Peter, for his seemingly practical ministry and understanding was more in sympathy with their ups and downs. But there was a fourth group who insisted the others were divisive in their interpretations. These proudly insisted: "We are of Christ—you are wrong—we are the only ones who are right, for we follow only Christ." So they were selecting gifted men for themselves (as the center) without seeing all these men and their ministry in relatedness to that spiritual Body He is building.

Oh to forget our divisions and factions! Paul would remind us that all God's servants belong to the whole Body. This means Luther is not only for the Lutherans, but he belongs to all. So with Calvin, Wesley, Finney, Moody – all these belong to you, but only as you keep them properly related to HIM.

Similarly the Corinthians were relating blessings, gifts, the Lord's table and liberty to themselves as selfish centers. Little

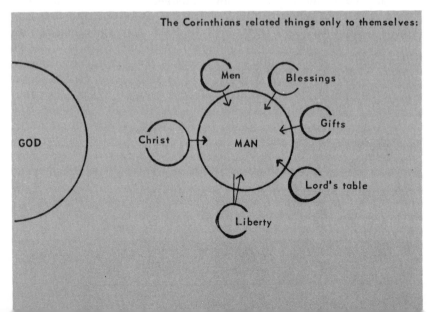

The Corinthians related things only to themselves:

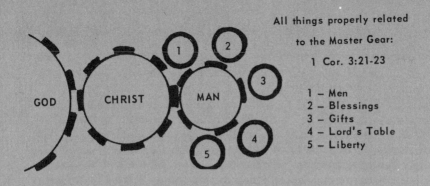

All things properly related
to the Master Gear:
1 Cor. 3:21-23

1 — Men
2 — Blessings
3 — Gifts
4 — Lord's Table
5 — Liberty

wonder we use the Corinthian Church as the example of spiritual cancer. As with the little cell in our body, so with us as cells in His Body. The first law of spiritual life is this: We must lose our life to find it. If we seek to find it by centering on ourself, our blessings, our gifts or our liberty – in no matter how religious a way – we will lose it. Life will crumble when it gets beyond the stream of His authority.

To become off-centered is to be out of the *spiritual stream*. Whether moral, physical, spiritual or celestial, the laws of the universe do not support that way of life. There is but one stream of power and authority. Only as we discover how every gear is to properly mesh into our life and how we are made to mesh into THE MASTER GEAR, can we find the proper relatedness and ultimate meaning in life.

THE PSALMIST GIVES THE ANSWER

In union with God, the Master Gear, we find in Him all we need to fulfill what He designs to have from us. In religious circles men have become so power and knowledge conscious as though by their pleading and praying God would send them a package marked power, knowledge or wisdom. Not so! God has designed something far better than merely giving us these as a package. God's way is so different! He would bring us into a vital union with Himself. This means our gear is once and for all enmeshed into the MASTER GEAR. In this union with Him we do not need to ask for things; they automatically become operative. Surely the Psalmist (in Ps. 31) explains what it means for God's will to become our will. It means He does not give us a mere package of knowledge or power, *but He becomes our continual flow of all we need*. As we shall see, He becomes the *how*, *where*, *when* and *why*.

THE HOW: "...for thou art my strength. Into thy hand I commit my spirit..." (vs. 4, 5). What a day it is when we recognize that His gear turns ours. He becomes our continual strength and power. How often we have sought for resources from Him without being wholly enmeshed. If we could, we would have pushed ahead by our own strength to drive the Master Gear. And when we knew that we had the right answer, our little gear got so anxious — we did not wait for Him, His timing and His placing. So often it is not a matter of our doing the wrong thing, but simply the matter of "doing it on our own"; thus it turned out wrong. It is this bent toward acting independently—the living by what we know—instead of learning with the Psalmist that "all my springs are in Thee." As we have said before, we are *to live in the will:* HIS WILL!

THE WHERE: The Psalmist also knew, "...thou hast set my feet in a large room" (vs. 8). Those who want their own freedom to enjoy boundless direction and their own placing, soon discover that it becomes the way of narrowness and limitation. Because they imagined that God would confine them, they ran from Him, only to be locked up in the prison house of their own selfishness. Yet those who have accepted what seemed like dependence and limitation in God, have found it was really God's desire to enlarge them. "The widest thing in the universe is not space; it is the potential capacity of the human heart. Being made in the image of God, it is capable of almost unlimited extension in all directions. And one of the world's worst tragedies is that we allow our hearts to shrink until there is room in them for little beside ourselves." (A. W. Tozer) [10]

Indeed there is nothing like the direction and largeness which God gives to that life which is fully enmeshed in His plan. Hear this remarkable testimony: "Fifty years ago I thought I was accepting the life of bondage and limitation in yielding myself wholly to God; yet now I see what an enlarging experience it has become—far beyond my expectation. If I had been allowed my own selfish way, I should have died having seen only my little farm or at the most, my own small state of Nebraska. But in God's great purpose He has sent me around the world several times to visit almost every country in the world. How can I ever doubt the Psalmist's words: 'thou hast set my feet in a large room.'"

THE WHEN: The Psalmist also found, "My times are in thy hand..." (vs. 15). Who else but God can understand the proper timing in His universe? It was not in Moses to know as long as he was on his own. Knowing that he was called to be the deliverer of the slave people from Egypt, he rushed ahead of God and got out of the *divine timing*. Only when God had worked at both ends of the line—first in preparing His deliverer by forty years on the backside of the desert and next in making Israel so sick of her slavery in Egypt that she began to cry out for help — yes, only then had the right timing come. Then His deliverer could deliver. This is the way God's timing works. Moses was ready, he thought, forty years earlier; but the people were not ready to leave Egypt.

How blessed to leave our anxious will enmeshed into His own will and know in reality that "there is a time and season to every purpose under the sun." Surely He who sets the timing of the universe will keep me in perfect timing as I live in union (enmeshed) with Him.

THE WHY: Finally, the Psalmist explains that which is all-important: "...therefore for THY NAME'S SAKE lead me, and guide me" (vs. 3). How significant for the Psalmist to start with this — saying in effect: "I am in gear with Thee for Thy glory, for Thy purpose and for Thy satisfaction." It becomes evident that the secret of *living in His will* is living wholly for His glory. What beauty and harmony when the Corinthians could keep every lesser gear related to them as they were rightly related to Him. And so shall we then announce to the Master Gear, if we are properly enmeshed — even as the Psalmist announced: "Lead me and guide me." And we shall better understand Thomas Aquinas: "It is clear that he does not pray, who, far from uplifting himself to God, requires that God shall lower Himself to him, and who resorts to prayer not to stir the man in us to will what God wills, but only to persuade God to will what the man in us wills."

SECTION
FOUR

Moving . . .

UNTO FULL STATURE

in

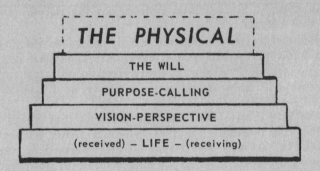

While many believers ignore the need for a proper attitude toward their body, still others have so overemphasized the physical as to make it everything. In moving unto full stature we shall see:

IN CHAPTER 13: What is the difference between a "touch from" and a "vital union with" the Lord?

IN CHAPTER 14: How do we avoid the extreme positions regarding health and healing? How do we discover God's position?

IN CHAPTER 15: How shall we answer those zealous workers who would have us "burn out for God"?

IN CHAPTER 16: How does Paul picture God's highest glory in our body in Romans eight?

THIS QUESTION COMES:

"Even in the midst of so much emphasis today on healing, it seems to me there is an increasing bewilderment and misunderstanding regarding divine health and healing. More people are needing physical help, but too many are becoming bitter.

"I have never been able to go along with these great healing campaigns, but I do believe it is God's desire to bring His people into a fuller conception of healing as revealed in the Scriptures. On several occasions I have seen the Lord 'touch' a body and restore it. Yet the question that continues to puzzle me is that so seldom does this healing work bring any real transformation in the deepest spiritual life of these as we would wish to see. Is it because in their seeking healing for themselves there is no real giving of themselves to Him for Himself?"

THE DIFFERENCE BETWEEN A "TOUCH FROM" AND A "VITAL UNION WITH" THE LORD

WE REMEMBER while He was on this earth how many thronged the Lord Jesus and received a "touch from" Him. We see His compassion as He put forth a healing virtue to meet their physical needs. In Him the "Living God" was manifest and working in a general kingdom ministry meeting physical needs.

How often we have pondered why there was not a greater evidence of spiritual work wrought in their inner lives. Was there something of an inward work wrought – something actually accomplished even though we could not see it outwardly? In some instances, as with the lepers who failed to show any gratitude for their healing, it would seem they received little more than a touch upon their outward physical being. There was no evidence of any inner spiritual work which would have manifest itself in praise or thankfulness. Why?

I never felt I understood this general kingdom ministry until one day I realized what was involved in Christ's death, burial and resurrection. I saw through our union in His death and resurrection we could experience a *vital life-union with* Him, which was far more than a mere *touch from* Him. Thus we have the distinctive ministry of the Apostle Paul as he interprets for us how a new and unique privilege becomes available since Christ arose as the resurrected and ascended Lord. We can have more than a package from the "Living God"—more than a "touch from" Him; now we can enter into a "vital union with" our Lord and share in His divine life. For years I had sensed this general kingdom ministry of Christ, but had not realized that it was distinct from Christ's unique ministry to His Body since His resurrection and ascension.

I have always been extremely cautious in sharing those things which seemed to be a private unveiling to me until there has been divine confirmation through some other servant. I believe this is proper order when we truly love the unity of the Body of Christ. Then when I found in a little booklet by Witness Lee, Chinese co-worker with Watchman Nee, this very real confirmation I rejoiced abundantly in God's wonderful timing and ways. Perhaps it will lend more authority if I quote several portions directly from him, as he makes this important distinction between *receiving a touch from the Living God* and *experiencing a life-union with the God of Resurrection:*

" . . . why do we stress the distinction between the *Living God* and the *God of* Resurrection? Because, while the Living God can perform many acts on man's behalf, the nature of the Living God cannot blend with the nature of man. When, on the other hand, the God of Resurrection works, His very nature is wrought into the nature of man. Brothers and sisters, please note carefully that even when the Living God has performed some act on your behalf, after that act as before it, He is still He and you are still you. The Living God can work on behalf of man, but the nature of the Living God cannot unite with the nature of man. On the other hand, when the God of Resurrection works, He communicates Himself to man by that which He does for him. Let me cite two illustrations:

"When the children of Israel were in a hopeless plight in the wilderness, the Living God opened a way for them across the Red Sea. The dividing of the Red Sea was a miracle which demonstrated to them that God was the Living God, yet that miracle performed for them did not bring any measure of the *life* of God unto them. They witnessed many other divine acts in the wilderness – e.g., God gave them bread from heaven and water out of the rock – but despite those and other wonders performed for them, nothing of God Himself was thereby imparted to them.

"In contrast to this, the Apostle Paul testifies to knowing not only the Living God, but also the God of Resurrection. Paul was so sorely tried that he despaired of life, but it was thus he learned to trust in the God who raises the dead. When the God of Resurrection acted on his behalf to raise him from the dead, that divine act not only accomplished something for Paul; it also communicated God's own nature to Paul.

"Brothers and sisters, do discriminate here. The miracles wrought for Israel in the wilderness were acts of the Living God; but despite the many miracles wrought for them, nothing of God was wrought into their constitutions. The miracles wrought for Paul were wrought by the God of Resurrection, and each fresh miracle wrought a fresh measure of God Himself into the life of Paul. Alas! though generations have passed since the Resurrection, many Christians are almost ignorant of the God of Resurrection, and are only interested in the Living God. Let me try and bring this matter home to our daily lives.

"A brother becomes seriously ill. His case is considered hopeless, but God has mercy on him and works a miracle on his behalf so that he recovers. Thereafter, he testifies to the fact that God is the Living God. Yet within a short time of his recovery he plunges right into the world. Even when he is living in the world, he still remembers that God is the Living God and that God preserved his life from death. But he has experienced no increase of divine life; he has only experienced a miracle of healing.

"Another brother becomes ill. Day after day passes without a vestige of improvement. For long he keeps hovering at the edge of the grave. Then, when he has completely despaired of life, in the depths of his being he gradually becomes aware of God. Resurrection life begins to work within, and he awakens to the fact that this resurrection life is a life that can overcome all affliction and can even swallow up death. He is still conscious of much weakness, and is sorely tested; nevertheless the realization deepens that God is not working to make His might known in external acts, but is working to impart Himself.

"Light breaks upon him gradually, and gradually health returns. This brother does not just experience healing; he comes into a new experience of God. The other brother could testify to a miracle wrought in his body, and shortly after could plunge right into the world; but if this brother gives a word of testimony there is nothing sensational about it, and there is no stress on the healing; yet, you meet God in his life.

"Let me tell another incident to illustrate this further: A brother who was engaged in export business had arranged a consignment of goods by a certain ship. Somehow the goods were delayed and were forwarded by a later ship. Shortly afterwards he learned that the boat by which he had originally planned to send the goods had been sunk. How he praised God for His overruling grace! 'Oh God,' he said, 'how perfect your guidance was! You are indeed the True and Living God.'

"Some time later this same brother contracted tuberculosis, and to complicate matters, he developed digestive trouble as well. The T.B. called for a nourishing diet while the digestive complaint forbade it. He was in a sore plight, but his wife comforted him and said: 'Don't you remember the episode of two months ago when God saved that consignment of goods? Oh, our God is the True and Living God.'

"But on this occasion God seemed neither true nor living, for the more that couple prayed, the more the brother hemorrhaged; the more they prayed, the worse his digestive complaint became. He was perplexed. Finally he gave way to doubt, and his wife began to question too. A few months later his business came to a standstill. His health steadily deteriorated and his financial resources steadily dwindled, till both he and his wife reached the verge of despair.

"In their extremity they rallied all their united faith and prayed once again: 'Oh God, you are the Living God. We believe you will yet be gracious to us.' But the next day the patient had a further hemorrhage, and neither he nor his wife could exercise faith any more. The Living God vanished from their horizon! Friends and neighbors pronounced the brother's case hopeless, and the doctor's verdict confirmed theirs.

"However, that was not the end of the story. A crisis took place in the inner life of that brother. It began to dawn upon him (though he could not then define it as we are defining it now) that while he knew God as the Living God, he did not know Him as the God of Resurrection. He knew the doctrine of the Resurrection, but he did not know the reality of Resurrection. He knew in experience that God had come into his life, but he did not know in experience that he had come into the life of God.

"It became clear to him that from his conversion right up to that time he had possessed the life of God, but he had not been living in the life of HIM. He saw that even his faith in God had been *his* faith, his reliance upon God had been *his* reliance. He saw all his efforts to please God as something apart from God. He was filled with remorse. He abhorred himself. His healing ceased to be a question. His one question was himself. He became overwhelmingly aware that what he had regarded as his most spiritual service had been something apart from the divine life. No one preached to him, but the Holy Spirit gave him a deep registration of his individualism. He judged himself unsparingly and ceased to entertain any thought of improvement in health or circumstances.

"At that point a strange thing happened — his health began to improve. No one knew when or how healing took place. There was just a gradual increase of strength until he was quite well. At an earlier date he could bear witness to God as the Living God and all the while be living his life in independence of God; from that date he knew the God of Resurrection and began to live in dependence on resurrection life." (From THE GOD OF RESURRECTION.)

In this extended quote we have been describing how many believers may go along for years — testifying to some very real miraculous acts of God in their behalf — and then suddenly God allows them to go into the deep valley. They cannot understand why God does not respond as before. But it is for this reason: That He may lead them into a separation from the old source and dependence — because only in death can they be cut loose that they might truly experience the vital union with the God of Resurrection.

All of this would emphasize clearly two levels of life: Those

who enjoy an occasional "touch from" God are most often still
secretly wishing to use Him for their own ends; whereas God
desires to bring each one into this vital life-union with Himself
that ours is a continuous participation in Him. Such a life can
only be experienced as we live unto Him and His pleasure. On
the first level the attitude is *escape for us;* on the higher level
it is a life of *fulfillment for Him.* Once we sought deliverance
only, but now we cry for inward development first.

Now as we further understand two levels of ministry we shall
see how there is a proper place for this divine "touch from the
Lord." There is the *building up ministry within the Body* that
there may be the *flowing out ministry unto others.* Let us take a
closer look at these two. It will help us to remember that in His
general kingdom ministry our Lord often gave the healing touch—
even so He would use His servants to act in His behalf today.
This is the *flowing out* ministry unto the unbeliever or even for
the unenlightened believers in the Church who have not yet
experienced what it means to participate in the vital union with
the Resurrected Lord. But God's first order is that the members
who have shared in this living-union-participation in His Body
should also know the unique ministry of *building up* the Body in
love. Only when this *innermost spiritual kingdom* becomes operative will there be an effectual flowing out in a *general kingdom
ministry.*

Is it not evident that as individuals we cannot have any effective ministry flowing through us until there has first been a
spiritual building-up within us? Even so in the corporate Body
of Christ, there will come this effectual flowing out – the touch
of God upon lives – as there is a spiritual building-up of the
corporate Body. And in God's own time, those who have been
"touched" will come to also experience their vital participation
in living union of the Body of Christ.

How often as we encounter folk who are facing the bitter
experiences of life, do we hear them insist: "Oh, I'm trusting in
God." And we are sure, for the measure of light they have – this
is true. But God wants to press each one to a much different
relationship than merely trusting Him for things. He wants to
give us a vital union with Himself. As we have seen, this was
God's plan from the very beginning – not because Adam sinned –
but because in His master-design He has desired for us to live
by the life of the Lord Jesus – thus enjoying all things which
includes health – not merely healing.

A PASTOR QUESTIONS:

"It seems to me there are two extreme views as regards our body. Many a church is torn by opposing convictions and conceptions. One group will almost worship the body as though physical well-being were the summum bonum of life; while the other seems almost to worship suffering and pain as though the body were only made for such. There are those who are positive and adamant that everyone should be healed, while others seem almost to glory in affliction as God's only means of instruction. There are those who seek to escape any pain as though it should not so much as be recognized among God's children, and still others who almost seem to glory in any opportunity to suffer. One group would take the body up and make it a part of the divine, and the others—seeing only evil in it— would seek to get rid of the body. In avoiding these dangerous extremes, is there any balance clearly indicated in God's Word?"

RECOGNIZING EXTREME POSITIONS
BUT ALSO THE SCRIPTURAL BALANCE

I N ONE OF HIS little books[11] Oswald Chambers explains the error of two extreme attitudes. He calls them the *Cult of the splendid animal* and the *Cult of the sick attitude.* In describing the first he says:

"There always have been and always will be people who worship splendid, well-groomed health. This verse (in Psalm 147:10) which reads '...he taketh not pleasure in the legs of a man,' reveals that God places health in a totally different relationship from that which is put in by man. The modern name for the worship of physical health is Christian Science. The great error of the healthy-minded cult is that it ignores a man's moral and spiritual life."

Of the second cult who manifest the sick attitude, he says:

"A great many people indulge in the luxury of misery; their one worship is anguish, agony, weakness and sensitiveness to pain. The cult of the sick attitude is well established in human history by the fact that most of the great men and women whose personalities have marked the life of their time have been to some degree deranged physically. Amiel, a highly sensitive and cultured man, almost too morbid to exist, was a lifelong invalid, and he wrote thus in his Journal: 'The first summonses of illness have a divine value, so that evil though they seem, they are really an appeal to us from on high, a touch of God's Fatherly scourge.' Now the healthy-minded (cult) do not agree with that attitude, while the people (of the sick-cult) are inclined to worship it.

"Is it not true: the people who accept the fact of being sick are inclined to have a jaundiced eye for everything healthy? For a man to make health his god (as many unwittingly do) is to put himself merely at the head of the brute creation."

Thus we have two extreme attitudes, but before we consider the proper Christian attitude, let us look at two other extremes which have often become manifest in some of our fundamental churches. There are those who insist that the Christian faith should be primarily occupied with the saving of the soul and getting it ready for heaven. Others, perhaps in reaction, have come to overemphasize the needs of the body as to almost exclude the spiritual preparation of the inner man. In the midst of these two extreme emphases, what is the proper Christian attitude? One has put it thus:

"Let it be said straight off that Christianity is not a healing cult; its primary purpose is not to keep our bodies in repair. God is not a cosmic convenience, dancing attendance on our bodily comfort. That would make us use God. And we can't use God; God must use us. And incidentally it must be said that Christianity is not a happiness cult. Its primary purpose is not to make us happy, as many happiness cults would imply or state. Happiness does come through the Christian faith, amazing happiness beyond description. But if the end of the Christian faith is to make us happy, then we are again using God — we are the center, not God. This means self-idolatry. Happiness is a by-product of God's using us."

So the Christian faith is not a success cult, a happiness cult, or a healing cult as so many today have sought to make it. Its

central purpose is – having redeemed man from his fallen condition – to bring man into that fullest participation with God in
that ultimate intention He designed in the beginning. Of course
in realizing God's highest, man will enjoy (as by-products) true
happiness and true health. But if we seek health first – or anything else – we shall lose it – it will evade us; but if we seek
first the Kingdom of God, then all these things will be added
to us.

In the past twenty years we have constantly been confronted
with these extreme and dogmatic attitudes as we have moved
among all kinds of churches. It has driven me to ask: What is
the proper Christian attitude as revealed in the Bible? As we
have said in the first chapter of this section, we can insist upon
a concept of healing which we gather from the general ministry
of the Lord Jesus and yet be left hanging in the hour of severe
physical crisis. All the theory, doctrines and bold affirmations
of our faith go down the drain in a hurry – when they do not work.
We have all witnessed this again and again, even in some of the
greatest exponents of healing. It is all the outgrowth of developing a doctrine without understanding God's larger and higher
intention for us to share a *living union* with His Son.

Again we turn to our pattern-man, and consider what God has
revealed through him. It was not until I understood what Paul
meant by LIVING IN HIS POINT OF VIEW, that I could appreciate the proper attitude of the believer toward his body and
health. Listen as Paul prays for the Colossians:

"We are asking God that you may SEE THINGS, AS IT WERE,
FROM HIS POINT OF VIEW by being given spiritual insight and
understanding. We also pray that your outward lives, which men
see, may bring credit to your Master's Name, and that you may
bring joy to His heart by bearing genuine Christian fruit, and
that your knowledge of God may grow yet deeper.

"As you live this new life, we pray that you will be strength-
ened from God's boundless resources, so that you will find yourselves able to pass through any experience and endure it with
courage. You will even be able to thank God in the midst of pain
and distress because you are privileged to share the lot of those
who are living in the Light" (Phillips – Col. 1:9-12).

We have quoted this translation because perhaps it gives a
new and fresh light as to the inner groaning of Paul. Here in this
one short passage we have at least five things which forms the
foundation for the proper Christian attitude:

FIRST: it is imperative that we · SHARE HIS VIEWPOINT. Apart from this how can we expect spiritual insight and understanding?

SECOND: as we become God-relating instead of self-relating we live to bring joy to His heart by bearing fruit.

THIRD: we can most surely count on God's boundless resources of grace for enduring whatever we are called to pass through. While it most surely works for our inner development, we are most concerned that it furthers His purpose.

FOURTH: we learn to be thankful (not necessarily *for* but) in the midst of pain and distress.

FIFTH: we can expect that pain and distress will surely be the privilege of all: "the lot of those who are living in the light." This does not mean that we embrace a suffering complex, nor do we invite pain, but we know how to accept tribulation and pressures when they come.

We have been realizing that we can only share the full measure of His life as we also learn to share in His attitude and viewpoint. We are convinced that God wills health. It is a part of His straight-line purpose. Disease is a coming short, a dip or moving off from that line and is not the first will of God. Furthermore, disease of the body is no more the will of God than is disease of the soul. God is out to get rid of all its ugly forms. "The evil of the mind is error; the evil of the emotion is suffering; the evil of the body is disease; the evil of the soul is sin. And He is out to root out all evil from all of life, including the evil of the body, disease."

However, when we say that "disease is not the will of God and that He never sends disease, we must clarify a bit. Indirectly He does. For He has made a universe of moral and material law. These laws are His preventive grace saying: 'Keep off — danger.' If we break these laws, we don't break the laws: we break ourselves upon the laws. We get hurt — physically, spiritually, morally. We get the consequences in ourselves.

"If we work with the moral universe, we get results — the moral universe will back us, sustain us, and further us. We will get results. But if we go against the moral universe, we will be up against it, frustrated, hurt. We will get consequences. Some people go through life getting results; others get consequences. But we get one or the other. And those results or consequences are passed on to others, for we are all bound up in a bundle of life together for good or ill. We have the power to hurt or to help one another, and that through succeeding generations. 'Just as the individual enjoys assets he is not entitled to as an individual, so he is called on to suffer liabilities which he does not individually merit.'

"So God, having made the laws, is remotely responsible for our suffering if we break those laws through the misuse of freedom. He is responsible for making us free and hence is responsible, remotely, if we misuse our freedom and suffer. God accepts that responsibility and discharges it at the cross. There He takes on Himself everything that would and does fall on us and suffers with us and for us. There the world's sin and sorrow 'were forced through the channel of a single heart.' There He provided an open door of release from all that hurts and hinders us in any realm of life." [12]

Now through the Cross and the resurrection God has provided something almost completely missed by even the majority of believers. The blinds have too long been over our eyes. If we have had a bad heredity physically, here is God's answer — straight from above. There is imparted to us a divine nature, a new creation heredity that cancels out or controls the lower heredity. We are to enjoy a union from above. So we are not caught in the unchangeable conditions; there is an open door upward, always. We must learn to walk into that open door into radiant health.

While so many would thrust off any responsibility for their condition, I like the counsel of Oswald Chambers: "My personal experience is this: I have never once in my life been sick without being to blame for it. As soon as I turned my mind to asking why the sickness was allowed, I learned a lesson that I have never forgotten, viz. that my physical health depends absolutely on my relationship to God. Never pin your faith to a doctrine or to anyone else's statement. Get hold of God's Book, and you will find that your spiritual character determines exactly how God deals with you personally. People continually get into fogs because they will not take God's line; they will take someone else's line. God's Book deals with facts, not fancies. There are cases recorded in the Bible, and in our own day, of people who have been marvelously healed — for what purpose? For us to imitate them? Never, but in order that we might discern what lies behind, viz — the individual relationship to a personal God."

Finally we must recognize two other extremes. There are those who say that all disease has a physical origin — they are the materialists. There are others who insist that all disease has only a spiritual or mental origin – they are the mentalists. To hold either extreme is to be like a bird with one wing. Again we quote:

"To hold that all disease is mental in origin is to alienate the whole scientific movement for health. To hold that all disease is physical in origin is to alienate the whole spiritual conception of health. Both extreme positions have filled graveyards as a result of their half-truths. Many people have died repeating the slogan that disease was all in their minds, when a surgeon could have applied a physical remedy and healed them. But, as Dr. Joseph Hersey Pratt says, 'bushels of tonsils and teeth have been taken out of people who needed to be delivered from fears and self-centeredness and resentments in order to be well.' "

It was Hawthorne who said, "A bodily disease which we look upon as whole and entire itself may, after all, be but a symptom of some ailment in the spiritual part." True. And just as truly a soul disease which we look upon as whole and entire may, after all, be a symptom of some ailment in the physical part. There are many people who are castigating their souls and loading them with guilt when they should attend to their nutrition, or have an infected tooth out. If the nerves are starved on account of lack of vitamins, they will kick back in spiritual depression in exactly the same way that a starved soul will kick back in bodily depressions.

In all of this there are those who will wonder why we have not taken some definite position regarding this aspect or that. We have studied in vain to find some position which the Apostle Paul formulated regarding all being healed, or all living in full health. We have concluded that he lived *in a Person* instead of *in a position*. Now this seems difficult for many! They have such a doctrinal bent, they cannot imagine one having no exacting position from which or for which to argue.

But it brings such a relief and inner rest to know that our faith rests, not in an articulately phrased position – but rather in a Person, the Lord Himself. Perhaps some day the full import of that reality will reach our own heart in a way it has not, and we shall more fully understand that God designs for each of us to be informed and so we shall be more balanced Christians. Thus balanced – we become the most beautiful handiwork of God. Life living in Him and fully expressing Him. This is FULL STATURE.

A MISSIONARY QUESTIONS:

"For years I had glibbly announced before congregations that I would rather burn out than rust out. With many others I had been caught in the *spirit of emergency* — insisting that our dedication to God should be demonstrated by a willingness to "burn out" for Him, even in a few years if He so desired. Refusing the counsel of wiser and more mature men I disregarded many natural laws, and now my body is reaping retribution. I have since come to realize I was just mouthing words without much spiritual understanding of how God is to realize His highest glory through our body.

"Now I am convinced that God will not only help us to heed the moral and physical laws of well-being but He will so make the spiritual laws operative in us that after 80 years of poured-out-service we may stand, even as Moses, as a glorious monument of God's lifelong handiwork."

LIVING AT THE POINT
OF EXHAUSTION

IF I HAD ARRANGED the chapters of this book in sequence according to the most vulnerable or weakest level in our quest for full stature, perhaps this problem of physical well-being should have come much earlier. Here is the haunting question: How shall we escape this modern tempo of religious programming and the false conceptions imposed by men and organizations (not God)? Among many things, these are primarily responsible for keeping pastors and Christian workers at the point of physical and nervous exhaustion.

How can any church hope to establish proper home life when it insists on keeping its members in church almost every night in the week? Consider a church which boasts that its doors have been open at least five or six nights in the week for the past ten

years. I know there are many who reason: "If we don't keep folk
occupied with divine things (?) they will be snared into other
things." It is true, once we have discovered the "life in the
Spirit" we have learned to "burn the oil" and not the wick. But
what about the vast majority in the church who are still burning
only the wick? We are sure these folk need, not an increased
programming schedule, but God's message revealing THIS NEW
KIND OF LIFE.

Or consider the pastor who, because he knows what is happening, weeps over an impossible schedule which has kept him from
a proper home and family life for months, even years—until he is
a virtual stranger to those he should be molding. We must honestly face it! So many are held like a helpless gear in a vast
religious machine. We must, absolutely must, understand and
rectify certain wrong conceptions which are presently producing
this harvest of ulcers, frustration, delinquency and nervous
breakdown in God's children.

CALLED: NOT TO "BURN OUT" BUT TO "SHINE FORTH"

If our controlling conceptions are wrong it is because we have
not truly passed through the rectifying work of the Cross. Apart
from a Calvary *crushing* and *seeing* no one will give up his little
kingdom building or ego feeding to be released into that new
plane of physical quickening by God's Spirit (Rom. 8:11).

Please! Bear with me. Even though every reader should become enraged and lay this book aside at this point, I must be
faithful to Him in exposing and rectifying according as God has
given light. There is a plane of life—quickened life—which the
more spiritual talk much about, yet hardly know in reality and
experience. It is most disheartening to realize that scores who
read this will acknowledge the truth, yet continue right on in
their vicious tempo of religious activity serving some machine.
They will admit they are caught! But what a price must be paid
to get free! The price of passing through the Cross in its deeper
detaching work!

Those who have known me best will affirm that I have not yet
arrived at any full rectification or realization of these principles
I am about to share. But they will also be the first to rejoice in
what God (and only He could do it) has wrought to slow down a
driving, promoting, steam-roller type of personality which has in
the past kept everybody and everything in a perpetual high-speed
turmoil.

God has wrought! And He is continuing to *tear down* and
rectify so He might build that built-in stature of Christ He intends. For this I am eternally grateful.

What about our controlling conception? Do we have the in-
ordinate itch to burn out as a meteor blazing its way across the
sky or do we long to shine forth as His brilliant star? God has
not designed us to be meteors, falling out of our orbit and burning up as we madly rush through space. There is much greater
glory for Him if we "shine forth as the stars" for a lifetime, than
if we attract attention as a blazing meteor for a short season.

Once again (in the diagram) we must show how the eternal
perspective will help us keep every emergency properly related
to the highway of God's ultimacy.

We could wish that there had never been any downward dip
(w-x-y) and that all we needed to consider is the Father's straight
line (a to z) of eternal purpose which He will realize in Christ
Jesus. But since that awful disaster in the Garden when Adam
turned to his own way (w - x), sin *has* brought an emergency. This
emergency is upon us and will be here until the final hour of
restoration.   Nothing will ever be returned to that original
normalcy.

Only as we see how this *emergency* is incorporated into *God's
highway of ultimacy* can we appreciate how God intends for us
to walk.   Before the Fall Adam was faced with the glorious
urgency of opportunity. Since the Fall every fallen son in Adam
is confronted with emergency: "Now is the accepted time; today
is the day of salvation." The Bible clearly indicates there can
be no rest for the wicked. They are like the troubled sea, which
cannot rest. Therefore the *urgency of crisis* is constantly staring

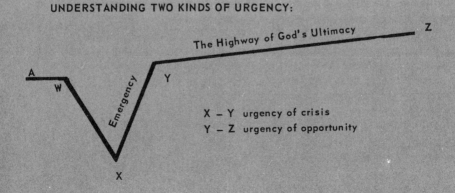

UNDERSTANDING TWO KINDS OF URGENCY:

The Highway of God's Ultimacy

Z

A

W

Emergency

Y

X – Y urgency of crisis
Y – Z urgency of opportunity

X

them in the face. However, once we have passed through the redemptive work of the Cross, we can move onto God's highway of ultimacy, living for the fulfillment of His pleasure and glory. Immediately we should have moved into the new sphere, living with the *urgency of opportunity* before us. I say we "should have," for it must be recognized that far too many believers who have trusted Christ and His finished work on the Cross are still in the throes of emergency living. It is no glory to God that they have not been fully rectified in their conceptions. Once we have truly moved out of the *now* of crisis, we shall appreciate what it means to live in that *eternal now* from whence the Father could speak "This day (eternal day) have I begotten thee." What day was that? It was that "eternal day."

NOT FRUSTRATED "BUSYNESS" BUT SPIRIT-DIRECTED FRUITFULNESS

We return to consider the missionary's testimony given at the beginning. One thing is evident: there is no honor to God to abuse or burn out our body for Him. Our willingness may be admirable, indeed! But there is real difficulty in answering the natural logic of those who would impose a burden upon us which He does not intend. And we are sure to fall victim unless we understand this difference between the urgency of *opportunity* or of *crisis*.

In view of the extreme emergency of this present hour many would plead for immediate, total dedication to meet the desperate challenge in the closing seconds of this dying dispensation. With what fervor, zeal and enthusiasm they would convince us it isn't fair to tell men here twice until all have heard at least once. It is a fact; no one can deny that many modern-day believers have gone soft and accepted an easy way. They are without passion or real concern for the tragic plight of the lost. Let no one assume he is beyond the temptation to settle down and only enjoy the gospel for himself when he should be pouring himself out in a sacrificial sharing. We can testify that unless the Cross is constantly operative in a life one is sure to settle down and "live by his tastebuds and glands" and even find a most logical reason for so doing.

Here is the point of danger. While it is necessary to turn men from "sparing themselves" there is something more basically wrong in imposing a conception which pushes so many into a frenzy of activity, exhaustion and frustrated "busyness." Is it

by natural reason or logic that we motivate men? Is it by sheer
soul-force that we compel men to action? Could it be that
some of our "specialists" who have learned to move men and
impart their own vision and burden are *themselves* thrusting
laborers forth into the harvest field? There is an important difference between guilt that is self-induced or man-imposed and
that which is Spirit-imparted. What a rectifying word it was to my
own heart when the Lord quietly whispered to me one night:
"Son, I am the Lord of the harvest. It is not your job to thrust
forth laborers. 'Pray ye the Lord of the harvest that HE MAY
THRUST FORTH LABORERS...'" Then I saw! There is so
much power of personality, power of persuasion, power of natural
logic which is seeking to thrust men forth, but it is not the
thrusting forth of the Lord. Then I realized how often it is men
who impose upon themselves the *urgency of crisis* and live in a
constant frenzy of busyness. It is of their own doing, not something imparted by the Holy Spirit.

But there is a proper sense of urgency if we live the Spirit-
controlled life. The Spirit will keep us continually alert to the
urgency of opportunity, and in those special times of need use
us in the *urgency of a crisis.* Last evening in the service I saw
a dear mother mightily laid hold of by the Spirit of intercession.
What groaning and travail! What urgency was imparted by the
Spirit. Was it for some loved one? Was it some crisis she might
never understand that called for such urgency of Spirit? I do not
know. But of this we are sure, it is God who takes the initiative.
When we are under the lordship of the Holy Spirit we shall never,
on our own, drum up any feverish excitement and frenzy of activity. Like our lovely Lord we shall always be ready for every
emergency, yet ever living above that pull or drag upon our body
which would cause physical exhaustion.

ONCE CONTINUAL TENSION . . . BUT NOW SPIRIT
CONTROLLED ACTION

I recall one night at the close of a service how a dear little
mother in Israel slipped a piece of paper into my hand as she
slipped out. No doubt she had watched my tense striving and
breathless pace in working for Him, and she simply added: "This
may be a help to you."

It was! Like a sharp shaft it was Spirit-directed to my need.
In my zeal I was completely ignorant that I was abusing my body
by disregarding the natural laws God had established. Her ex-

hortation which I copied on the fly-leaf of my Bible has continued to speak to me through these years. It was a legend about the beloved Apostle John who was supposedly in the midst of writing that sublime and profound revelation given to him while on the Isle of Patmos. As the incident goes, someone who approached John was quite surprised to find him not in prayer or in deep spiritual meditation, but instead amusing himself with his pet parrot. Whether or not the legend had any possible truth, indeed the author's point does: "The bow that is always strung will soon lose its strength."

How this crossed up my natural reasoning! If the whole world was lost and doomed, who could possibly rest? Surely we are expendable; the message must go forth at any cost. But then I read how the Lord Jesus rested. Surely it was not the Lord's plan for continuous tension. In all His universe there is a built-in design: A time for work and a time for rest. And He goes so far as to help enforce it by taking the sun out of the sky when it is time to rest.

It was venerable Henry Ward Beecher who announced that he could do a year's work in eleven months, but he could not do it in twelve. John Wesley's advice to young preachers was, "I take care of my body just like I do my best horse: so as to get the most work out of it."

NOT FIGHTING HIS LAWS . . . BUT CO-OPERATING

There is only one way to live: GOD'S WAY. Since the first century the Christian way has often been called "the Way." "If this means anything, it means that the Way is written not merely in the Bible but also in biology—the demands of religion and the demands of life are the same. The Way, then, is written in our nerves, our blood, our tissues, in the total organization of life. If we live according to that Way, we live; if we don't, we get hurt. So the Christian Way is written not merely in texts of Scripture but in the texture of life. It is the way we are made to live." (E.S.J.) [13]

If we ignore the laws of the physical or moral kingdom, is it right to expect that some higher laws of the Spiritual kingdom should intercede to keep us from receiving retribution? No intelligent Christian would jump from a fifth story window and expect some spiritual law to abrogate the law of gravity, yet that same person will allow the sand of hate, fear and animosity to upset the delicate inner mechanism of the body, and when the inevitable retribution follows, plead with God to over-rule.

What did Jesus mean: "Blessed are your eyes, for they see, and your ears for they hear"? Could it also mean blessed is youɪ stomach, your heart, your nerves, your blood – blessed is every organ within you if it is fulfilling its intended function through living the Christian way? But woe be to the stomach, the heart, the nerves, or the blood when they are forced to work against the laws of the body. They are made for a glorious cooperation.

You may have read one author's unique way of describing an imaginary convention of bodies who met to discuss their inhabitants. One body stands up and says: "I wish the man who occupies me knew how to live. He doesn't, so I'm tied in knots half the time. He doesn't know how very sensitive I am, inherently so, to his letting in fears to take possession of him. I go into a spasm every time he lets one in. But he entertains them and I go on a strike."

Another body stands up and says: "The woman who inhabits me is afraid to live. She's always inventing ways to escape living. When I start to drag because of late hours and improper food, she feeds me more pills and tranquilizers. Then when I further protest by a reaction of dullness and lethargy, she whips me up again with another dose. But it's all a losing game—we are under the law of decreasing returns. She has to whip me up more to get out the same result. It's a descending spiral—and some day I'm going to quit protesting. She even teaches in church from the Book in which my Creator explains how I work best, but she doesn't seem to have read or understood those pages. It's too bad that these humans don't know how to cooperate with God's laws – and really live."

Another body stands up and says: "Look at my condition. I'm all black and blue inside, and I'm showing it on the outside too. The person who lives in me has become resentful toward life and has a chronic grouch. You see how my gastric juices refuse to flow under these conditions. And now this silly person is dosing himself with medicines and running from doctor to doctor, who can't find a thing wrong with me. I know what is wrong: I don't work well with resentments. I am made for love. One is sand in my machinery and the other is oil."

If our bodies could talk, what wouldn't they say! But they are talking—talking in the only language they know, the language of protest when we refuse to cooperate with His laws for our body.

TWO WRONG CONCEPTIONS:

Is our humanity to be shucked off like a peanut husk in due time? While it is true believers will discard this earthly tabernacle which has only been intended as a temporary abode, and we do groan to be clothed upon with our new house from above, yet we shall not discard our humanity. We have been saying that manhood or humanity is a Divine conception which had its origin in the mind of God. There is nothing in the Scriptures to indicate that God at some future time is going to finish this order of things and replace humanity with an angelic order or some higher creation conceived in His mind. Our humanity is a very noble thing in the Divine planning and occupies a very great and high destiny. Even the Eternal Son has robed himself in humanity—not merely for a season but forever— and now sits in the heavenlies in His glorified humanity.

While our temporary tabernacle has been made subject to mortality and corruption for the present, yet the hour is coming when we shall put on immortality and incorruption. Then our humanity shall be beyond the powers that now seem to hold it in bondage. THE BURNING QUESTION IS THIS: Just how much of the redemptive and quickening work of the Spirit is available now for our mortal body? How do we appropriate this work so as . . .

TO REALIZE GOD'S HIGHEST
GLORY THROUGH OUR BODY

THE MORE ONE OBSERVES how God's children are being pushed like mere pawns, pushed beyond their natural measure of strength, carried along in this mad rushing tempo of our day, the more one is amazed that there is not more physical, emotional and mental breakdown. Apparently these children have not considered what it means to observe His built-in laws or to appropriate divine resources for realizing His highest glory through their bodies.

In all this mad rushing and breakdown God is crowding His children into that place where He might unveil His purpose and His ways for their body. Many are discovering that as long as they are still carving out their own religious kingdoms, or promoting the work they would accomplish for Him by their own methods, He must allow them to crumble and falter in their own strength. Apart from a very real death to selfish purposes, ambitions and methods, there can be no understanding or appropriation of that Life in the Spirit. God will only supply His energy for His work done in His way.

In the heading we have mentioned two conceptions which need correction. First, our humanity will not be discarded for some higher kind of angelic form. God has planned for a glorified humanity which will express the dignity, beauty and majesty of His intention. Second, and this will comprise the main subject of this present chapter, we must correct the all too prevailing idea that since man's body is subject to mortality and the bondage of corruption, the very best we can hope for now is to put up with this "limitation" and eagerly wait for another body. How we use this body or abuse it has not seemed too important.

We have considered the fact that God has designed His universal kingdom to function according to built-in laws. In the heavenlies we have the planets and the constellations following exact laws of their orbit. All around us there are hundreds of laws in operation. A father was explaining that Newton's Law of Gravitation held things together, when his son asked, "Well, Dad, what held things together before they passed this law?" Just as Newton did not pass the law of gravitation, but discovered it, so we do not pass the physical or moral laws written into the constitution of things; we discover them. We must honor these built-in laws just as we have learned to honor the law of gravitation. If not, we shall be broken. We do not break these laws, they break us.

God has written into the very structure of our being, into our tissues, our nerve cells, our blood stream, into the total organization of our life certain laws which govern our mortal body. Indeed sin has invaded this little kingdom of our mortal body and sought to upset these laws and the way we are made to live. What is so completely alarming is that so many of God's children seem ignorant of these laws, or unconcerned about honoring those they do recognize. Indeed God has provided a redemption which allows forgiveness because we have broken these laws. But it is surely not a redemption which allows one to continue breaking these laws of our mortal being at our own whim without paying the penalty.

In the glorious eighth chapter of Romans, Paul is primarily concerned with how this redemptive and quickening work of the Spirit is to be operative in our mortal body. He unveils a level of spiritual reality which even the most spiritual have hardly grasped or appropriated in their daily living. I know that others have had a glimpse into this *life in the Spirit;* therefore I am not alone in presenting something which seems most revolutionary. There is something far beyond a mere "touch from the Lord" or claiming a package of healing; there is a moving into that which God originally intended for Adam and his family even if he had not sinned.

One who has most surely known much of this eighth-chapter-reality has said: "In my lifetime I have seen so few who knew how to continually abide by God's built-in laws so that they might draw from divine resources to sustain their physical life. Some of these had learned to finish great amounts of work which would exhaust the average individual. Their vitality and rebound so challenged me I determined to know their secret. It seemed they were free from the strain and anxiety of trying to know God's will. Because they knew – and were sure that they knew – they could confidently face impossible obstacles which had swamped other men. Why were they so vibrant with surging life? Watching them created intense longings within me to also share in this flowing stream of His Life. Then I realized they had learned the reality of Romans eight. To them it was no mere doctrinal passage. I also realized that what has seemed so extraordinary should actually be normal for every life who would realize God's highest glory through his body."

In this brief space there is too much to cover, but let me enlarge on five little phrases in this eighth chapter and trust they may take on new meaning:

1. Living with "no condemnation."
2. Living according to the "law of Life."
3. Living by the "Spirit of Life."
4. Living as though our "body was dead."
5. Living in that "glorious liberty."

First, how many really live with "no condemnation?" I do not mean that we should be free merely from a conscience that condemns, but also from a heart that condemns. To understand the value of Christ's Blood as the Father values it is wonderful. By revelation we understand that His precious Blood accomplishes a legal satisfaction. Our conscience will not condemn us. This is very important for the child of God. Yet I believe there is another condemnation which arises from our own heart. John says: "Beloved, if our heart condemn us not, then have we confidence toward God" (1 John 3:21). This gnawing in the inner heart drives men; it is not a question of legal satisfaction, but the "assurance of our heart before Him" (3:19).

There is only one answer for this heart condemnation. Those who are completely identified with His mind and purpose – who have come to live in the eternal perspective where they see both the urgency of opportunity and the urgency of crisis–can "know that they are of the truth" and have "assured hearts." And this is the consolation: "God is greater than our heart, and knoweth all things." God does more than remove the condemnation of our heart; He gives the Spirit of assurance and Sonship. This is far more than merely being free from condemnation. There is that inward witness to pleasing God which Enoch enjoyed as he knew he pleased God. What complete harmony and attunement that one day he should walk too far–yes, walk right into the very presence of God!

Beloved, be sure of this: where there is "no condemnation" but rather a glorious "heart of assurance" it is like being free from all the grit and sand which usually hinders the delicate mechanism of our body.

SECOND, there is much more than we have realized in living according to the "law of life." A railway engine is made to run on tracks, and if it remains on the tracks it finds freedom, pulls its loads, and gets to its destination. But if, in order to gain its freedom, it jumps the tracks, the result is not freedom, but ruin to itself – for it has missed the laws of its function. To further illustrate: A little boy had listened attentively as his father explained the natural laws which God had built into the universe. He was especially fascinated by the law of gravity. A few minutes later as they were walking in the garden, he questioned his father, "Why do those leaves on that plant point up when gravity is surely pulling them downward?"

As they stood looking at several plants the father explained, "It's because God has built a higher law of life into that plant which lifts its leaves upward to the sun. This law is not exactly defying gravity, but in some strange way is transcending that downward pull. You see, this next little plant has one leaf which failed to draw from the plant's resources and has become limp;

therefore the law of gravity has taken over. Only God really understands how the plant's metabolism lives according to the law of life and thus transcends the law of gravity.''

The same is true in our bodies. God has designed us to live according to a strange and wonderful law of life which is not something imposed upon us from without, but is built into our very being. It merely requires that we be yielded to Him as His tender plant. Even as the plant is alive to the sun, so every petal and leaf of our being should continually be living unto Him. When this is so, our whole physical being is transcendently over-riding every downward pull. As the *law of Life* is constantly operating within we are vibrant by sharing divine resources. As surely as our physical turns from its "Sun" it will as surely become limp and succumb to the downward drag. Might we suggest that most failure or breakdown is simply proof that we have not heeded the divine *law of Life* and the resources which become available?

THIRD, we are seeing there is much more provision for living by the *Spirit of Life* than we have usually appropriated. Paul insists that God has not only given us the *law of Life* as an inward regulating power, but also the *Spirit of Life* as the abounding resource. The two will always work together, for they are inseparable. Thus Paul writes: ''... the law of the Spirit of Life. ...''

We have asked the question: Just how much quickening can we appropriate for our mortal body? For many it has seemed easy to excuse themselves from this kind of reality by insisting that this quickening is to be available at the time of the rapture when we receive our new house from above. But notice, this quickening by His Spirit is for our "mortal body" not our immortal body This is a provision we can enjoy *now.*

Have we not at times had a wee taste of this quickening? You know what it is after an exhausting day of labor to drag your weary body to midweek prayer service. While you were there something strange happened! You sensed an inward quickening—a flow of His life into your dragging body. By the close of the service you were renewed. The Spirit of Life working according to the law of Life had produced a quickening. That which had been limping and dragging suddenly became alive. Like the plant which turns its attention to the sun, so your attention was upon THE SON, and that wonderful law of Life cooperating with the Spirit of Life had infused a vitality and vibrancy you could not explain. Now if God can do this for a couple of hours, can He not do it continuously?

FOURTH, it is no small thing that God counts our "body as dead because of sin." This means that God has looked down the corridor of time to see that sin has already reached its full harvest. Death is that full and final harvest. Thus when God looked upon His Son hanging on the Cross He reckoned the full harvest of sin and death wrapped up into His dear Son and placed in the tomb. So when Christ died there, He carried in His body the full harvest. Since God reckons "our body dead because of sin" He waits for us to realize this glorious truth and also reckon the same thing. This means that as we have moved through the Cross and the tomb into His resurrection Life, we have a deliverance from the bondage and callings of the physical; that is, we have this deliverance as we reckon upon this "sentence of death on our body" and yield to the Spirit of Life.

This means living as though our "body was dead." At first glance I know how strange this statement seems. Some will insist, "Even though I have reckoned upon my union in His death and resurrection, my body seems very much alive; in fact, its appetites are constantly calling out and become very demanding." That may be true, yet as surely as we have reckoned the self life into its place of death, so we must recognize that our body was also included in this death. We can only reckon as we have new light.

Is it not true that there have been those rare hours when the Spirit of Life seemed to be reigning in such measure that you were lifted out, above and beyond the calling of your body so that you did not even hear or were not responsive to its demanding voice? You were quite surprised that three hours had slipped by while you were in prayer and your knees or physical had not reminded you of any weariness or of any appetite. In those hours "things which had seemed so important were no longer important at all." It is no small thing to "become alive unto God" and find yourself moved along in a whole new occupation—occupied with Christ Himself. In this union there is a flowing of life which automatically cuts off the old occupation.

Perhaps this will illustrate: One Fall when I decided to rake the leaves in our yard about half of them were still hanging to the oak trees. I could have wished for some way to knock them off so I could rake all the leaves at once, in fact I seriously considered how I might reach them with a long pole. But they continued to hang there throughout the winter months.

In the Spring when the sap began to flow into the branches of the tree, the old leaves quite naturally fell off. Surging life had its own way of cooperating with the law of Life. Then God opened my eyes to see His ways. I realized how often we have taken after God's little ones with our poles. We have sought to strip off the dead things from their life. But after we have pretty much stripped them down outwardly and conformed them to our wishes, we still have nothing but a barren tree, seemingly dormant and fruitless.

If we can only see that God considers our "body as dead"— even as the leaves — we shall turn our attention then to the glorious Spirit of Life which is surging within, working according to the law of Life. We shall not need to be occupied with the "knocking off" or the putting to death of our body. We reckon this as accomplished and become occupied with Him and His surging Life; the rest follows automatically. How often have we heard folk announce as they entered this reality of Roman's eight that it was like the entrance into springtime in their physical being. He who has known even a taste of this needs little explanation. He who is prejudiced or ruled by a carnal mind will accept no amount of explanation. Now we must go on to the last phrase.

FIFTH, there is much more in this "glorious liberty" (vs. 21) than we have even imagined. How shall we explain this maturity of liberty? Like the wiggling worm which finally burst forth as a butterfly! We have all rejoiced when some introvert has suddenly been set free from the shackles, inhibitions and bondages to enjoy the release of their personality. But if that seems great it is only a small glimmer of that glorious liberty which God intends for all His children.

I shall always cherish the remembrance of such a liberation, I

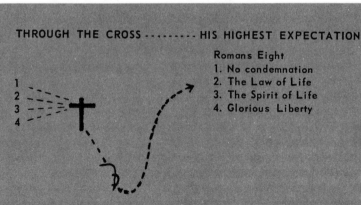

THROUGH THE CROSS ········· HIS HIGHEST EXPECTATION

Romans Eight
1. No condemnation
2. The Law of Life
3. The Spirit of Life
4. Glorious Liberty

recall one afternoon how a staid, queenly Presbyterian grandmother, well beyond eighty years of age, stood and shouted at the
top of her voice: "Well, glory! For more than eighty years I've
been in this cage and He's set the bird free." She wept and she
laughed! "No one has ever heard me pray aloud, for I've been
afraid of my own voice, but now I'm alive unto God instead of
others." And with lifted countenance toward Him she shone with
a glory which was the reflection of looking into His lovely face.
She was never again the same. The old veneer was removed, and
the personality was released to express His loveliness. If God
can liberate such a starchy, reserved old grandmother at eighty,
surely He can break up any old patterns and veneers which have
bound us.

Again there are those who make this liberty to be something
mostly future. Indeed there will come an hour of glorious liberation for which all creation is now groaning and travailing. Yet
there is a glorious liberty which is now available. Paul reminds
us: "... where the Spirit of the Lord is, THERE IS LIBERTY.
But we all, with open face beholding as in a glass the glory of
the Lord, are changed into the same image FROM GLORY TO
GLORY, even as by the Spirit of the Lord" (2 Cor. 3:17, 18). So
this change FROM GLORY TO GLORY is not something in the
distant future, it is even now being wrought in those who move
along the highway toward full sonship.

Finally, we are saying this liberty is *the life of glory!* Instead
of living merely to "burn out" so as to quench that inner gnawing
and condemnation, there is a shining forth of His glory and one
 has that inward assurance He is pleasing God — even as Enoch.
Instead of struggling to keep mere laws there is a cooperation
with the Spirit of Life, and the law of Life becomes automatic as
we become wholly alive unto Him. Instead of frustrated busyness
we become relaxed in His Spirit-directed fruitfulness.

Words are utterly inadequate to explain the reality Paul is
presenting in this eighth chapter of Romans. Yet the one who has
tasted of the quickening of his mortal body by the Spirit will
understand that it comes because our heart throbs as one with
His heart, and our mind has come into full harmony with His mind.

THIS IS THE LIFE OF GLORY! It is the life of continuous
union. We have sought to show that as we live in the reality of
these five phrases God realizes His highest glory in our body.
Then because we have not sought any glory for ourselves, but
only for Him, He is delighted to allow us to share in the spot-
light OF HIS GLORY.

Moving ...

UNTO FULL STATURE

in

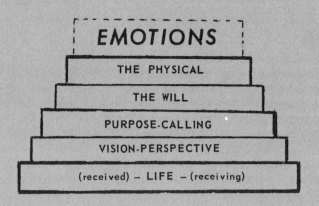

Perhaps nothing so reveals immaturity as pouting or emotional outbursts. In adding the next level of our stature we must see God's purpose in giving us the capacity for emotion:

IN CHAPTER 17: What are the "druthers?" Is it really possible to control the emotional stream?

IN CHAPTER 18: Should Christians "fall in love?" Since love is the highest emotion, what is God's design for our "love-life?"

IN CHAPTER 19: Did God intend for our deepest emotions to be repressed or expressed? Why has He given us the nine windows of the soul?

✳ WE HAVE ALL known individuals who excel in the intellectual, yet who seem like dwarfs in their emotions and will power. They can arrive at profound conclusions, yet cannot rise above their hurt feelings or selfish preferences to choose what they know is right. At the center of almost every acute problem, whether personal, social, economic, political or international is this basic emotional immaturity. Observing this has caused Dr. R. Beard to say: "The problems and possibilities in almost every situation have outgrown the persons. The consuming illness of our times is our immaturity — our refusal to grow up."

We have all known individuals like the man who boarded the Pennsylvania in Washington, walked into the dining car and ordered anchovies. There were no anchovies. He announced to the steward, "I am the Anchovy King of America. I spend $75,000 a year shipping anchovies on the Pennsylvania Railroad, yet when I come into your dining car, I cannot find a single anchovy. Is that a good business relationship?"

As soon as the train got to Baltimore, the steward immediately telegraphed ahead to Wilmington: "Rush Anchovies!"

They put anchovies on at Wilmington, had them already to serve at Philadelphia. But when the Anchovy King saw them before him, he said, "I will not eat them; I'd druther be mad."

UNDERSTANDING WHAT CAUSES
THE "DRUTHERS."

RECENTLY WHEN A PASTOR unfolded the problems he was facing in his home and church, it became evident by his attitude and remarks that he was very much like a little boy in his emotions. He was allowing his feelings to rule; his mind to be colored and his will to be numbed. Like the Anchovy King he was nursing hurt feelings and enjoyed his wounds. I could only remark quite frankly, "Your problem is that you have the druthers."

"And what is that?" he asked.

I explained. "You don't really want a solution; you want sympathy. You'd *druther* have your little circle of friends feel sorry for you, than allow the truth to set you free and thus liberate all the others who are somewhat justified in their opinions about you."

Thank God, he faced it! God had been preparing him to recognize that his selfish feelings were sitting as king. The self one has to live with can be one's own greatest punishment. To be left forever with that self which we hate, is hell.

The moment he honestly faced up to his hurt feelings and admitted that he was controlled by the *druthers,* he was ashamed; how self-pity had colored his glasses and caused him to relate things only to himself. Then as we drew this diagram he understood what feeds and controls the emotional stream.

UNDERSTANDING WHAT FEEDS THE STREAM

Someone has likened our emotions to that deep flowing river of feeling which either runs black or white, depending upon its

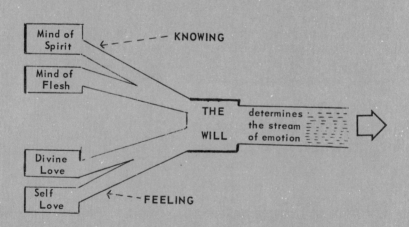

source. It is the flowing of this river which either helps or hinders all genuine communication. It either assists or makes void all that our intellect has stored up for use. How often you have seen some calm, cultured person completely lose his poise and self-control by an outburst of the emotions. Like a flooding torrent the black river has seemed to overcome the mind and will which are intended to govern and control.

In the diagram we have pictured four little rivers which pass through the will and become the main stream. It will help us to understand the three faculties of the soul: the mind for knowing and calculating, the emotions for feeling and loving, and the will for choosing and governing. We have shown the two little rivers which feed the knowing: either the mind of the flesh or the mind of the Spirit. But there are also two little rivers which feed our feeling: the black river or the white river. (James 3:11) Now these little rivers flow into the mixing room where the mind, the emotions and the will determine what kind of stream will flow out of us. Since we have already considered the mind and the will, let us now concentrate on the black river which has its source in the self-life and self-love and on the white river which has its source in Divine life and love.

Calmness and serenity are the beautiful jewels of a rich emotional life. It is the result of long and patient Spirit-directed self-control. Its presence is an indication of ripened experience, and of a more than ordinary knowledge of the laws and operations of thought, feelings and will. A man becomes calm in the measure that he understands himself and the working of his inner being. As he approaches an enlightened understanding and sees more and more clearly the internal relations of things by the action of cause and effect, he ceases to fuss and fume and worry and grieve, and remains poised, steadfast, serene. This is God's standard of full stature as so beautifully manifest in our Lord.

"The calm man, having learned how to govern himself, knows how to adapt himself to others; and they, in turn reverence his spiritual strength, and feel that they can learn of him and rely upon him. The strong, calm man is always loved and revered. He is like a shade-giving tree in a thirsty land, or a sheltering rock in a storm. Who does not love a tranquil heart, a sweet-tempered, balanced life? It does not matter whether it rains or shines, or what changes come to those possessing these blessings, for they are always sweet, serene, and calm. That exquisite poise of character which we call serenity is the last lesson of culture; it is the flowering of life, the fruitage of the soul. It is precious as wisdom, more to be desired than gold—yea, than even fine gold. How insignificant mere money-seeking looks in comparison with a serene life—a life that dwells in the ocean of Truth, beneath the waves, beyond the reach of tempests, in the Eternal Calm!

"How many people we know who sour their lives, who ruin all that is sweet and beautiful by explosive tempers, who destroy their poise of character, and make bad blood! It is a question whether the great majority of people do not ruin their lives and mar their happiness by lack of self-control. How few people we meet in life who are well-balanced, who have that exquisite poise which is characteristic of the finished character!' [14]

How does God accomplish this in us? First we must understand how it is the uncrucified self which causes the river to run black. With all its pent-up emotion, anger, frustration, hostility or resentment the old self comes flooding out with a head of pressure. Sometimes it is a long time in building up pressure, for the dam (will) holds back. But when it comes forth it stings, it hurts and it burns whatever it touches. Invariably it produces an immediate reaction in others; they can hardly help but throw up defenses and will retaliate unless the deepest inner working of the Cross has prepared them for such blasts.

In times of such pressure the sane judgment of the mind seems almost numbed into inactivity. The participants seem to each set up a battle line. The wife tells her husband for the first time not only what she is thinking, but what she has been feeling deep within. The thermometer rises, the breathing becomes shallow and rapid, and the husband replies: "Well, now, let me tell you a thing or two," and he pulls the tailgate on his load.

What a disgrace! Yes—that such should happen in Christian people. But let no one pretend that he is any different. Such a river flows in every individual who has not experienced the Cross in its deepest working in his life. It is the black river flowing out of its carnal source. The feelings are under the control of self; the fleshly mind is ruling, and the will is helpless until broken and then fortified by God's own will.

But we must also understand how the white river flows. God has so planned our inner being that our personality can express His own lovely Person. Much more than a cold calculating machine we are able to extol the warmth, compassion, enthusiasm, zeal — and a hundred more facets of His Being. And what is the source? It is never self. It is God who sheds His Life and Love abroad in our heart by the Holy Ghost.

It is in the life of the Lord Jesus that we see this most wonderfully expressed: "And Jesus went forth, and saw a great multitude, and was moved with compassion toward them, and He healed their sick." Note the proper relation of intellect to feeling and feeling to will. When Jesus saw their need and understood — the mind of the Spirit fed into the doorway of the will. But He was also moved with the inner compassion which initiated the Spirit of love. He had knowledge, but He had more. He had deep feeling, not merely a fleshly sympathy — but His own feelings were under the control of the Father's deep bowels of mercy and compassion. To more fully appreciate this white river which was flowing in our Lord, let us turn to Colossians 3 where Paul exhorts: "put on ... bowels of mercies, kindness...." A study of the Greek word translated bowels, suggests it is the deepest, innermost source of true feeling. It is in this area that the Holy Spirit sheds abroad divine love—and as it flows it becomes a fruit of the Spirit. It is by this union with Him that divine love and compassion flow through us. Thus we read how Jesus knew their need, felt their plight with a deep compassion and so he acted: He healed them.

What if we had no emotions? What if we had no warmth of feeling, no capacity for jubilation, no power to express enthusiasm? We have all observed such individuals. Some have gone through great shock to become passive, stoical and expressionless. Others have imagined it was wrong for their emotions to function, and have become cold, calculating persons. Without His radiant personality expressing through us, we should all be warped and lack that beauty God intended.

With his typical keen analysis the late Dr. A. W. Tozer shows the important function of the emotions: "We must not forget that a state of emotion always comes between the knowledge and the act. A feeling of pity would never arise in the human heart unless aroused by a mental picture of other's distress, and without *the emotional bump* to set off the will there would be no act of mercy. That is the way we are constituted. Whether the emotion aroused by a mental picture be pity, love, fear, desire, grief, there can be no act of the will without it. What I am saying is nothing new. Every mother, every statesman, every leader of men, every preacher of the Word of God knows that a mental picture must be presented to the listener before he can be moved to act, even though it be for his own advantage." [15]

WHILE MARY was home from Bible college during the summer months she explained how she had "fallen in love" with Johnnie, a young fellow she was trying to help spiritually. She told how the attraction had developed so gradually she was not fully aware of all that was happening. First, she had witnessed to him about the Lord. His interest grew and in due time he accepted the Lord as His Saviour. Then Mary tried to instruct him in God's Word that he might be established. Since there were so few Christian young people in their little town, she tried to fill his need for spiritual fellowship. It seemed quite natural when he needed help to seek out Mary. In fact no one else seemed really interested in him or capable to help.

By the time Bible college was ready to start in the Fall, they had (to use their terms) fallen madly in love. In great haste they married and moved off to school to prepare for Christian service. But by the end of the first term, they were in great confusion. Johnnie had quit school, in fact, he was so bitter he even refused to attend church. He insisted there was nothing to his conversion. A real breech of misunderstanding had developed between them. Mary was broken; John was without purpose or direction. Mary's original dream and dedication to Christian service and the mission field had come crashing down. What had happened? Where had she missed God's will? The enemy had set a snare; what was it?

SHOULD CHRISTIANS "FALL IN LOVE"?

ONE OF THE MOST revealing weaknesses in our schools and churches today is the lack of clear instruction regarding our emotions and our love life. Mary and John — with varying details — have their counterpart in hundreds of young people. It seems tragic that young people could attend a fundamental church or a good Bible college, and yet fall into this snare set by the enemy to sidetrack their future ministry and effectiveness for God.

We must face this question: Has God intended that a Christian should *fall in love?* Without doubt it is a serious misunderstand-

ing of the emotions when we assume it is right to *fall in love.*
For those outside God's grace and the help of the Holy Spirit,
it might seem necessary for people to be gripped by an animal
magnetism and so *fall in love.* Apart from that powerful magnetism, there might come an extinction of the human race. But for
those who have been enlightened by the Holy Spirit and have
come under the government of a new Lord, it is unthinkable that
they should follow the ways of the world.

It seems there are two false notions that dominate the world's
thought about love. First of all there is the fatalistic notion as
expressed in the phrase "fall in love." The very expression
seems to suggest that love is a sort of trap into which one falls,
and, having fallen in, one is a hopeless victim unable to extri-
cate oneself.

Second, love is thought of as an irresistible power that may
overcome a person at any time. And, willy-nilly, you have to love
a certain one regardless of circumstances and conditions. If
things are such that you cannot get the one you have fallen in
love with, then your fate is tragic. As the romance lyrics picture,
you must pine away in regrets and unsatisfied longings. It is this
warped notion of falling in love that has ruined homes and married couples. It accounts for the scandalous record of divorces
in our nation.

Recently we read of a prominent playright who, as he married
his second wife, agreed with her that if love should ever depart,
and either one of them should fall in love with anyone else, one
would not seek to hold the other. He is now married to a third
wife, and she, if I remember rightly, is a divorced second wife
of someone else. Only the judgment of God can rest on such a
travesty of marriage.

Thank God, love is not some cruel, unseen despot who plays
with its victims. God does not intend that a Christian should
marry simply because he has *fallen in love.* In his love he should
be just as definitely guided by the Holy Spirit as in any other
experience in his life. So we should choose to love the one to
whom the Holy Spirit guides. With the renewed mind under the
direction of the Holy Spirit, one can deliberately *live in the will*
and live above all the animal magnetism of the flesh.

Now we are not implying that Christian people do not *fall in
love.* Oh no! Perhaps the word *fall* explains exactly what they
do. As we have pictured in the diagram, there are three levels of
love: *eros* is passion and animal magnetism, *phileo* is a very

high soulish fondness or natural affection often confused with divine love, *agapa* is His divine love which is shed abroad by the Holy Spirit. It is not that these two lower levels should not exist; no, God has planned them and built them into our being. But He never intended that either *eros* or *phileo* should be dominating or controlling. It is when the Holy Spirit is controlling to shed abroad *agapa love* that the phileo love and the eros love are in their proper function.

Thus we can understand these infatuations which people call love. They begin with the imaginations of the fleshly mind, combine with the affections of the nature and arise to create what seems like an irresistible power. The world calls it love! But it is not God's highest design. Because of these infatuations many young (and alas, older) are led astray. Those who have not known their abiding position in His death and resurrection cannot reckon upon the sentence of death which God places upon our fleshly affections which have become warped in the Fall. They are apt to find themselves strongly attracted as a strange magnetic infatuation grips the soulish mind. This is what they describe as *falling in love;* it is falling from that higher plane which God has intended.

Notice how fleeting and passing these infatuations may be. Here is a young man who can hardly eat or sleep because he is thinking only of a certain girl. He chooses to be occupied with only her. Then comes a day when she does something to hurt his ego. Perhaps she disappoints him and goes off with someone else. Lo and behold, the spell is broken and the infatuation is over. Suddenly he can see all kinds of things in her that he doesn't like—things he never saw before.

Of course we have learned that when a young person is in the midst of such an "infatuation spell," it is almost impossible to reason or show him anything. If we are wise, we shall give instruction before the hour of need so as to forewarn. He who has learned to *live in his will* will not be the ready victim of these soulish whims.

There are many who have experienced love only in the second plane. They have discovered a soul-mating because they have a union of ideals and values. But what happens when their ideals or values change? Others whose goals and plans were miles apart have experienced only passion and physical union. They assumed that sex appeal was all there is in love; and when the sex appeal seems to have shifted or waned, they imagined that love had left. It is lives who have built upon these shallow notions who can expect sin and sorrow and wrecked homes.

How necessary that our conception of love be rectified. Many who have not known much of the mental or spiritual aspects wonder why the physical aspect of love cannot hold them. They cannot understand how the Bible can command a husband and wife to continue to love each other as long as they live. If love were merely a physical or emotional thing that could not be possible. But God intends that love be something which the spirit and will controls. We are to thoughtfully and by a deliberate action of the will choose to love. This love is not something one merely *falls* into. A Christian who understands this conception of love could never even think of ceasing to love the one to whom he or she is married.

It was an undeniable fact that the wife with whom I was counseling had suffered through more than twenty years of married life. Her drunken, inconsiderate husband had seemed to increase in his irresponsibility. Now she wanted a legal separation. She insisted that her love for him had gone long ago and that her home situation was unbearable.

As I listened and as we prayed it seemed the Lord gave insight into her real problem. During most of these twenty years she had developed a secret bitterness toward her husband; but she had also harbored a bitterness toward God because He had (seemingly) allowed her life to be ruined by such a wretched man. Why didn't God answer her prayers? Why didn't He fix up this husband and relieve her frustration? Suddenly she saw two things: first, that she really only wanted to use God to remedy this home problem. She was not concerned for what God might realize through her life—she only wanted to use Him for her own benefit. Second, she saw how she had been running—running away from her ordained place as a wife. She didn't want God's will; she only wanted release. Whereas God wanted her to accept this difficult place "as His will" and trust Him to work an inward grace in her heart, she wanted escape – not fulfillment. She wanted release, but God wanted to rectify her life unto Himself and then through her get at her husband.

When I read God's Word for this situation it was like a shaft of light breaking through. She admitted: "I'm through running. This is the will of God in Christ Jesus concerning me."

Then I continued: "Are you sure what God's will is for you and John?"

She was quick to reply, "I'm sure that in God's purpose John is truly my husband and I vowed to take him 'for better or for worse!' I will accept God's will and go back to John—with a new mind and spirit."

I showed how this meant allowing the mind of the Spirit to send the right knowledge into the stream; whereas before she had been compromising with vain reasonings of the flesh.

"But that is not all," I continued. "God also wants you to love your husband, not just put up with him. This is the real difficulty. You are sure you cannot turn love on just as you would a faucet. All the pent-up bitterness, feelings of resentment and hatred rise up to justify you in your self-pity and would once again seek to over-ride what you know is God's will."

"I know what God's will is," she continued. "But I don't see how I can work up love or confidence where there is none. I can *will* – but how can I *perform?*"

"That is where God's part comes in," I returned. "If you will simply will, as you would open a door, then you can trust God to move through to do the performing. You do not perform it. You simply set your will on His side—in harmony with all that He desires for Himself in your lives. By this deliberate choice you can expect God to send the flow of His own love and His own knowledge – as rivers into your will.

"Furthermore, you must reckon that when you died in Christ upon the Cross, that God dealt a death blow to all of the old mind of the flesh and the feelings of pity in the self-life. Claim that the Cross has been placed over these two rivers so that they will not be the source from whence flows carnal reasonings and feelings." So we drew a cross over the two rivers, thus indicating they were to be rendered inoperative, (crucified).

We considered how this was but a crisis, and in the hours and weeks ahead she must continually reckon upon the cross-work as stopping the old sources of flow and count on God's feeding both the mind and the emotions from the proper source. I could assure her, "If you do this, God will impart His own love in your heart and will help you to see, through a renewed mind, some of the good qualities in John you have so long completely missed."

With an enlightened smile she left, announcing: "I can see now why you place so much emphasis on the continuous act of the will. I shall do it."

Because it had happened in so many others I could confidently insist, "God has far more design for our will than most of us have realized. If you *will* to accept God's remedy (the old life has been rendered inoperative at the Cross), then God will start the right flow of His own love and compassion through your emotions."

She returned to the meetings every day for the next two weeks. She seemed like a new person with a new inner glow and of course a new testimony. "I thought it was my husband, but I was the key to our home difficulty. God is allowing a new flow of His own love through me."

I am glad to report after seven years that the home is completely changed. Her husband is not only a believer, but has become a truly spirit-filled leader in their church. She has become a loving, submissive wife who knows her place and gladly accepts it.

THIS *FALLING IN LOVE* CONCEPT HAS BROUGHT CONFUSION

How often we have heard the confession of some confused heart: "I just don't love the Lord as I know I should." Because the world's sentimental notion of love has been imposed upon the church, many seem unable to manufacture that kind of religious emotion which they so often hear about in songs, sermons and writings. And they imagine, perhaps after all, they have only an empty profession and are not truly a believer. Now the very fact of their genuine longing to love Him would seem to indicate they have encountered Him as Lord and trusted His finished work on Calvary. Why then, does this love which the Scriptures so emphatically command, seem to consistently elude them?

Dr. A.W. Tozer has asked and then answered this question. "One of the puzzling questions likely to turn up sooner or later to vex the seeking Christian is how he can fulfill the scriptural command to love God with all his heart and his neighbor as himself.

"The earnest Christian, as he meditates on his sacred obligations to love God and mankind, may experience a sense of frustration gendered by the knowledge that he cannot seem to work up any emotional thrill over his Lord or his brothers. He wants to, but he cannot, the delightful wells of feeling simply will not flow.

"To find our way out of the shadows and into the cheerful sunlight we need only to know that there are two kinds of love — the love of *feeling* and the love of *willing*. The first lies in the emotions, the other in the will. Over the one we may have little

control. It comes and goes, rises and falls, flares up and disappears as it chooses, and changes from hot to warm to cool and back to warm again, very much as does the weather." [16]
This emotional love surely was not in the mind of Christ when He told His people to love God and each other. But the love which Jesus introduces is not the love of feeling; "It is the love of willing, the willed tendency of the heart." (AWT) When we understand the difference between the two Greek words (phileo and agapeo), we realize how discriminately the Holy Spirit has used each in the Word of God. And we see more clearly that God never intended that man should be the plaything of his emotions or feelings. Indeed the emotional life is a proper and noble part of the total personality, but it is by its very nature to be secondary. And since the fall of man it must be rectified through the work of the Cross. The man who would learn to walk with his spirit controlling his soul faculties and with his body in subjection, must learn to LIVE BY THE WILL. The will becomes the rudder that keeps the boat on course.

On what level is our loving? If it is anything less than agape-love, it is sub-Christian. The lines are pretty clearly drawn between agape, phileo and eros love. If we merely find a union with others in similar goals, ideals, and values—however high and noble or cultured—it is merely phileo-love. It is still a love that loves for what it can get out of it. It is loving people for what they give us in return. When there is no return, then love ceases. How truly the term *falling* describes this level; for it is falling short of that which God intends.

And when love has fallen from the phileo to the eros level, it becomes lust and uncontrolled passion which would use another's body for his own satisfaction. How aptly the worldling expresses this level of *falling in love*. He sees something in another—maybe beauty or physical attractiveness—which would bring a satisfaction to him. He sees and lusts for another as that one would meet a need in him; therefore sets out to acquire that one. Indeed love has fallen—fallen from God's high standard.

But what is more tragic is to realize how often in the church—love has fallen. "God, too, comes under the acquisition urge. We make God a means to our ends. He saves us from trouble, heals us of our sickness, gives us success in life, provides us a heaven hereafter; therefore we serve Him." While we seek to use God, we are the center and God is pulled into the sphere of our interests. All this may be very religious, but it is pure ego-centricity.

We expect to get something out of our loving God. We go to church, we pray, we pay to church and charitable causes, we are faithful in our duties; therefore, we feel that God is under obligation to us—to shield us from harm and danger, ward off our sicknesses, provide us with plenty of material goods, and give us a home in heaven.

While this theme has secretly slipped into many hearts in the church, how much more boldly it is the emphasis of the "peace of mind" and "happiness" cults. They unashamedly insist, "If I will serve God, repeat certain slogans, obey certain rules, I'll have *peace of mind* and *happiness*. What I give all comes back to me. I'm the center of the universe. Everything, including God, comes to my beck and call — revolves around me." Now what is so dangerous is that these are working principles which will go a long ways toward realization if actually practiced. But they will finally fail because they are wrong at the center.

God's final word is that as His children we are not to fall, but to rise into the divine level where His agape love is flowing. The Lexicon gives this meaning of agape-love: "...it chooses its object with decision, and self-denying compassion. This is love in its fullest and highest form. It has its source in God. The verb form stands for kindliness toward its object and has reference to the *tendency of the will.*" So when we are exhorted in His Word to love God and others with all our heart, it is that we choose (will) to allow His own love to flow through us.

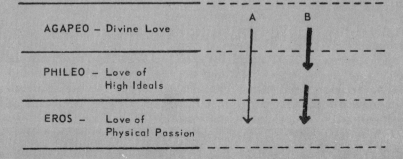

THE THREE LEVELS OF LOVING:
A Falling to a Lower Level
B High Level governing Lower Levels

AGAPEO — Divine Love

PHILEO — Love of High Ideals

EROS — Love of Physical Passion

THE STORY HAS BEEN TOLD:

When Jenny Lind first came to America to sing on the stage, there was an admirer in the audience who confided to his companion by his side: "What a lovely voice; what possibilities! But she will never reach the highest and most lovely expression until there has come a deep crushing and breaking in her life." He continued, "I'm going to marry her and break her heart; then she will sing from a new inner depth instead of mere surface feeling."

How tragic the thought! But that is exactly what he did. The details of this heart breaking experience are not known but her audiences immediately knew that something had happened. Out of deep sorrow and brokenness her singing began to express a new depth of feeling and compassion.

There is perhaps, a counterpart of this in the lives of many Christians whom God has allowed to be broken and crushed by the most tragic circumstances of life. Many who cannot understand God's way of releasing the fragrance of Himself through our life by stripping away the false veneer we build up, are always asking: "Why does God permit such?" If we have imbibed the carnal attitude of the modern church, of course we cannot understand. But if we have embraced the way of expressing HIM at any cost, we shall rejoice that in the crushing of the rose the most lovely fragrance can come forth.

THE NINE WINDOWS
OF OUR SOUL

W HAT AN AMAZING privilege for us that the God of the universe should design to express Himself through us! That the all glorious Father should purpose for a vast family of sons as the means of His expression throughout the universe!

For several weeks I have been strangely checked in writing

this chapter which closes this section on full stature of emotions. But now I understand why. We have just met one of God's choice vessels who has translated into living expression what I have so longed to share!

Others have agreed that once you have met this dear brother, you can never be the same. For you sense in meeting him, you have truly met HIM — Christ who lives and flows through the deepest recesses of the personality. I have marveled at his gracious manner in opening up another's life. While he does not use these words, it is almost as if he were asking everyone, "Are your windows open today?" We all know that to be with some folk is to sense the closing of our windows, while to come into another person's presence is to sense the opening of our windows.

Somehow we have come to a new appreciation of the rich emotional depth which should flow out in full expression from every life. We become aware that God could never have intended a suppression of our deep emotions, but instead designed them as a glorious means for a nine-fold expression of His own personality through us. We begin to ask, "What if we had no emotions?" How drab, how colorless, how monotonous are those beings who express no personality.

How wonderful then, that God has fused our inner beings in such variety as to make us completely different. But there has been good reason. For He who designs to express Himself through us is so infinitely beyond full expression that were there a million windows in every one of us it would still be impossible to unveil all the shades, the hues, the warmth and the depth of His own lovely Person. Furthermore, what seems almost beyond our comprehension is that through all eternity we shall continue to behold in His sons, new and glorious facets of His Being. We shall forever be making new and deeper discoveries in Him. Who can fathom?

As we have said, there are infinite possibilities of expression, yet for our purpose just now, let us consider these nine windows of the soul.

(1) What are these windows of the soul?

(2) Why do so many insist on putting up blinds?

(3) How will God make us as a house with open windows?

First, these windows are the lovely capacities built into our soul which enable us to express love, joy, peace, longsuffering, gentleness, goodness, faith, meekness and temperance. Immediately you recognize this is the nine-fold fruit of the Spirit. In His lovely intention to express His Son, God has selected these nine varieties of expression in showing the different shades of His loveliness. Whichever window you look in, you simply see Him, our Lord Jesus, in His indivisible loveliness. What a delightful way the Bride in the Song of Solomon expresses this fact: "My beloved . . . looketh forth at the windows, showing himself through the lattice" (S. of Sol. 2:9).

Now we must be careful to see that the windows of the soul are those natural built-in capacities. We need only look at the human houses designed by God to realize that these windows allow the deepest expression of our soul. We are designed for the expression of love, joy, peace, etc. Yet when we look into the natural window and see only a feeble light, we realize this individual is trying by his own efforts to manufacture love, to be joyous, to be at peace, etc.

We have on rare occasions observed individuals who developed their soul until there was a natural loveliness to behold in the window. They had discovered some of the natural laws for producing love, joy, gentleness, meekness, etc. Yet for everyone who has attained this natural mastery there are ten thousand who have put up blinds over their windows. By this their soul is saying: "Please don't look in. I am ashamed that you will not see love, joy, meekness, etc. My natural factory has become bankrupt. I am forced to defend myself with these blinds. Please don't look in my windows!"

This leads us secondly to see why so many insist upon putting up blinds. Whenever you see a drab, stoical, unexpressive person,

WIDE-OPEN WINDOWS FOR HIS EXPRESSION

LOVE	LONGSUFFERING	FAITH
JOY	GENTLENESS	MEEKNESS
PEACE	GOODNESS	TEMPERANCE

you are usually looking at a life that has somehow become disappointed, disgruntled and warped in their soul by wrong conceptions. Circumstances have seemingly dealt a severe blow and
the soul has become passive. The mind cannot be challenged into
thinking; the will has become inert and refuses to make choices;
the emotions have become unexpressive. The blinds are the
mechanism of the self life which insists upon wearing a mask to
hide the emptiness and barrenness of the inner soul.

There are many who admit, "I am caught in a web of circumstances that have put blinds over my windows; it is like being
in a dungeon. I can't see out, and I'm not willing for others to
see in. Is it really possible under such circumstances to live
with open windows?"

In answer I refer you to this passage which explains how God
would use the dungeon to work His inward graces. It would seem
if you find these inner graces at all it is through the crushing,
the breaking, the darkness. Like Jeremiah, you will "find grace
in the dungeon " (Jer. 31:2 Moffatt).   It is not abnormal to be
caught, that is, to find yourself unable to get out of the dungeon.
So often that is God's way — His hour of opportunity. In that
moment of complete despair as He offers us His grace we discover He is getting the dungeon out of us. It is when HE comes
in to bring HIS Life, Light and Love that the old blinds will
come down and there will be a glorious expression out of our
inner being. Thus wherever we are there is light. He is that Light
which changes every dungeon circumstance.

There is no running away from some situations. A Christian
lady had a very slow maid. Though an excellent girl in every
other respect and very valuable in the household, yet her slowness was a constant source of irritation to her mistress who was
naturally quick and always chaffed at her slowness. This lady
would consequently get out of temper with the girl twenty times
a day and twenty times a day would repent of her anger and
resolve to conquer it, but all in vain. Gradually her life was becoming more miserable by this conflict, so she put up blinds to
cover her lack of joy, gentleness, longsuffering, etc.

Then it dawned on her that in praying for fruitfulness unto
God, she had not realized God's blessed windows by which He
could demonstrate meekness which "doth not behave itself unseemly and is not easily provoked." Anyone can express natural
joy, temperance, gentleness, amid the easy circumstances of
life. But here was God's opportunity for that Divine expression.

Her old blinds came down. It was like announcing to the whole world that her own natural source had gone bankrupt, but now she had discovered the Divine source which would henceforth send forth the expression of HIS glorious joy, peace, meekness, etc.

A girl of twenty was confined to her bed for a year with a bad heart. The first week was spent in bitter rebellion. Then she read CHRIST AND HUMAN SUFFERING, and it opened some windows. She saw the possibility of not merely bearing suffering and frustration, but also using it for an expression of His long-suffering. What a revelation to her! The remaining fifty-one weeks of that year were beautiful; the best of her life. She arose out of that year awakened in heart, and with open windows in her soul. No one could visit her bedside without having their own windows opened. Out of her inmost being was flowing an expression of Christ, and it conquered wherever it flowed. Here was something far more than natural love, longsuffering, peace; it was a spiritual flowing of love unexplainable and utterly conquering; of joy unspeakable and full of glory; and of peace indescribable which passeth understanding. Like the Bride she could say: "There is Another standing at my lattice windows showing Himself." His lovely stature was coming forth in full expression.

AN HOUR OF OPEN WINDOWS

How often during the years we have concluded a week of meetings with *an hour of open windows*. But it often took a whole week before we could arrive at that hour of sharing when lives would permit such an opening. In the beginning of the week it seemed so many in the congregation were closed and unreceptive. Thick, heavy blinds challenged anyone's entrance. And I am shamed in admitting that perhaps my own windows often were so closed there could be very little outflow of His Spirit. In such times we had little more than the annual week of spiritual emphasis. But things began to change when I found that our open windows will produce open windows in others.

So in the closing service we would have *an hour of open windows*, often even staying over one more night to allow hearts that had been opened to share their victories and discoveries in Christ. We have all known that when one is outgoing and loving, when our windows are open and the Holy Spirit is freely expressing Himself from our inner heart — what a difference! Yet how little it is practiced.

Every facet or window of our soul is designed for this over-flowing expression, this outgoing fellowship, and this all con-quering love. And we shall soon realize that where everybody receives, there is always a creative fellowship. Such a group has its own redemptive powers inherent. Individual growth may be growth lopsidedly, but this group growth is by its very nature corrective. But we must ever be careful that it does not slip into merely *natural expression* as from our own light, but that there is the glorious expression of CHRIST HIMSELF. Where there is true humility, honesty and the honoring of the Holy Spirit, He will safeguard such fellowship of open hearts and windows.

In the diagram we have pictured the sixth story as our emo-tional stature. We have been showing how God designs to mani-fest Himself through these nine windows by the nine-fold fruit of the Spirit. When this fruit is "flowing from our windows" indeed it will be blessing for others and glory for God. Paul described this kind of sharing or outflow as "an odor of a sweetsmell, a sacrifice acceptable, well pleasing to God."

Now since this fruit is actually the loveliness of Christ Him-self flowing forth out of the deepest emotions of our being, it will not seem strange if we suggest that through each window we will also see the facets of Divine love as described in the thirteenth chapter of First Corinthians. When the windows are open and God is expressive through us, we shall see how:

LOVE – is the sum total.

JOY – "rejoiceth not in iniquity, but rejoiceth in the truth."

PEACE – "envieth not" – which is peace with others; and "vaunteth not itself" – which is inward peace.

LONGSUFFERING – "suffereth long."

GENTLENESS – "beareth all things."

GOODNESS – "thinketh no evil . . . hopeth all things."

FAITH – "believeth all things."

MEEKNESS – "doth not behave itself unseemly . . . is not easily provoked."

TEMPERANCE – only when there is self-control is there ability to "endure all things."

We have been saying that love is the highest emotion, and in moving unto full stature we shall be manifesting more of Christ who is LOVE.

Moving . . .

UNTO FULL STATURE

in

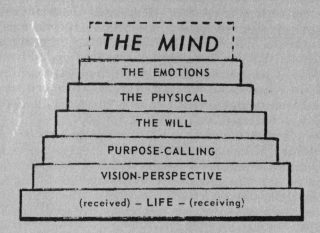

In moving unto full mental stature we must distinguish between self-development or His-development. In yielding our mind to the Holy Spirit for His-development He will work in these seven areas of our mind:

IN CHAPTER 20: (An awakened mind) The Master awakens our mind.

IN CHAPTER 21: (A balanced mind) Learning to cooperate with the Holy Spirit.

IN CHAPTER 22: (A discerning mind) We shall surely be sidetracked without a discerning mind.

IN CHAPTER 23: (An enlightened mind) Self-introspection or His unveiling, which?

IN CHAPTER 24: (A garrisoned mind) The three-fold garrison of the mind.

IN CHAPTER 25: (An occupied mind) Occupied with "other things" and missing Him.

ONE PASTOR ANNOUNCES:

"Suddenly I seem to have come awake! What a renewing and illumination has come to my mind since I passed through the Cross into a God-centered viewpoint. Now all things have become new. I am wondering if others have, even as I, experienced such a radical overhauling and rectification in their mind. Though I had been a Christian for years, I am now realizing how I've been almost asleep as compared to the potential God planned for our mind. I've been much like the violin in a private collection of a wealthy family which lay unused on a velvet pad for many years. When a violinist of great distinction acquired this valuable Stradivarious, he said: 'The violin is asleep, and I must play it until I wake it up and bring it to its proper form. It will have to learn its own beauty and power all over again.'"

WHEN THE MASTER
IMPARTS HIS MIND

PERHAPS WE CAN use the violin to picture the two fundamental needs of every mind. First, there must be a fundamental change of ownership; second, there must be an awakening or renewing as we are wholly given into the hands of the Master for whom we have been designed. Thus we shall be like the violin which suddenly discovered the hidden power and beauty it did not know existed.

In this sense the Apostle Paul was emphasizing "Present yourselves" and "...be ye transformed by the renewing of your mind..." (Rom. 12:1, 2). Here are those two fundamental needs. It is not enough to become His property by an initial crisis; we must also know His continual playing upon the strings of our mind by which there is a glorious awakening, or renewing. Like the pastor in the heading of this chapter, there are many who have known a change of ownership for years, yet have not moved beyond what is merely "good" or what is "acceptable." Only by the most drastic awakening can they ever "prove" what is the perfect will of God.

It may seem to some that in getting at the root matter we should emphasize the change of ownership. This seems all important. Indeed it is so fundamental as to produce a drastic change as the mind receives a whole new mainspring, a whole new source from which to draw. While this crisis of ownership must never be overlooked or minimized, I believe there is just as great a need for believers to recognize this continual renewing of the mind.

Let us consider how this progressive renewing allows the fuller impartation of His mind. Our Heavenly Father has faced this very problem in bringing each of us to appreciate His will, His ways and His purpose. A friend of mine who had been caught with the glory and privilege of his high calling as a father, explained how he was awakened to this problem in training his sons. He said, "The more I understand my relationship as a son unto my Father, the more I understand how to properly represent Him by being the father I should be. In training my two boys, now six and fifteen, I have found the importance of sharing not only my will, but also my mind and purpose. I call it sharing the *what,* the *how* and the *why.*"

He continued, "One morning when I asked our fifteen year old to clean out the garage I knew he was not too impressed; therefore, I was not surprised that evening when he insisted he had forgotten. He had disobeyed, but I also realized I was somewhat at fault in failing to give him proper directions. As we went to the garage I explained carefully *what* should be done, but also *how* he could do it best. Then I told him *why!* His face lit up when he heard I was bringing home a new car that evening. This was the inspiration he needed. Immediately after school he was home making room for the new car."

Perhaps there are some implications here we should guard against, but at least consider this primary point he is making: "It was thus the Lord showed me how often I lagged in fulfilling His desires when I only knew *what* He wanted, but did not know the *how* or *why.* I further realized that this is the difficult process of renewing our mind to appreciate His ways that we might understand the *how,* and to appreciate His purpose that we might know the *why.*"

How wonderfully we are designed in our mental makeup. To know the ways and the purpose of the Lord is to enjoy a special kind of motivation. This is what we so often fail to transfer to our children or to those who serve the Lord. Yet there is much more involved.

"The next day," he continued, "I realized we did not think alike, nor did we have the same goals or final purpose. When I announced that grandmother was coming for a visit and that I wanted my younger son to put the basement in order, there was little enthusiasm. It was evident he had little appreciation for *what* I wanted, and the *how* and *why* which I offered were no inspiration. I realized how much more difficult was God's problem with us than I had first imagined. Though I might exercise my right to force him to do my will against his own desires, still I had not imparted my mind or purpose to him. How wonderful and important is this renewing of our mind which permits the impartation of His mind and purpose."

As we observe those of our own acquaintance, or even look at those lives described in the Scriptures we arrive at this conclusion. Very few have allowed the impartation of His mind and purpose as easily as did our Lord Jesus. He "learned obedience by the things He suffered." The great majority have learned only by the pathway of trial and error, affliction and distressing crises. Whatever may be necessary, we are convinced that this renewing of mind is most imperative. It is God the Father bringing His sons into such intimacy in sharing His desires, His mind, His purpose, His deepest longings that these finally become theirs. Then we shall respond as His only begotten Son: " I delight to do Thy will."

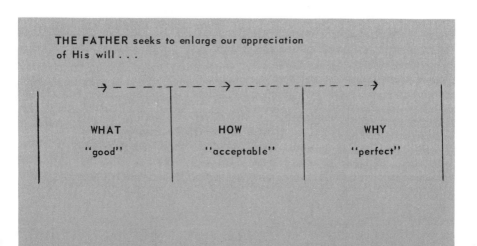

THE FATHER seeks to enlarge our appreciation
of His will . . .

WHAT "good"   HOW "acceptable"   WHY "perfect"

As we have indicated in the diagram, most of the time as His children we are inclined to stop with knowing His will; knowing *what to do*. It is no wonder there is little delight and enjoyment. As we groan and struggle in fulfilling His will, our headstrong self-will makes it difficult for Him to impart the *how to do it*. Our minds are usually made up to do it in our own way, according to our own natural reasoning of what seems best. All we really want is His blessing.

Let no one assume this hard way is the only way; it only becomes necessary that through heartache, affliction, and trial and error we finally come to prove His way is best. If we had just waited to learn *how* at the beginning!

Yet even when we know the ways of the Lord our service can seem overshadowed with drudgery or burden. All this while our Father is inwardly preparing our inner eyes to appreciate the glorious *why* in all His doing. Is there some key we have missed which might have allowed us to receive this purpose sooner? I only know that until we are wholly one with Him in His inmost longing we shall hear a hundred times, yet not appreciate nor delight in His purpose. Until then we can hardly appreciate how the full renewing of our mind enables us to prove not merely the good and acceptable but the perfect will of God.

Now we can understand why Paul so deliberately takes us step by step through Romans five, six, seven and eight. It is all preparatory. Finally as we enter chapter twelve he makes this all-out plea: "I beseech you, brethren, by the mercies of God, that ye present your bodies a living sacrifice, well pleasing to God, which is your REASONABLE (rational, intelligent) service and spiritual worship"   (A.N.T. Rom. 12:1).

Did you notice that phrase, "intelligent service?" While it may often seem necessary, God is really not after our blind obedience or service. There are times when that is all He can expect from our unrenewed minds. Yet God is always using every means to crowd us to intelligently appreciate and delight in His will.

As His little children our minds have been so closed, so unreceptive to any way or will but our own. To reason with such a mind is almost impossible. And those who refuse to accept the fuller *how* and *why* of His will can only expect the emphatic "this do, and thou shalt live," or "do this, for it is right." Of course implied in these words there is always this fact, that some day you will have matured enough in mind to appreciate and accept the ways and purposes you now reject.

Is this not exactly what Paul is saying in Ephesians 6:1, "Children, obey your parents in the Lord (as His representatives), FOR THIS IS JUST AND RIGHT"? (A.N.T.). As God has dealt tenderly and patiently when He could, so we must deal with our children. But when it is necessary because they will not reason, we can only deal firmly and emphatically: "Obey! for this is right."

If this seems like hard and arbitrary action on the part of the parent, let such a one consider that he is a part of this brainwashed generation which has grown up undisciplined and unspanked and he is now producing similar offspring. It is time to learn God's ways. How else could a parent deal with a child-is. mind that was closed and unreceptive to good judgment. As God has insisted upon obedience to His will, so must we. The whole record of His Word demonstrates how stubborn men faltered in the pathway, and reaped a pitiful harvest because they would not heed Him.

Finally we must realize that in our relationship unto God as we have been transformed by a renewing of our mind and have proved His will for ourselves, so we shall be more effective in imparting our mind and will to others. So Paul continues in the second verse: "...but be ye transformed (changed) by the (entire) renewal of your mind—by its new ideals and its new attitude — so that you may prove (for yourselves) what is the good and acceptable and perfect will of God, even the thing which is good and acceptable (in His sight for you)" (A.N.T. Rom. 12:2).

Again we must be careful lest we seem to imply that chastening is the only way God can bring us into full stature of mind. To infer such is to overlook those rare examples who wholly yielded themselves to God, thus affliction and chastening were unnecessary. They heard their earthly father insist: "Do this because it is right; God says so, and I stand with Him." And in their learning obedience to an earthly father, they were prepared for obedience to their Heavenly Father. Such obedience and reverence is the beginning of wisdom; it is every father's unhindered opportunity to share himself.

IN OUR CHURCH . . . .
we seem to have two groups who are so very different.
Because of their mental makeup and outlook, they tend to
emphasize an opposite extreme. The one group has put so
much emphasis on cold, intellectual reasoning they have
given very little place for any revelation or illumination of
the Holy Spirit. But the other group, perhaps in reaction,
has so emphasized the necessity of the Spirit's work of
revelation in imparting wisdom and knowledge they seem
almost to belittle anything which requires mental exercise
on their part. While the first group is most diligent in study
and clear articulation of terms, this later group has seemed
to become both lazy and hazy in their thinking. Surely
there must be a proper balance in God's divine order."

LEARNING TO COOPERATE
WITH THE HOLY SPIRIT

THE BABE IN CHRIST will not have
read very far or studied intelligent-
ly in his Bible until he comes upon passages that appear to
contradict each other. Even after he has consulted all the study
helps, perhaps even reading the text in the original languages,
he will be forced to acknowledge these seeming contradictions.
Try as he will, he cannot avoid or escape them.

It is at this point that his particular bent or cast of mind will
become evident. Aside from quitting in despair and concluding
that he can never understand the Bible, he will probably turn
toward others in whom he has confidence. The voice he is inclined to heed will demonstrate the special cast of his mind.
Should he consult some of the rationalistic-orthodox theologians
who are not ashamed to admit that they have every verse properly
exegeted and neatly tucked into its proper pigeon-hole, he may
fall into the snare that has caught a multitude. Because they
assume everything in the Bible should be understood and ex-

plained immediately, they have removed anything that savors of the supernatural from religion. There is no mystery — nothing to wait for. All that is there can be understood and explained now.

In characteristic prophetic voice, Dr. Tozer warned: "The pitiable attempt of churchmen to explain everything for the smiling unbeliever has had an effect exactly opposite to that which was intended. It has reduced worship to the level of the intellect and introduced the rationalistic spirit into the wonders of religion. This is sure to be fatal to true spirituality, for the whole heart attitude of these expositors is wrong and they cannot but lead their disciples astray. They belong to that class of persons mentioned by Cicero, who 'fear nothing so much as to appear to be in doubt about anything.' They proceed on the false assumption that everything in heaven and earth can be explained." [17]

On the other hand, at the opposite pole from the rationalistic interpretation, are those who overemphasize the mystical interpretation. Those of a certain cast of mind will incline toward spiritualization. It is important to be aware of both extremes and to seek the interpretation of the Spirit, rather than either that which will satisfy the natural mind or that which is an intrusion into mysteries not yet revealed.

It is to be regretted that in most every church there are individuals who manifest and follow to an extreme the cast of their own mind. So the battle rages between those who have often bypassed formal education and tend to belittle the need for disciplined thinking. Having seen the dangers of rationalism and cold intellectualism, they drift into an almost unintelligible mysticism, using words loosely and spiritualizing everything to fit their little system of theology.

What is the answer? Surely if we are to reach the full stature of mind which God intends we must make room for mystery, but also for disciplined thinking. We must settle one thing immediately: The Holy Spirit must be Lord of our mind. The same Spirit who controls the mystery must also bring our minds into severe discipline. As the Spirit of revelation, He imparts knowledge which is beyond our natural powers of discovery; as the Spirit who disciplines our thinking, He will lead us into wisdom by illumined thinking. The answer then is to humbly acknowledge that our only hope for clear insight into the Scripture is through cooperation with the Holy Spirit. It is good for us to find there are many things in heaven and earth that we shall never be able to understand. In fact, until we reach the humble place of pupil,

eagerly pursuing a course of learning laid out by the Teacher
Himself, we will dart ahead into this and that avenue of thought
"Tossed to and fro, and carried about by every wind of doctrine."

As we submit to God's teaching through the Holy Spirit we
become gloriously alive to truths He makes real in our own experience day by day as He prepares us to receive more and more
of His unfathomable universes of knowledge and wisdom. The
Psalmist has described this lovely balance between the rational
and the mystical: "The meek will He guide in judgment:" (this is
the Spirit's discipline) "and the meek will He teach His way"
(this is the Spirit's mystical impartation).

In this mad rushing age, we *must stop to think!* Either forget
about reaching any spiritual stature in your mind, or slow down!
Deliberately set aside special times for meditation and waiting
before God. It is not easy to learn the Spirit's discipline. Much
of our "spiritual exercise" is simply a flitting from one flower
to another, because we are attracted by first one and then another intriguing idea or train of thought. This is not discipline.

The real purpose of disciplined thinking is to teach us how to
shake ourselves free of created things and temporal concerns and
enter into a conscious and loving fellowship with God. Such
fellowship brings a two-way flow — to God flows the praise and
honor and thanksgiving and love which are His due, and to us
flows that sufficiency that only God can give. In this withdrawal
from exterior things—the activities, the business, the thoughts
and concerns of temporal existence — our mind comes under the
discipline and tutelage of the Spirit.

The supreme goal of all disciplined thinking or meditation is
to produce in us greater *likeness to* and *love for* God. Whether or
not this concept seems satisfactory, of course, depends on what
one means by loving God. Meditation has not done its work when
it has brought you to *say* you love God or to *feel* you love God.
Nor is it to bring to us some interesting idea or fresh understanding of Him. To strengthen all our spiritual convictions and
give them a deeper foundation and understanding is one of the
elementary purposes of meditation on the things of God, but
really this is only the beginning. Meditation should become fiber
in us—that constant, open channel for spirit-union with God. "As
a man thinketh in his heart so is he."

"Since contemplation is the union of our mind and will with
God in an act of pure love that coincides with the knowledge of
Him as He is in Himself, the way to contemplation is to develop

and perfect our mind and will: this is disciplined thinking. Infused contemplation begins when the direct intervention of God raises this whole process above the level of our nature; and then He perfects our faculties by seeming to defeat all their activity in the suffering and darkness of His infused light and love." (T.M.) [18]

Who can deny that Spirit-disciplined thinking is a most essential step in reaching mental stature. Hear the words of one who learned its importance and could thus become a mighty champion in exhorting others to take time to meditate and think. A.W. Tozer described its importance thus:

"I believe that pure thinking will do more to educate a man than any other activity he can engage in. To afford sympathetic entertainment to abstract ideas, to let one idea beget another, and that another, till the mind teems with them; to compare one idea with others, to weigh, to consider, evaluate, approve, reject, correct, refine; to join thought with thought like an architect till a noble edifice has been created within the mind; to travel back in imagination to the beginning of the creation and then to leap swiftly forward to the end of time; to bound upward through illimitable space and downward into the nucleus of an atom; and all this without so much as moving from our chair or opening the eyes – this is to soar above all the lower creation and to come near to the angels of God.

"Of all earth's creatures only man can think in this way. And while thinking is the mightiest act a man can perform, perhaps for the very reason that it is the mightiest act, it is the one act he likes the least and avoids the most. Aside from a few professionals, who cannot number more than one-tenth of one per cent of the population, people simply do not think at all except in the most elementary way. Their thinking is done for them by the professionals." [19]

If we are to intelligently cooperate with the Holy Spirit, passivity of mind should be studiously avoided. We must next recognize our own particular cast of mind—if we have one—and claim God's protection from extremes. We must claim that He will accomplish that divine balance where there is room for mystery, yet room for discovery; where there is relaxed meditation, yet deliberate concentration; where there is the expectance of Spirit-imparted knowledge, yet the delight in Spirit-disciplined thinking. When we are wholly in His control God will perform this balance.

ONE OF OUR CO-LABORERS HAS DISCOVERED:

"How often during a week of ministry there are those first-timers who become jubilant in the hope that this is the sure method of self-development and self-realization which they have been seeking. They are most attentive and as long as one is presenting mere principles and philosophy, they will enthusiastically embrace what you teach. Just here is the most crucial issue in every ministry. The very moment you present THE PERSON, the Lord Jesus, and insist that He will live in us to become these working principles and this controlling philosophy — that moment many folk are through. They want knowledge, but not Him; they want development, but not the Developer; they want a meaningful philosophy, but not the One who will make that philosophy operative; they want maturity but not His FULL STATURE formed in them."

In every generation since the early church this has been the most subtle snare: The danger of allowing mere knowledge to become the substitute for the reality of the Living Person.

WITHOUT A DISCERNING MIND
WE SHALL SURELY BE SIDETRACKED

THERE WAS AN INVASION into the early church, even as there has continued to be throughout the centuries since, by a movement attempting to take over Christianity. By using Christianities' names and forms but rejecting its substance, the movement called Gnosticism has always been a subtle enemy of the gospel.

Gnosticism, coming from the Greek gnosis ("to know"), is simply an attempt to gain full stature by seeking to know God through principles and philosophy, yet all the while by-passing the real Lord Jesus. One has described that first-century Gnosticism: "You didn't need to go through Jesus to God; if you had the key, the *gnosis,* you could know immediately. Gnosticism supplied mysterious formulas and passwords which gave one

access to the higher world and (they thought) brought about perfect union with the Divine ... So Jesus was taken over, not as
God becoming man, but merely as a revealer of the secrets of
Gnosticism — another Jesus. Gnosticism was the word become
idea." [20]

We can seem to recognize that Gnosticism of the early church,
but it is alarming how many are unaware that a modern Gnosticism in new garb is now making a subtle invasion in our churches.
Only the discerning eye can detect what is wrong, for the same
Bible terms are used, in fact the Bible is revered as a most
significant textbook on successful living; therein they seem to
find the important laws of life. Their message exhorts every man
to have faith (in himself) and to cooperate with the kingdom
around him if he would achieve. There are multiplied thousands
who have proven these laws of the kingdom to be absolutely
trustworthy. They boldly acclaim that anyone who will "believe
in himself" can use this knowledge (gnosis) to realize his selfish goals. But just here is the crucial issue. They are heralding
the importance of "another jesus" for they have seen no real
need for personal submission to the crucified and resurrected
Lord Jesus.

Perhaps some of our readers are not aware of the inroad this
modern Gnosticism is now making through books found on shelves
in many of our book stores. If it were not for the Christian friends
who attend our meetings and their constantly referring to the
things they have learned in reading these books, I would not be
alarmed and speak so emphatically. But too many are being
"taken in."

For example, one of the newer books, rapidly rising to the
best-seller level is entitled YOUR THOUGHTS CAN CHANGE
YOUR LIFE. A careful observer of human nature is forced to
admit there is much truth in this. One's own experience can
verify it.

Then again the significant words of William James are often
quoted: "The greatest discovery in my generation is that men
can alter their lives by altering their attitudes." We know how
this is demonstrated for us in nearly every facet of our living. In
fact, whole systems of religion are based upon the premise: *As
your thoughts are so shall your health be.*

Another writer has reminded us that "The dominant trend of
your secret thoughts will either make or break your ministry (or
work). It will beautify or mar your personality, and it will render

you radiant or repressive." Here again we can recognize a facet of truth.

But especially in the business world it would seem religion has made its invasion. Business experts love to boast that they have laid hold of "Biblical laws." They point to their ventures which are skyrocketing to success in the terms of the dollar sign; all because some executive begins to practice the book he has read: THINK AND GROW RICH. Amid all these exploits it is quite amazing how God is allowed to share in man's glory—at least they would like to impress us so.

Now the question before us is this. How much of this modern emphasis is Christian? How much of it is subtle substitute? How much of it is simply Gnosticism dressed up with a twentieth century appeal? The believer who insists on living a life adjusted at the Cross and wholly for the glory of the Lord is asking, "What does God's Word teach?"

To understand this basic error we must go way back to the beginning. Adam, and all men since have faced the one issue whether to live by the light and knowledge imparted by God or develop their own natural powers in feeding from the tree of knowledge. It is a matter of source. The two trees which Adam faced at the gateway of choice simply represent these two different sources. The tree of life meant a dependence upon God in receiving spiritual resources; the tree of knowledge meant independence and the self-development of one's own soul powers so as to grasp for knowledge by cooperating with the laws of life.

Indeed the issue has not changed one whit since that first hour. Would Adam develop his own natural mind, or choose rather to share in the mind of God? His choice meant either seeking full *natural* stature or it meant allowing the Holy Spirit to realize full spiritual stature. Men are still facing these same two trees. However, they now stand in a different setting. It is either the old rugged Cross or the modern smooth cross. But they are the same trees. The first tree offers death and through it divine life and light are imparted. The second tree offers a new philosophy which is so similar that apart from discernment many are sacrificially giving themselves to a new way of life so as to gain and achieve success, but all the while they are escaping the ignominy of the old rugged Cross and the lordship of Jesus.

How subtle is this modern Gnosticism. It uses terminology like the true message; outwardly the likenesses are superficial, but basic differences are fundamental. Gnosticism has an amaz-

ing appeal to the intellectual mind for it offers all the laws of
success and achievement without any of the embarrassment
which comes in the demands of the old rugged Cross. Thus the
modern Gnostic prides himself in vast discoveries of knowledge
in the laws of the mind, of believing, of cooperating with God,
but they are always for his own ends which are often disguised
as humanitarian and benevolent, yet basically selfish at root.

Surely the great sifting and testing is upon us. Many believers
who could hardly be tempted to gross sins or to indulgence in
fleshly habits are being tested as to whether they will live by
the natural resources of the old life, or live only by a divine
union with HIS NEW LIFE.

Consider the present psychical invasion into certain religious
groups. Many do not understand this new soul-power they are
using, but they are quite amazed at their power to dominate
others. But what power are they using? What resources are they
tapping? It is either one tree or the other. If it is the human personality drawing upon all the well ordered soul-powers, however
amazing the results, it is still *of man*. There may be great
changes in the personality of those who respond, but there is no
deep spiritual change.

We must go back for a closer investigation of God's Word to
see His answer to this subtle invasion. The Bible does have a
great deal to say about this modern, yet ancient error. "The
reason the Bible is so explicit in its instruction about a proper
thought-life is that our thinking is so vitally important to us;
the reason evangelicalism says so little is that we are over-
reacting from the "thought" cults, such as New Thought, Unity,
Christian Science and their like. The cults make our thoughts to
be nearly everything, and we counter by making them very nearly
nothing. Both positions are wrong." (A.W.T.) [21]

In His day we see how Jesus challenged the Gnostic who
taunted Him on every hand. While the blind Pharisees and Scribes
were clinging religiously to the Scriptures, Jesus warned them
of their knowledge without reality, of their form without power.
It is true that any casual observer, unless he had discernment,
could hardly have helped but commend them for their astute
devotion and profound concern for accurately interpreting the
Scriptures. But Jesus could see through their guise and He did
not hesitate to lay it bare before them. What value was their
knowledge, their principles, their doctrinal correctness if they
lacked reality, moral rectitude or missed THE PERSON who
could make it all real? He warned them: "Search the scriptures;

for in them ye think ye have eternal life: and they are they which
testify of me. And ye will not come TO ME, THAT YE MIGHT
HAVE LIFE" (John 5:39-40). What an exposure!

In his day the Apostle Paul faced the Gnostic faction in the
Corinthian church. These were puffed up in their knowledge; they
had grasped their liberty to eat meat which had been offered in
sacrifice at the heathen temples, unconcerned what it did to
others. They had *knowledge;* to them that was all important.
Smug in their insistence that their correct interpretation allowed
them liberty, we see Paul did not discredit this right, but chided
them for their lack of inner grace and inward reality of love. How
could they know God as they ought and knowingly offend or hurt
those weaker brethren who did not have the fuller knowledge?

And in our day the same problem confronts us. This indictment
of our Lord and Paul is true in many Bible churches who are
proud they are letter perfect in their orthodoxy even though they
lack His flowing Life. How often in our Bible colleges and
seminaries there is a diligent searching of the Word, yet scores
and hundreds are graduated who have hardly tasted the Living
Word or know the reality of Love.

Let us be sure of the source from which we feed. Is it spiritual
or soulish? Does it develop our spiritual capacity or develop
our soul-powers? Paul must have anticipated Satan's attack upon
the mind and the need for spiritual discernment when he wrote to
the Philippians. In this one letter he has concentrated most of
his teaching on the mind and its proper spiritual function. As no
other writer, Paul seems to give us God's highest intention for
full spiritual mental stature.

If there is anyone questioning which source is operative in
their mind, let him check by these characteristics of the mind of
Christ as Paul presents them in Philippians:

Living together "...with one mind..." 1:27
"my joy...that ye be likeminded" 2:2
"...of one accord,...of one mind..." 2:2
"...in lowliness of mind let each esteem..." 2:3
"Let this mind be in you which was..." 2:5
"For I have no man likeminded..." 2:20
"...as many as be perfect, be thus minded..." 3:15a
"...and if in anything ye be otherwise minded..." 3:15b .
"...let us mind the same thing..." 3:16
"...be of the same mind in the Lord." 4:2
"...shall keep your hearts and minds..." 4:7

A DISCERNING BIBLE COLLEGE PROFESSOR ADVISES:

"There is a very real need for discernment in this hour. Of course there has always been that need, but specially now God's children need to realize that searching their own soul can never accomplish what the Holy Spirit's searching can do.

"Those who would search by their own light, will soon discover what an abortive and barren effort it is to attempt revival in this way. No place in God's Word—if we interpret rightly—do we find this exhortation to *search ourselves*. Instead we are to cry 'Search me, O God!' How different is the light which the Holy Spirit uses in unveiling to us the hidden areas of our life."

SELF-INTROSPECTION OR
HIS UNVEILING, WHICH?

WE ALL HAVE, in our longing for revival and a more intimate fellowship with the Lord, tried some special times of searching our soul. We have read how God's choice saints through the centuries were always very sensitive to the slightest infraction of His will. This created such a longing in our own heart for a new measure of honesty and brokenness before Him, that we determined to use a fine-tooth comb on our inner life. Yet, when this attempted inner searching was all over, we discovered, along with multitudes of others, how empty, barren and unfruitful the effort was.

We must understand how that which is self-induced will always end up as another *works program* which God will not approve of or cooperate with. How natural it is for man to look within, to differentiate, to discriminate, to analyze his inner workings. and in so doing merely complicate his problem. This

most common experience is really dangerous to spiritual growth,
for inward knowledge will never be reached along the barren path
of self-introspection or self-analysis.

It was a confirmation to our heart to find this same admonition
given by Watchman Nee in THE NORMAL CHRISTIAN LIFE:
"We are never told in the Word of God to examine our inward
condition." In his footnote he explains these two apparent ex-
ceptions:"(1 Cor. 11:28, 31 calls upon us to discern ourselves as
to whether we recognize the Lord's Body or not, and this in a
particular connection with the Lord's table. It is not concerned
with self-knowledge as such. The strong command of Paul in
2 Cor. 13:5 is to examine ourselves as to whether or not we be
'in the faith.' It is a question of the existence or otherwise in
us of a fundamental faith; of whether, in fact, we are Christians.
This is in no way related to our daily walk in the Spirit, or in
self-knowledge.)

"Self examination leads only to uncertainty, vacillation and
despair. Of course we have to have self-knowledge. We have to
know what is going on within. We do not want to live in a fool's
paradise; to have gone altogether wrong and yet not know we
have gone wrong; to have a Spartan will and yet think we are
pursuing the will of God. But such self-knowledge does not come
by our turning within; by our analyzing our feelings and motives
and everything that is going on inside, and then trying to pro-
nounce whether we are walking in the flesh or in the Spirit.

"You remember how in Psalm 139:23 the writer says: 'Search
me, O God, and know my heart.' You realize, do you not, what it
means to say 'search me'? It certainly does not mean that I
search myself. 'Search me' means 'You search me'! That is the
way of illumination. It is for God to come in and search; it is not
for me to search. Of course that will never mean that I may go
blindly on, careless of my true condition. That is not the point.
The point is that however much my self-examination may reveal
in me that needs putting right, such searching never really gets
below the surface. My true knowledge of self comes not from my
searching myself (nor anyone else searching for me) but from
God searching me."

In turning our attention next to Psalm 36:9, Watchman Nee
points out: "'In Thy light shall we see light.' There are two
lights there. There is 'Thy light,' and then, when we have come
into that light, we shall 'see light.' Now these two lights are
different. The first light is the light which belongs to God, but

is shed upon us; the second is the knowledge imparted by that light. 'In Thy light we shall see light': we shall know something; we shall be clear about something; we shall *see*. No turning within, no introspective self-examination will ever bring us to that clear place. No, it is when there is light coming from God that we see.''

LEGAL CONVICTION AND HOLY SPIRIT CONVICTION

Through the years there have been certain occasions when a sudden spurt of conviction and confession would fall upon a group of young people or a congregation. One after another would rise to confess certain wrongs they had committed in their life, and like a spreading fire it would seem that soon everyone was smitten. Quite often the unveiling was so electrifying as to convince some folk it was truly a spiritual awakening: revival was here! But what had come suddenly left just as suddenly.

What was the reason? It was many years before I discovered what earlier men of God have written about, namely, that there is a very real difference between *legal conviction* and *Holy Spirit conviction*. One is sure to confuse these unless he recognizes that in legal conviction the *conscience* is working to accuse or excuse according to the law. The purpose of conscience is to convict me of *what* I have done that is wrong. It deals with the branches and the fruit on the tree.

By contrast, it is the Holy Spirit who uncovers *the motives*, the selfish purposes and pursuits of the heart thereby revealing *why* I do what I do. As we have pictured in the diagram, the conscience's sphere of working is above the surface on *outward issues*, while the Holy Spirit goes deep into the hidden recesses to uncover the *root issues*.

One can usually discern in a meeting whether it is a true spirit of — or just a spurt of — conviction and confession. Conviction will either be on the legal level of the conscience, or it will be in a deeper area wrought by the Holy Spirit. Those who are confessing things they have done are merely seeking relief and release from a conscience. Those who have had deep unveiling of themselves will surely cry out: ''Oh wretched man that I am.'' In their own light they have seen things, but in His light they shall see themselves. Thus we see the work of conscience and the work of the Holy Spirit. We can usually discern the difference. We observe that the deeper the Holy Spirit plows in any life, the slower will be the outburst of confession.

Another sure evidence of Holy Spirit conviction is that it has such a deep lasting effect and continues to be real in lives. But where an electrifying surge of legal conviction has swept through a group it is not uncommon to see those very individuals back at their old ways before another week has passed. The branches and fruit were pruned, but the root system remained the same. It is so with any kind of surface soul-searching. One could not say it would never have any place, yet it has brought far more superficiality and emptiness into lives and churches than we shall ever recognize. This is often the enemy's way of sending a substitute to turn folk aside from the deep lasting, penetrating work of the Cross as the Holy Spirit unveils a life.

GOD HAS SENT THE MASTER PSYCHIATRIST

I am thankful I am not alone in my concern about the present trend among evangelicals to encourage believers to visit the "cot of the psychiatrist." We would not deny that many need help in their deep mental, emotional and personality problems. For those living in the world who will not submit to God it may seem the only recourse, but this is not for those who have the Holy Spirit. If there is to be any exploring of the subconscious faculties, God has reserved this right for His Master Psychiatrist, the Holy Spirit.

In this day amazing discoveries have been made not only in exploring the outer universe, but also in the inner universe of the human soul. Even though man has gained this deeper knowledge of his mental workings he is still haunted with the fact that self-knowledge is not enough. Recently I counseled for several hours with a patient in a mental ward who gave me the most detailed explanation of his problem as he had learned it from his psychiatrist. But with a deep sigh he could only admit: "While I understand my problem I'm still helpless to control my mind."

It has been my experience that whenever I have tried to fellowship believers who have had their inner soul-workings unveiled, they have often been evasive; tending to disregard any working of the Spirit. They find it too easy to revert to some abnormality because of a childhood experience. Instead of honestly facing their own responsibility now, they have accepted the modern delusion that environment, parents,– everything else is really to blame. This attitude is alarming! They have learned it from men who pose as spiritual counselors, but who are mere explorers of the soul.

A YOUNG MISSIONARY CONFIDES: "My first days on the field away from friends and co-workers were dreadful. What awful depression and darkness enveloped my mind. Suddenly I realized how unprepared I was; all the doctrine I had learned in Bible college seemed almost useless. I had never really entered into a Spirit-wrought reality such that the Blood and the Word of testimony could be my garrison against the enemy."

A YOUNG MOTHER DISCOVERS: "After giving birth to our second child my body was so depleted my mind and spirit seemed like open windows for the invasion of depression and imaginations of the enemy. While I had known the value of the Blood as a garrison, I now discovered how imperative it was for my body to be strong so it would not be a drag on my mind and spirit. I am sure dozens of my friends fail to realize that full protection from the enemy demands that our whole being—body, soul and spirit should be strong and under the Lord's dominion."

THE THREE-FOLD GARRISON
OF THE MIND

A S ONE MOVES TOWARD spiritual stature he will soon recognize the need for the garrison of the mind. An intense battle for the mind is underway today, perhaps as never before. The increasing deluge of printed matter and the intrusion of radio and television into the hallowed chambers of the home have converted many Christian minds into entertainment halls packed with thoughts both good and bad. But there is an even more severe attack than this carnal invasion.

That believer who determines to press into full overcoming will experience a spiritual onslaught directly from the enemy. All renewing, balancing, disciplining, developing and discerning of the mind will seem wasted until one has learned to claim the three-fold garrison of the Blood, the Word and the Spirit for protection.

Paul, having faced Satan's persistent attack, knew how every child of God needs to know that " . . . the peace of God which surpasses all power of thought, be a GARRISON to guard your hearts and minds in Christ Jesus" (Phil. 4:7 Weymouth).

This three-fold garrison of the mind is pictured in Revelation 12:11. In the day when the accuser of the brethren steps in to accuse and cast down, John says, "they overcame him by the blood of the Lamb, and by the word of their testimony; and they loved not their lives unto the death. Therefore rejoice. . . ."

THE BLOOD is always effective in the legal or governmental realm. The Father has placed great value on the precious Blood of His Son, and we must accept in confidence what it means to Him. Even the enemy recognizes this judicial significance of the Blood. Wherever its covering is claimed or announced, it immediately becomes a garrison which all the hosts of darkness must honor.

THE WORD is effective in another sphere — to affirm our experience. Notice in the great temptation how Jesus did not trust in His own words, but The Word — "It is written!" Even so, the "word of our testimony" is significant only as it is our affirmation that we are wholly in harmony with His Word. As we testify to the victory the glorious Emancipator has wrought in the finished work of the Cross, we announce that this is our victory — our emancipation now. We allow our voice to cut the atmosphere where the enemy is "the Prince of the power of the air." These are no idle words about what we hope, or feel, or wish. The testimony that overcomes stands only on the ground of His Word — our testimony in full agreement with *His testimony*.

THE SPIRIT is also our garrison. But in connection with this, we must understand what "not loving our lives unto the death" signifies. We are told that the last enemy to be overcome is death. As long as the enemy can find a beachhead for frightening us about losing our life, we are in bondage to the spirit of death and fear. The Spirit of life and victory is not reigning to accomplish full peace as a garrison over our hearts and minds until this fear of death is banished.

How perfectly this is revealed in the Lord Jesus.. By the Spirit there was a unique link between His inner being and His Father God. They were in perfect oneness of Spirit. From this hidden spiritual union flowed the motivating purpose of His life. The Spirit served as a garrison to protect Him from outside invasions. All His guidance came by that link, and He did not act on other lines of guidance common to men – advice, counsel, coercion, custom, expectation, nor even sympathetic appeal. Even appeals that were made to Him out of the highest motives and desires for His own good were refused; even his mother's appeal (Matt. 12:48). From inner union with God He took His guidance – the yea and nay for everything He did.

I hope we can see how this complete union with the Lord is involved in this three-fold garrison of the mind. Many readily claim the Blood, as they would wave a fetish to secure peace of mind, yet they have no real concern for coming into a harmony of testimony and a harmony of inner spirit with God. A stool will not stand on one leg when the other two are missing, nor will the mind be garrisoned when our spirit is not in union with His.

How many dear souls have entertained fear for a moment and then allowed it to capture them. The heart begins to palpitate and fear begins to take hold; soon the very thing that one so greatly feared has actually come upon him. (See Job 3:25) What should one do? Simply reckon on the legal ground of the Blood. But also affirm your reckoning openly as the word of your testimony. Then you must not only stand on Calvary ground, but your daily walk must be in accord or your testimony will sound like a weak whisper against the lion's roar and he will sneer, "Jesus I know, and Paul I know; but who are you?" (Acts 19:15). Our testimony will cut the atmosphere just as emphatically as we know our inner life is wholly attuned to His heart. When we can stand strong in the Spirit, it is because we are one in Spirit.

In this pressing hour when every newscast describes unrest on the national and international scene, there is need to be alerted but not alarmed. Some "little children" will push the *panic button* and allow the waves to swallow them up in fear, although they *could* be walking on those very waves with their eyes steadfast on Him. Others will begin to see every new pressure as another call to prayer and intercession. It is imperative to know God's Word and understand what God is allowing and what He is doing in these closing moments, as the age of the Gentiles ends in utter confusion. In these perilous times, God's children should know the facts, yet they should also know how to keep their hearts and minds garrisoned so they are at peace in the midst of the storm.

I believe only eternity will reveal how many times God's children, thus garrisoned, have stood in the breach in the hour of disaster or crisis. I recall the Friday morning service in Medford, Oregon, when news of President Kennedy's assassination came. We had just given the benediction. Everyone stood stunned and breathless. Then a spirit of intercession came as deep groaning and weeping swept over the entire assembly. We fell to our knees, as one person, beseeching God to have His own way, to protect and rule over all. It has come to my attention that this very same travail came upon many others — perhaps thousands were smitten in that crucial hour — all around the world. As we arose from our knees, one could sense the inner peace and calm that had begun to reign in hearts which only a few minutes before had been bombarded by the enemy's attack.

Now that many facts regarding the assassination are coming to light, we can easily trace Satan's master design; but we can also rejoice in God's amazing protection. He still rules supreme over the designs of men. I will always believe it was the intercession wrought by the Spirit among God's saints which turned the tide and caused the most unexpected apprehension of the assassin. Can you imagine what might have happened if Lee Oswald had not been caught? It seems almost conclusive that right-wing patriots might have been rounded up from coast to coast. Only moments after Kennedy's death the "Voice of America" beaming its message into Russia, blamed the "reactionary' right wing" for the President's death. And despite all facts to the contrary, the attempt is still being made to lay the blame on the doorstep of the conservative right wing.

These tactics have been used before. In the first century when the despised Christians had made such an impact upon the Roman empire, it was Nero who masterminded the plot to blame the believers for burning Rome. And we must expect as the battle becomes more intense in the closing hours of this dispensation that Satan's master plan will include continued and increased insinuations against Christians.

Does this enrage your mind or stir your emotions? It is futile to start your own hate campaign by warring against flesh and blood. Rise up to see where the real battle is raging. What we see from here is merely the puppets controlled by evil powers in the heavenlies. God will give us calm hearts and cool heads if we learn to live in His garrison. Spiritual stature is not attained without a growing understanding of the peace of God that keeps our hearts and minds through Christ Jesus.

How many times in crises I have witnessed the value of the Blood. When minds are being incensed and emotions are about to overrule, we have simply appropriated His Blood as a covering over minds; as a protection from the onslaughts of the Evil One. That Friday morning we have just alluded to, this was once again so evident. As we openly announced "by the word of our testimony" that His precious Blood was to be a garrison for all our minds, it was almost like dew falling from heaven. Peace and inward serenity began to reign. The flood of distressing thoughts and emotional outburst were set at naught.

Yes, in this hour when emotions are like a tinderbox in so many communities, it is imperative that men and women of full stature rise to demonstrate His peace of mind in the midst of calamity. But we must know the value of the Blood, and how to announce our word of testimony in complete accord with His Word.

What about those times when physical exhaustion has left one's being with windows open and doors broken down? To the young mother mentioned in the beginning of this section and to others in a similar plight, we give this word of counsel. Our body, soul, and spirit function as one unit. If we could understand the intricate interworking, we should realize how important is proper nutrition and rest. To the amazement of many, I have sent certain folk home from meetings. In their intense hunger for spiritual reality they would attend every night for weeks, only to discover they were helpless to appropriate because of body fatigue. I have ministered to some congregations who needed a good night's rest far more than they needed the truth I would share. The present truth for them might be: How the body affects the mind and spirit.

So there must be a rebuilding process in many bodies while they claim the garrison of His Spirit as a continual protection when they are not even strong enough to plead the Blood or declare their word of testimony. But where there is no obedience to the light which the Holy Spirit is giving regarding care of the body, where there is no gradual rebuilding of the walls, doors and closing of physical gaps, there can be little faith to trust the Blood or the Word. What a helpless state ensues. We have observed it so often.

There is one final step in bringing our mind to God's intended full stature. It is to know the proper occupation of the mind. The prophet said, "Thou wilt keep him in perfect peace whose mind is STAYED (occupied) on Thee because he trusteth in Thee" (Isa. 26:3).

THIS TESTIMONY COMES:

"For years I was like a butterfly flitting first to one and then another spiritual (?) attraction. Once it was a dynamic leader, then an experience, next a movement and then a message or emphasis of truth. It is true I learned much in moving about these centers, but all the while I was missing THE CENTER. Now I want to know if there is any way to help others who are going through this same wandering? I see so many who, in their first flush of zeal to fulfill God's purpose, rush into activity and programming. They have *seen* — but it has been a *seeing* things only as related to themselves. They see God's purpose *for them* and how He is related to *their calling*, but seem unconcerned about God's Eternal PURPOSE FOR HIMSELF."

It is usually true in "initial vision" that, somehow or other, the individual is seeing himself as quite central in the picture. He begins with great zeal to promote his work for God. Then when God seems to withhold His blessing and resources, for He dare not cooperate with things out of line or focus, such individuals become discouraged. They try other promotions, other methods, and greater zeal. They have not recognized God's way of bringing them through adjustment into fuller vision — the way by which He will eliminate self from their working. God will patiently, persistently and painfully dig down into the recesses of self, more and more to fully reveal to us just what we are, and are not, in ourselves.

We can tell others about this process but it will usually fall on deaf ears. There is a divine timing involved! Until they see themselves — their motives and their fleshly energy — as God sees them, they will hardly cease living for "other things."

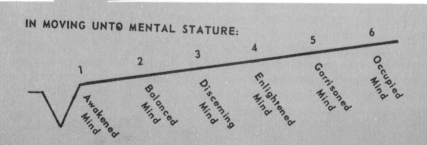

IN MOVING UNTO MENTAL STATURE:

1 Awakened Mind
2 Balanced Mind
3 Discerning Mind
4 Enlightened Mind
5 Garrisoned Mind
6 Occupied Mind

IS OUR VISION OCCUPIED WITH MERE THINGS AND ALL THE WHILE WE HAVE MISSED HIM?

HAVE YOU EVER been in a relentless search for a church home that would fully satisfy that indefinable hunger in your heart? Finally you find one. After attending a couple of Sundays you say, "Bless the Lord—at last—this is IT! At last I have found a pastor and people where I feel at home. My deep hunger is satisfied!" But then after attending a few months you are aware that the hunger is still there. Once again you become restless and start your search for a church that will *really* satisfy. But you become weary in your wanderings. IS THERE NO ANSWER?

In your insatiable hunger for the *truth,* have you ever discovered some doctrine, some message or phase of truth, and then said to yourself, "Bless the Lord—this is really IT! At last I'm satisfied. 'Cease your restless wanderings, O my soul.'" But somehow after weeks or months went by, this "IT" which you thought to be all you ever needed is no longer satisfying. WHAT IS THE ANSWER?

Ever feel dry, barren and restless in your soul and spirit? Looking, longing for something, but you do not know just what? Maybe that *experience* that you have heard others tell about is the answer and final end to the insatiable yearning in your innermost breast. So you begin to inquire. It sounds like "IT" all right. You begin to seek that experience. Others encourage you saying, "This is IT. Keep seeking! Hang on! Trust God! Fast! Let go! Pray more! Give up! Let loose!" So everybody cheers you on to that glorious experience.

Alas—"IT" happened! That glorious feeling, wonderful blessing, mountaintop experience! You said then to yourself, "This is IT.' This must be IT! I have never felt like this before. This *has to be* IT!'"

But ere long, disillusionment comes again when the experience wanes as the emotions change. Instead of heart rest there is still that indefinable restlessness.

Now what has been the matter? Why this continued gnawing and recurring search for more? You were sure that each "thing"

was "IT" all right, but it *wasn't* HIM. That was your trouble.
Yes, these were blessings, truths, experiences from God, but
not God HIMSELF. [22]

Could the basic cause of this restlessness be that we have a
most refined kind of ego-centricity — relating everything to ourselves — so that even in our "dedication" we are yet seeking to
acquire, grasp and get? The church we seek, the truth we pursue,
the experience we enjoy — all become peculiarly *ours* to be
horded and added to. Should we not rather be motivated by a
divine desire to share, serve and give? We are created in the
likeness of God the Father who gives and shares. This is what
God intended us to do, and we can only know rest and satisfaction as we are fulfilling this purpose.

Is it not true that our greatest moments of frustration are when
we are seeking to get, grasp and hold? And our greatest moments
of satisfaction are when we are giving, sharing and scattering?
Even in spiritual things, to seek to get for ourselves and to
relate everything to self will leave us with an awkward sense
of incompleteness and gnawing. This gnawing is God's way of
reminding man that he has stopped short of THE CENTER and
has allowed himself or other things to become a pseudo-center.
The great religious fallacy of our day is that we seek God for
"what He can do for me" rather than to KNOW HIM for who He
is — the eternal Father. "This is Life eternal, that they might
know Thee the only true God, and Jesus Christ, whom thou hast
sent" (John 17:3).

Let us examine the pathway of most believers as they keep
moving from one center to another. It is true each new center
appears to be THE CENTER, only in a short time to be eclipsed
by something else new which seems even greater.

It usually goes like this: after trusting Christ as Lord, it is
quite natural that we should become salvation-centered. One
thing becomes all important: *getting others saved.* But it is not
long before we see how "others" are hindered by the faulty walk
of professing Christians. So as we search God's Word for more
light we are apt to become "separation-centered." That is, we
become preoccupied with the cutting off of old worldly practices,
habits and unwise friendship so as to be more useable and victorious in our walk and witness.

As we move on we will become more conscious of certain
doctrines such as baptism, Lordship, sanctification, the Cross

or the second coming of Christ. You see, beloved, there are
numerous things – doctrines, subjects, themes and teaching.
There is "the kingdom of God," and there is "sanctification";
there is "eternal life" and there is the "victorious life"; there
is the "overcoming life" and "the second coming of Christ."
These are but a few subjects or themes which have been taken
up and developed from the Scriptures. Alas, so often they have
become mere things –"other centers" with which people have
become very much occupied. Thus certain people hive off around
a sanctification interpretation and they become the sanctifi-
cationists – it becomes another "ism." Others hive off around
some interpretation of prophecy; and others are bounded by their
hedge of second adventism, mode of baptism or interpretation of
church truth. Thus each group has found some emphasis as *their
center.*

Still others will feel their lack of power and anointing in
service and will hive off with some experience as their center.
Or they will, perhaps without realizing it, become Spirit-centered
or gift-centered. So every group who would hold their people,
must envision with their distinctive message. Whether they
recognize or admit it, they must have some center as paramount
around which to gather and challenge their people. So it has been
with every new movement. The founders believe they were raised
up by God to recover and emphasize their distinctive message,
but the next generation lives in the glory of what they have

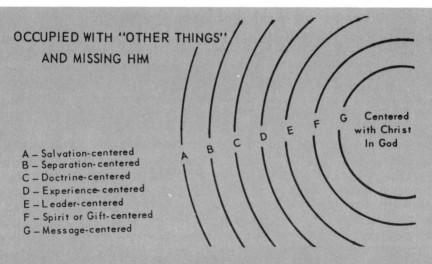

OCCUPIED WITH "OTHER THINGS"
AND MISSING HIM

G Centered
with Christ
In God

A – Salvation-centered
B – Separation-centered
C – Doctrine-centered
D – Experience-centered
E – Leader-centered
F – Spirit or Gift-centered
G – Message-centered

A B C D E F G

heard, while the third generation ·hardly acknowledges or remembers that which was once distinctive — and so seeks to
emphasize a more balanced message.

As we have pictured in the diagram, how prone we are to move
from one center to another. Yes, each new center becomes more
involving and gratifying — more enticing and subtle in its capti-
vating us. Even though for the time we have walked with the
Lord, we should have our spiritual senses exercised to become
more discerning — yet we still often allow spiritual leaders to
capture our affections and impart their vision so that we become
leader-centered, or we become so overwhelmed and gripped by
the imperative necessity for a message that is indeed ultimate
that we (unwittingly) become *message-centered.*

Now someone will at once get jittery, thinking that I do not
believe in recognizing certain messages, honoring certain leaders
whom God may use, or believe in certain crisis experiences or
unveilings of truth. Surely there is a proper place for certain
genuine experiences such as salvation, identification, filling of
the Spirit, healing or consecration. But to *stop* with any one or
all of these is to become stalled with *another center* and miss
THE CENTER. Anyone who is off-center, however little, is still
eccentric, and like a revolving wheel which is heavy on one
side he is apt to "shake things to pieces" wherever he goes.
There are some folk like that. This is *the problem* throughout the
church-world today. People who have their *private emphasis* are
moving around shaking — shaking others who have their own little
"off-centered emphasis."

Now all of this has been leading us to this one thing. If God
could have His full way with us — He would take us immediately
(past all this off-centered wandering) to THE CENTER which
our Father has given: Christ Himself. This is not more learning
about Christ, but *learning Christ.* Of all things to make plain and
clear, I have found this point one of the most difficult. It is
because the majority have become so preoccupied *with mere
things* that they have *missed Christ.* We could take up every
thing there is about Christ as doctrine, as teaching, but that is
not what we are after. God would *center us in Christ* Himself.

"He Himself is the living personal embodiment, the personi-
fication of all truth, of all life, and the Lord's purpose and will
for us is not to come to *know truth* in its manifold aspects, but
to *know the PERSON,* the living Person in a living way, and the

Person being imparted to us, and we being incorporated into the Person, all the truth becomes living truth rather than merely theoretical or technical truth" (T.A.S.). [23]

Here is the real test. When you have been sitting under some ministry where have you been left? With what are you occupied? What has become central? Is it the person himself who ministered or some system of doctrine he taught? Is it some experience we can obtain? Or some church-form which we should practice? When the Holy Spirit can lead us in His own way, He will always bring us to Christ. He will show us what Christ as a Person represents—how He is the way of meeting every situation.

We may need sanctification! Is it a doctrine? No, it is not an "it" at all. It is Christ. He is "made unto us ... sanctification" (1 Cor. 1:30). If you are in Christ and if the Holy Spirit is teaching you Christ, then you are knowing all about sanctification; but if He is not, you may have a theory and doctrine of sanctification—even a trip to the altar—but you will have *missed Him*. "It" will separate you from other Christians, and "it" will bring any number of Christians into difficulties. Probably the teaching of sanctification as a *thing,* instead of keeping *Christ* as our sanctification, has brought more Christians into difficulty than any other particular doctrine.

Now the Father's intention is to first bring us to Christ as THE CENTER where "we live and move and have our being"— for when we are truly centered *in Him,* we are also *with Him* centered *in the Father*—His purpose and viewpoint. Thus we can see with enlarged vision and perspective. Is it not sad that so many have followed the wandering course of moving from one center to another before finally arriving at Christ Himself as the Center? Only from this new center can we appreciate the series of crises through which, as hungry hearts, we have wandered in quest of truth. We see then how each experience or unveiling was not a goal, but an open door through which we passed (no one was a finality).

Now if we had started "with Christ" under proper teaching of the Holy Spirit (instead of following mere tradition and wandering) we could have knowingly surrendered to the purpose of each crisis; we could have kept every experience and unveiling in its proper focus as related to Him. We could come to " ... the knowledge of the Son of God, unto a perfect man, unto the measure of the stature of the fulness of Christ" (Eph. 4:13).

Moving...

UNTO FULL STATURE

in the

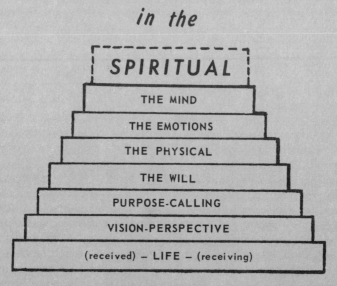

It has been our purpose through this book to show how the ministry of the Holy Spirit permeates through every level of our stature. Thus in this section, as we place THE SPIRITUAL as the capstone, we are merely demonstrating what should dominate our whole being. We consider:

IN CHAPTER 26: How the Spirit of Adoption moves us unto that full stature which the Father planned in the beginning.

IN CHAPTER 27: How the Holy Spirit must keep us stretchable in the inner man.

IN CHAPTER 28: How both inner graces and spiritual gifts are essential in a fruitful ministry of life.

IN CHAPTER 29: How our individual full stature depends upon our proper relatedness to the Body of Christ.

IN CHAPTER 30: How our full stature will fulfill the Father's delight.

PERHAPS YOU HAVE READ IN GREEK MYTHOLOGY...
...of the old sculptor who had yearned and longed for a
life-time that he might have a son—someone with whom he
might completely share himself, his skill and ambition. As
the years passed by he determined that the next best thing
was to carve out a life-size statue. Perhaps in this—even
though cold stone—he could embody some of himself, and
thus find some measure of paternal satisfaction. For many
years he molded and perfected this creation of his hands;
he loved it as though it were a living son who could respond back with love. And then the strangest thing happened! One morning when the old sculptor entered his shop
he found his statue had come alive. He was elated beyond
words! Now at last he could have that fellowship and
intimate communion which is the deepest craving of every
father-heart.

But in all his anticipation the hour of fulfillment turned
to an hour of untold grief. While his creative offspring
indeed shared the likeness and image he had imparted of
himself, he soon realized that this son had a mind and will
of his own. Like many an earthly father he was awakened
to see that fellowship could only flow between a father
and son who were one in spirit, mind, will, purpose, vision
and ambition. How could he ever bring about such oneness?

So it was a sad day when the son finally announced he
would stay at the shop with the old sculptor no longer.
The world was beckoning him to move out and fulfill his
own purpose in life. And the old sculptor, so we are told
—stricken with grief, yet continued through his remaining
years to dream of producing a son to whom he could extend
himself in fulfilling his unrealized purpose in life.

OF COURSE this story is mere fantasy; yet its reality
serves to condition our minds to grasp the deepest yearning of THE ETERNAL FATHER. It also awakens us to
see that what is impossible with man is gloriously possible with God, the Father. Indeed we shall rejoice to
see . . . . .

HOW THE FATHER WILL
REALIZE FULL STATURE

W E SHALL HARDLY understand or appreciate the Father's intention in "the adoption" until we realize it is *the way* by which He purposes to mature a vast family of sons so He can fully express and extend Himself, His life, vision, mind, spirit, purpose and goal. But we must be sure to start in the Eternal perspective to see the adoption in the ultimate framework, not merely in the redemptive framework.

It will, perhaps, help us if we ask, was the adoption necessary only because man sinned, or was it already a part of the Eternal purpose even if Adam and his posterity had never sinned? Either we shall be pressed into the importance of relating the adoption to the Eternal Purpose of the Father, or we shall continue blindly relating it to His redemptive recovery work.

In the diagram we have pictured the adoption as Paul presents it in Ephesians and in Romans. In Ephesians (shown by the solid line) Paul shows how the adoption was purposed in the Father-heart "before the beginning" as the means to maturing this vast family—and that—all apart from sin. "Having predestinated us unto the adoption of children by Jesus Christ to Himself, according to the good pleasure of His will" (Eph. 1:5). But in contrast with this straight line of Eternal purpose, Paul now indicates in Romans (shown by the dotted line) how after the fall and downward break the adoption is still unaffected and part of the original plan. (Consider Rom. 8:14-23 and Gal. 4:1-7.)

Since it is by adoption and full sonship that we arrive at full stature, we shall need to understand these four things:

1. The Eastern (or Biblical) picture of adoption.
2. The Indwelling Pedagogue of adoption.
3. The preparation for adoption.
4. The unique purpose of adoption.

1. HOW EASTERN AND WESTERN ADOPTION DIFFER

It would seem that much of the misconception and misinterpretation of adoption and sonship has resulted from assuming our Western custom of adoption is identical with the Biblical. In Eastern lands it was the practice of the noble-father to submit his infant male child to the tutelage and training of a trusted household servant or pedagogue. This was possible because many slaves were captives from conquered civilized nations. Educated, noble in character, and qualified to serve as pedagogue or child-trainer, such slaves were esteemed members of the household staff. It was into such custody that the infant child was entrusted for maturing and discipline until the time when he should come of age.

Actually then, the child though heir apparent, was no different from the servant to whom he must submit. During the long period of child-training and preparation for full sonship it was the tutor's task to bring the child into the ways, purposes and spirit of the father of the family.

Thus adoption, as presented in the Bible is the placing of one who is *already a child* in full sonship rights. Just here the Scofield Bible note is helpful: "Adoption (huiothesia, 'placing as a son') is not so much a word of relationship as of position. The believer's relation to God as a child results from the new birth (John 1:12, 13), whereas adoption is the act of God whereby one already a child is, through redemption from the law, placed in the position of an adult son (Gal. 4:1-5)."

It is indeed sad that so many have interpreted adoption as though it were the taking of a child outside the family into a new family. This is Western adoption, but not the Biblical or Eastern conception. The Greek, Roman, or Jewish father, adopted none as a son but his own child. Birth made him a child, preparation and discipline brought him to adoption and the full stature of sonship. R. B. Jones, scholarly theologian has written:

"To be a son is infinitely more than to be a child, and the terms are never loosely used by the Holy Spirit. It is not a difference of relationship, but in position. Every 'born again' child of God has in him the nature of His Father, and is a beloved member of His Father's family. Adoption cannot make the child any nearer or dear, yet it gives the child a status he did not enjoy before, a position he did not occupy. It is a recognition as an adult son, the attaining of his majority, the seal upon his growth to maturity of mind and character. A child is one born of God; a son is one taught of God. A child has God's nature; a son has God's character."[24]

In the present study we shall be primarily concerned with the growth, training, preparation and discipline which comes between our birth as a child and our adoption in full stature.

2. WHY THE INDWELLING PEDAGOGUE HAS BEEN GIVEN

Too often it seems the blessed Holy Spirit is looked upon as little more than a "blessing machine." In his self-relating, it has been quite natural for man to assume that the Spirit has been sent primarily to benefit and comfort man; but this is to miss the Father's full intention. He has sent forth the Indwelling Pedagogue to accomplish full stature in us and bring each child to the full adoption. So He comes initially at the new birth as the "Spirit of adoption" that He might actualize the believer's full sonship. "...God has sent forth the Spirit of His Son into your hearts, crying, Abba, Father" (Gal. 4:6). What the law did as child-trainer for Israel, the Spirit of adoption is to accomplish for·us.

"...if we do not doubt that the Son has perfected the work committed to Him by the Father, why then do we doubt that the Spirit will perfect the work committed to Him by the Son? The work of the Son is as comprehensive as the work of the Father. It does not go one whit beyond it, but nor does it fall one whit short of it. As great as is the work of the Father, so great is the work of the Son; and as great as is the work of the Son, so great is the work of the Spirit. There is not one particle of the work completed by the Son for us that will not be completed by the Spirit in us. All the fullness of spiritual reality that is in Christ will be imparted to us by the Spirit of Christ. Of Himself, Jesus said, 'I am the Reality,' and of the Spirit, 'He shall guide you into all Reality.'

"The question of coming into all the fullness of spiritual reality rests, therefore, not with us but with the Spirit. It is not a question of our capacity, or of our ability, but of the absolute faithfulness of the Holy Spirit of God. Can He be depended on to do all the work committed to Him by the Son? We must learn to trust Him. We must learn to count upon His twofold work, first of revealing to us the nature and the dimensions of divine reality, and secondly, of bringing us into every whit of the reality He has revealed."[25] (T.H. Sparks)

This emphasizes a very important distinction I believe we must make right here. It is true there are many who have experienced the working of the Holy Spirit within them in conviction, regeneration and illumination. Because they have received Jesus as Lord and Saviour, He is indwelling them. However they have never realized the importance of acknowledging and honoring Him in His own Person and Lordship, or recognized His distinct and unique ministry of bringing them UNTO FULL STATURE. This is a receiving Him in an official capacity *as a Person* in His own right.

Surely it does no dishonor to the Lord Jesus for us to honor and recognize the Holy Spirit as a very real Person – as the Indwelling Pedagogue. Both the Father and the Son expect us to do such. It is Their intention at this present hour that we who are born-ones (teknon) are to walk after the Spirit – which means that the Father is more and more embodying Himself, His spirit, mind, purpose and dedication in us. Now we must consider how the Spirit of adoption working within is leading us into a fuller sharing as we eagerly wait for the actual "placing of sons" (huiothesia).

3. THE TWELVE-FOLD SHARING AS PREPARATION FOR ADOPTION [26]

Just how does our Indwelling Pedagogue accomplish this preparation? It is: (1) by His revelation that we behold spiritual realities; and (2) it is by His loving discipline that these realities become operative within us. So whether for the initial revelation to our hearts of all that the Father waits to share, or amid the inward stretching whereby these become operative—we are always shut up to the Indwelling Pedagogue.

In the diagram we have listed the twelve-fold sharing which the Father has designed for His children in the beginning. Now

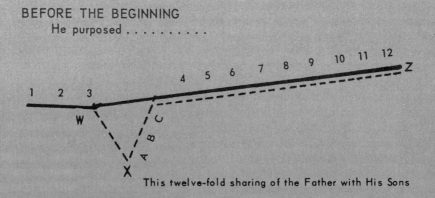

BEFORE THE BEGINNING
   He purposed . . . .

This twelve-fold sharing of the Father with His Sons

let us see how, even though the Fall necessitated the incorpo-
rating of redemption, this sharing continues unhindered.

1. IMAGE AND LIKENESS THROUGH ADAM: In the initial
phase of this sharing plan, God has used Himself as the pattern
after which man was created. Through Adam, the only created
son, the likeness and image is passed on to all of Adam's posterity. As we have already said, man was to be like God and to
represent Him on the earth. Through man's ingratitude and treason
this image of God was marred, yet there is full provision for
restoration "in Christ." It was in the Father's design that Adam,
who had human nature and created life, was to dedicate himself
to God's purpose and thus he could have . . .

2. DIVINE NATURE AND LIFE IN CHRIST: It is important
to remember that until Adam would give himself in obedience
and dedication unto God he could not share in the "tree of life."
This was God's way of representing that vital union with Himself
which He had planned. As Adam stood at the gateway of choice
he could either move along the high-way of divine purpose: (w to
z) or he could take his own way: (w to x). We know how Adam
chose to live by "another tree" representing complete independence of God. In his fallen condition we see how man's first
need is (A) justification and redemption. But man needs much
more. So that which Adam rejected and turned from is now made
available. In Christ and the work of the Cross man can now
receive (B) the Divine nature and life and also (C) a positional
righteousness and holiness. (1 John 5:11-12; John 3:16; 1 Cor.
1:30).

4. HIS SPIRIT AND FELLOWSHIP: You will observe in the
diagram that we have now reached that high-way of purpose. If
Adam had yielded to God in the Garden as he stood at the gateway of choice, we believe he could have entered into a living
union whereby he would have received (1) the divine nature and
life, and (2) the righteousness and holiness—all of which were
to be available "in Christ." Now that man has sinned and God
has provided the work of the Cross, man is at the bottom; we
must be sure that salvation, and hence maturity, does not come
by man striving to reach the top. It is God who comes all the
way down the ladder, meets man at the very bottom, and lifts
him by grace into a new position where he shares in the Divine
Spirit and fellowship.

Just here we must see how all religions fall into two types:
either man strives up through the Divine beckoning, or God comes

down to redeem us through the Incarnate Lord Jesus; either we attempt to go up to Him or He comes down to us; either we reach salvation and maturity by our resources or by His resources. So God has met man at the bottom rung and lifts him through (A-B-C) to that high-way where he can walk after the Spirit in an intimate fellowship with God. It is true that the Holy Spirit works regeneration, renewing, life, righteousness and holiness within us, but it is also true that until we have honored Him as a Person in His rights of Lordship there will be very little progress in that fuller sharing and moving toward full stature. (1 John 1:3; Eph. 2:19-20, 22).

5. LIGHT AND LOVE IN CHRIST: It could only be expected that if the Father were to have an intimate sharing with His children they must mutually enjoy one another in love and undimmed light. (Ps. 36:9; 2 Cor. 4:6; Rom. 5:5; Rom. 8:35-39)

6. PEACE AND JOY IN CHRIST: What a Father and what a glorious intention that this vast family of sons should all have the privilege of participating in His joy and peace. (Phil. 4:7-9; John 14:27; Gal. 5:22)

7. MIND AND SECRETS IN CHRIST: It would seem to many that it is only a distant hope that we are to share in the mind of Christ, when it can be a very present reality. And further, the fact that the Father has desired to share the secrets of the ages with those who are prepared and concerned to know – this is almost beyond our highest expectation. (1 Cor. 2:16; Deut. 29:29)

8. KNOWLEDGE AND WISDOM IN CHRIST: Indeed the Father withholds nothing from His children that is for His glory and their own good. When He can bring us into complete harmony with His own purposes, we shall enjoy the most glorious sharing of unlimited wisdom and knowledge. Has He not spoken of Abraham: "... Shall I hide from Abraham that thing which I do?" Now shall He hide from us, when we are moving toward full stature in our high calling? (Dan. 9:22; Col. 1:9-10; 2 Cor. 4:6)

9. GRACES AND GIFTS IN CHRIST: As we shall see in the coming chapters, there is a working of divine graces within us, while there is also an outworking of spiritual gifts whereby we have an effectual ministry unto Him. This also is God's working that we might be equipped unto every good work. (1 Peter 4:10; 1 Peter 5:5; 1 Cor. 7:7)

10. EARTHLY DOMINION, POWER AND AUTHORITY IN CHRIST: We remember how these were offered to Adam in the Garden, but he failed in their proper execution. Instead of

reigning with power and authority he became a slave to sin and
the Devil. Now in Christ these bondages are broken and man
once again is called to properly execute the will of God here
on earth.

Now this ten-fold sharing thus far is ours only by the inward
stretching and discipline, the crisis and testing which the Indwelling Pedagogue uses in preparing us for the adoption. But
we must press on to see . . .

THE UNIQUE PURPOSE OF THE ADOPTION

There is no clearer unveiling of the Father's unique purpose
in the adoption than when we look at the Lord Jesus. All that
could have happened in the First Adam moving along the straight
high-way of purpose is now demonstrated in the Last Adam as
He moves through childhood into that glorious position of. full
sonship. For the first clear indication of this, we turn back to
Isaiah's prophecy hundreds of years before Christ came to earth:

"Unto us a child is born; Unto us a son is given. And the
government shall be upon His shoulder . . . " (Isa. 9:6).

The prophet was, of course, giving us the Father's full purpose in bringing a son unto the adoption: That He might share
Himself and the governmental reigns of His vast household. How
beautifully the prophet distinguishes between the child who is
born in Bethlehem's manger and the Son who was openly recognized and given by the Father at Jordan River. It was there in
baptism the Son seemed to lay aside the old robes of childhood
and the Father sent His own Spirit like a Dove upon Him. John
heard the Father announce as from an open heaven: "This is my
beloved Son in whom I am well pleased." We cannot verify the
accuracy, but Jewish tradition tells us that it was most customary for every father to make this very announcement at the cere-
mony of "placing his child in full sonship privileges." Further
we are told that in Jewish custom it was at the age of 30 that a
father would place his son in adoption rights.

But there was another throne which also recognized the importance of this event at Jordan River. Immediately the enemy of
God realized that an Invader was now ready to challenge his
worldly kingdom. So the Lord Jesus was led by the Spirit into
the wilderness where the first great issues of government were
settled. Would Jesus sell out—as the First Adam had done in
the Garden? Or would He openly triumph over this archenemy of
God and in the most severe temptation make a way by which the

Father could share . . .

11. HIS THRONE AND THE PRIVILEGE OF JOINT-REIGN-
ING WITH CHRIST: "God's first call to man was to rulership
over the earth and His last call to him is throneship with Him
above the highest heavens. This is what the beloved Paul had
in mind when he said, 'I rush along the track for the prize of the
supreme call of God in Christ Jesus ' (Phil. 3:14). Thus we see
that the Eternal Father has purposed to share with man His
throne of power and glory above the highest heavens if he will
qualify for it. Rulership with Him is in God's purpose for His
vast family, but throneship with Him above the highest heavens
demands certain definite qualifications." (C.A.J.)

12. HEAVENLY GLORY AND SATISFACTION IN CHRIST:
Finally, we see how even sharing the throne is but a means to
a greater end: sharing in His glory and satisfaction. How strange
that those folk who so decry any kind of spiritual qualifying or
attainment do not realize how empty and meaningless is glory
where there is no sacrifice or effort. Who wants a trophy, however beautiful, if it has merely been purchased at the dime store
for a dollar? Even so our Father has allowed us the privilege of
entering into the sufferings and discipline of Christ that we
might be "glorified together." And what a day of glory it will be
for the Father when His Son and sons have the full exercise of
government upon their shoulders. Throughout the ages we can
conjecture there will be "the increase of His government." Of
course we are allowing our fondest imagination to project into
the vast universe which He is likely to populate and bring under
His glorious government. But here we must be cautious, lest we
move beyond that which is written. Yet if our mortal mind can
conceive of something so wonderful, we can be sure the Eternal
Father has something far greater to unfold before His Son and
sons. We must simply be content now to expectantly wait for that
hour when "all things shall find their consummation in HIM."
And to rejoice that we are "in Him."

Yes, what blessedness and satisfaction will come as the
Father's vast family enters into their full adoption to enjoy as
He enjoys. As we shall see this adoption is not of individuals
but of "One corporate Man."

That paternal and filial blessedness and satisfaction which
will be enjoyed by the Father will also be enjoyed by the Son
and sons. Indeed, there is so much we cannot grasp, for we yet
look "through a glass darkly." But we are confident that our

measure of participation will be exactly commensurate with our measure of FULL STATURE.

Surely J. B. Phillips was caught with the immensity of our calling to adoption when he translated Romans 8:18-30:

"In my opinion whatever we may have to go through now is less than nothing compared with the magnificent future God has planned for us. The whole creation is on tiptoe to see the wonderful sight of the sons of God coming into their own..."

"It is plain to anyone with eyes to see that at the present time all created life groans in a sort of universal travail. And it is plain, too, that we who have a foretaste of the Spirit are in a state of painful tension, while we wait for that redemption of our bodies which will mean at last we have REALIZED OUR FULL SONSHIP IN HIM."

"Moreover we know that to those who love God, who are called according to His Plan, everything that happens fits into a pattern for good. God, in His foreknowledge, chose them to bear the family likeness of His Son, that He might be the eldest of a family of many brothers. He chose them long ago; when the time came He called them, He made them righteous in His sight and then lifted them TO THE SPLENDOUR OF LIFE AS HIS OWN SONS."

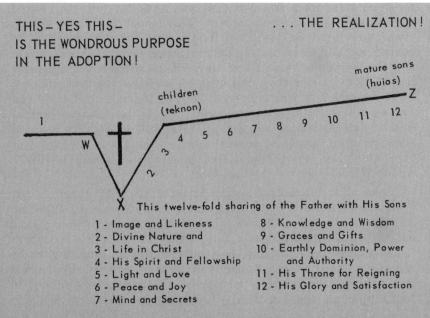

THIS— YES THIS—
IS THE WONDROUS PURPOSE
IN THE ADOPTION!

... THE REALIZATION!

mature sons (huios)

children (teknon)

This twelve-fold sharing of the Father with His Sons

1 - Image and Likeness
2 - Divine Nature and
3 - Life in Christ
4 - His Spirit and Fellowship
5 - Light and Love
6 - Peace and Joy
7 - Mind and Secrets
8 - Knowledge and Wisdom
9 - Graces and Gifts
10 - Earthly Dominion, Power and Authority
11 - His Throne for Reigning
12 - His Glory and Satisfaction

A MINISTER AT LARGE who has yearned for the building up of Christ's Body has said: "Among God's people today a great majority have settled for fixed positions while only a small minority have kept stretchable in their vision and experience. To many any spiritual stretchableness would seem as compromise or looseness of conviction, yet I am convinced that inward adjustableness is perhaps the outstanding mark of a life continuously governed by the Holy Spirit." Now we must see that reaching any spiritual stature involves . . .

THE CONTINUOUS STRETCHING
OF THE WINESKIN

WHERE THERE IS NO continuous governing of the Holy Spirit, whether in our personal walk or ministry, or in our church services or fellowship, there will be no real development of inner stature. Inward spiritual growth comes only as the believer or group gladly responds to that daily, fresh breath of the Spirit intended to govern the life. The result is a continuous inward stretching, adjusting and enlarging.

Is it not most evident today, that in most every circle of fellowship there are those who have "settled on their lees"? They are content with the gains the pioneers have wrought for them, and now feel called of God to simply hold to the old landmarks. What was good for their parents and grandparents is plenty good for them. No breath of vision, no reaching for new plateaus of experience is gripping them. And the result? Legalism, fixity of form, straining to retain meaningless patterns and empty letter-conceptions. They are in prison without realizing their captivity.

One who has discerned this predicament has evaluated: "The history of Christianity from the latter days of the Apostles is the history of prisons. Not literal, material prisons, though there have been not a few of these, but prisons which are the result of man's inveterate habit of taking hold and bringing into bondage. How many times has the Spirit broken loose and moved in a new and free way, only to have that way brought under the control of man and crystalized into another 'Form,' Creed, Organization, Denomination, Sect, 'Order,' Community, etc.! The invariable result has been that the free movement and life of the Spirit has been cramped, or even killed, by the prison or framework into which it has been drawn or forced. Every time we seek to express something Divine in word or form we at once limit it, and when that expression or form becomes the established and recognized formula we have in effect put fetters on the Spirit. God gives a vision, and every God-given vision has illimitable potentialities; but all too soon the vision is laid hold of by men who never had it in or of the Spirit, and the grapes of Eschol turn to raisins in their hands. So very many of the living fruits of the heavenly country have suffered in this way, and have become dried, shrunken, unctionless shadows of their early glory.

"Upon a living movement of the Spirit, born with fire in the heart of some prophet, successors, sponsors, or adherents build an earthly organization, and imprison the vision in a tradition. So a *message* becomes a Creed; a 'Heavenly Vision' becomes an earthly institution; a movement of the Spirit becomes a 'Work,' which must be kept going by the steam of human energy, and maintained by man's resourcefulness." (T.A.S.) [27]

Yet in the midst of this traditional pattern of confinement by men, God has always had His remnant in every hour—those who are pressing unto full sonship and stature. They know that inner stretching and adjustment of the Spirit, and even though painful seem to delight in it, for they realize that such an inward stretching is God's sure way of producing a spiritual elasticity, vitality and capacity they could not otherwise know.

As we keep under the government of the Holy Spirit, we never come to any fixed or final place as far as light and attainment is concerned. Of course we must distinguish between truth which is absolute, fixed, final and forever settled in God, and that which God unfolds before our eyes to be continuously appropriated and wrought out in life and experience. The great objective truths of our faith are fixed and settled. What Christ has wrought for the Father, what He is unto Him, and the work of the Son made available to us, never changes. So it is in the realm of our understanding, our apprehension, our knowledge, and our growth that we must remain open, ready for enlargement and expansion. In these there never can be any sense of finality either in our conceptions or attainment. And, as we remain stretchable, we may experience drastic changes both in our thinking, as well as our experience.

As we have indicated in the diagram, stretching brings the development of inward graces. These actually constitute our "inner spiritual stature," and it is the stretching of these graces which Peter describes in his second epistle. How well we know that such inward enlargement—that enlargement which causes us to be partakers of more and more of the divine nature—is most painful. Apart from "giving all diligence" we shall surely faint, and "settled on our lees," we shall find *reasons* for avoiding that stretching which is so necessary for the growth of faith, virtue, knowledge, temperance, patience, godliness, kindness and love.

First, let us consider the stretching of faith. Look at Philip. He was down in Samaria, and under the evident blessing and approval of the Lord. Wonderful things were happening. Then the word of the Lord comes to leave. What a stretching of faith here! We can almost hear him argue, "But Lord, You are doing such a great thing here. It doesn't seem reasonable that You should take me from this center of revival to a barren desert. Lord, this is where my faith is really strong and growing." But the real issue was in God's special word, "Go."

Immediately we can see this was really a question of being

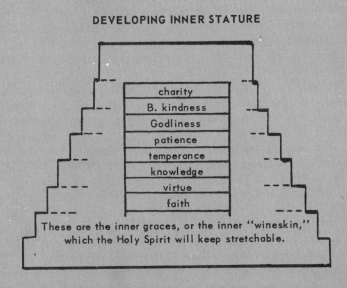

DEVELOPING INNER STATURE

charity
B. kindness
Godliness
patience
temperance
knowledge
virtue
faith

These are the inner graces, or the inner "wineskin," which the Holy Spirit will keep stretchable.

wholly under the Spirit's government. How often our locigal reasoning collides with God's reasoning at this very point. We think we see, but not as He sees. How much shall we allow God to stretch our faith? How much are we grooved in a fixity or finality of vision as to how God will use us, or where? Of course we can see now how much it meant to the Church that Philip was flexible. For while the desert may have seemed to be an end, it was, really, a gateway into that greater ministry which God intended. From that point there opened up for Philip a long story of ministry. You will find, that after this contact with the Ethiopian, some very vital things came into being through the ministry of Philip. And this all hung upon the matter of flexibility or adjustableness, on whether the Lord was free to have His way in Philip's life, or whether Philip would say, "No, this is where I am staying and this is how things are; this is where the Lord is working, and here I stay!"

Second, there is the stretching of virtue, or determination, as the word is more often translated. Perhaps we cannot make too much of the quality of determination, for the New Testament often emphasizes this matter of steadfast endurance as being set on going on: not being turned aside. We must see that while this quality is most admirable, yet it, too, must be flexible or stretchable. From the great battles of this past war comes this confession from a great leader: "The hardest test of generalship is to hold the balance between determination and flexibility. In this (referring to the Southeast Asia campaign) the enemy failed. He scored high by determination; he paid heavily for lack of flexibility."

Let us note this. When we have set our face with the steel of determination to achieve a certain task, this admirable quality can become our very downfall. All too easily our determination takes place of the Spirit's government. We decide on a certain course, and become so rigidly bound by it that we have no mind to listen to the Spirit when He speaks. We are prone to fall into the same snare which Paul nearly fell into, that is, to follow our plan through with inflexible determination. Paul, you recall, was set on going to Asia and Bithynia. It seemed the most logical course, and we admire Paul's determination to overcome every obstacle. But just at this point Paul is "forbidden of the Holy Ghost... the Spirit suffered them (him) not" (Acts 16:6,7). What if Paul had not been adjustable; what if this admirable quality of determination had not been stretchable? We all know what it has meant to Macedonia and Europe that Paul's determination was tempered by the Spirit with flexibility.

What a painful area of stretching in our inner wineskin! Like the enemy general mentioned, we, too, fail to be adjustable, adaptable, teachable. So often our inflexibility may manifest itself by our becoming completely demoralized if anything interferes with our plans. We are prone to be like the enemy general: "who was so lacking in adaptability that he had no resourcefulness with which to meet anything outside his program. Any slight deviation which turned him off his set course threw him into confusion."

How often we have witnessed this when a speaker could not follow his prepared message; a storm cut the electric power and without light he cannot read his script. Or suddenly the meeting was moved from the tabernacle to the waterfront, and the wind played such havoc with his notes that he was completely frustrated. Often a speaker has prepared a message to meet the needs of believers only to discover the majority in his audience do not know the Lord and his theme would be most inappropriate.

Yes, what stretching takes place when the life is completely governed by the Holy Spirit. God alone can keep one prepared for every emergency and situation. He can keep one properly balanced in determination and flexibility when the severe test is on.

Third, we have the stretching of knowledge. One can look at Peter and see that he had developed a fixed position regarding certain laws of the Old Testament and his interpretation of them. From his rigid, static position he argued, "Not so, Lord." Until he had "thought on the vision" he insisted,"Not so, Lord." He was neither stretchable, teachable nor adjustable. Yet what a tremendous advance, not only for Peter, but for the whole Church when, without giving away any steadfastness or determination, he adjusted to the new light that the Lord gave, and to a new knowing of the Lord and His ways. This ability to be adjustable to new insights of truth has been a problem throughout the centuries, not just with individuals but with groups as well.

History reveals how each new movement starts with a new and fresh glimmer of truth. The next generation lives to keep that truth bright and clear, and to perpetuate it. But a younger generation within the ranks is not content with God's manna of yesterday. There is a yearning for fresh manna, for the "present truth" essential for this hour. And when God answers by giving a fresh glimmer of light they seek immediately to include it within the "old wineskin."

How innocently the battle begins. Quickly the "old pillars" will rise up to reject any invasion of new light. They feel duty bound to stay by the "ancient landmarks" as interpreted by those who founded their movement. Without realizing it they are being sucked into a private whirlpool of fixed doctrine which leaves no place for that fresh flowing stream of living revelation which produces vitality, enlargement and true elasticity.

With real discernment one who "sees" has written: "Sooner or later any real or seeming departure or diversion from the 'recognized' and traditional order of Creed or practice will be heresy, to be violently suspect, repressed, and outcast. Too often what, at its beginning, was a spiritual energy producing a living organism expressing something that God really wanted and to which He gave *birth* has become something which the next generation has to sustain and work hard to keep going. The thing has developed a self-interest and it will go hard with anyone or anything interfering with it, or seeming so to do. The Spirit has become the prisoner of the institution or system, and the people become limited spiritually as the result. The refreshing breeze of the Spirit is lost—lost through self-protection." (T.A.S.)

And this brings us to the other inward graces which Peter mentions. Briefly we must consider the stretching of temperance (self-control) patience and godliness. God desires to add to the inner stature of both individuals and corporate groups. To be wholly under the government of the Spirit means a continuous stretching, thus increasing inner stature. No wonder Peter could exclaim "For if these things be in you, and abound, they make you that ye shall neither be barren nor unfruitful . . . " (2 Pet. 1:8).

Now the next question is: How do we allow and enjoy this inner stretchability in our own wineskin, yet be controlled and patient with those who are yet dragging their feet and fearful? While we may be jubilant in the divine operation wrought within us, there are others who cannot enjoy our delight. To them this hilarity and abounding overflow is only excess and extreme. How quickly they have forgotten that earlier day when God liberated them from their prison-house or fixed position. In that day they represented the "new work" which God was accomplishing and they groaned and suffered with those who feared any innovations wrought by man. Now they have become the *old* who are protective against the invasion of the *new*. To many it would seem there is no avoiding this conflict between the old and new, the fixed

and the free. It is just here God will accomplish a stretching in
our self-control, patience and godliness. We shall see how this
involves the difference between the permissive and the whole will
of God.

There are those times when we all can look back on our pathway and believe that certain steps which we took and different
courses we followed were in the will of God for us. Yet we have
now been forced to almost repudiate or drastically revise the position we took at that time. Here is the point of so much frustration. It does not mean that we missed God's will at the time we
took that step. It was perhaps all we could comprehend at that
moment. The Lord may, at one time, in His permissive will, lead
us in a certain way because that is the only way we could learn
certain things. Yet it does not mean that He intends for us to stay
there forever, nor that He had settled us there. Nor that in leading
us in that way at that time we dare not ever contemplate another
change. That is sheer bondage to a fixed conception. You and I
as sons should come to know liberty from such bondage. This
means that we keep teachable, stretchable, free for adjustments,
and not be bound to any position that would hinder the complete
government of the Spirit over us. Yes, it will surely require a
patience with ourselves and our seeming instability. Furthermore,
this self-control and patience will help us appreciate the same
stretching in other lives. Indeed he who is being stretched will
understand when others are groaning in the Spirit's stretching.

Then we must be prepared for the stretching of brotherly kindness. At times we all have found ourselves in a corner. We are
determined to be patient, controlled and kind unto all the brethren,
yet the Holy Spirit asks us to "plough deep" in some life or
group, to unveil almost unmercifully some hidden root which is
keeping that person from the fruitfulness he yearns for. Will we
allow this painful stretch, and under the Spirit's direction perform
the operation with a sharp scalpel? Even though it seems most
cruel to the natural eye, yet it is loving kindness.

There are those times when one seems to most utterly fail in
the common gesture of brotherliness. You are forced to leave
someone in the dark, to be almost mysterious in your failure to
answer a question. The Lord Jesus often faced this test of adjustableness. His brethren came to Him one day and said, "We
are going up to the feast. Are You going up with us? If You do not
go, people will wonder; You will prejudice Your interest." He
said, "No, you go up. I am not going."

Now when they had gone up, Jesus evidently received the
Spirit's witness that He should go up. He did not say, "I have
told them I was not going up: they will think I have played a trick
on them, that I did not want them." No, He did not argue like that,
but moved in the Spirit and left it all with the Father. He was not
bound by the considerations of people or what they would think
or say.

What an inward stretching this means—that even at an hour's
notice we should be free to follow. But just as important, we must
learn how best to keep from any position where we are bound to
contradict our word. Those who insist on binding us to something
definite will imagine we are not kind, thoughtful or considerate in
our relationships. Until they have experienced this same inner
stretching, it will be impossible for them to understand.

As the capstone of inner stature, we must add the stretching
of love. But first the question: What is all this inner stretching
really for? If we assume it is unto our own benefit and blessing
we have missed the point. Peter would hasten to remind us this
stretching is to insure abounding fruitfulness unto God.

Self-love will never allow any painful stretching. It can only
pity itself and flee from adversity or suffering or pressure. Yet
the stretching of divine love in us will help us to both suffer and
weep. It was this inner stretching of love which caused Jesus to
weep in compassion as He beheld Israel like little chicks who
could not hear the voice of their mother. How much He mourned
for those lost sheep who were following blindly without a shepherd. Yet when He offered Himself as THE SHEPHERD, they
turned upon His gesture of love and nailed Him to a Cross.

Shall we expect any different treatment when we are pouring
ourselves out in love? Such a stretching will produce a love that
understands even when others misunderstand, a love that gives
even when others reject our giving, a love that seeks not its own
but always the welfare of another.

Finally, what does Jesus teach us about the wineskins? He
would seem to say that either they will remain flexible by continuous stretching, or they will become hard and unflexible, and
by resistance to His will be usable only for old wine. When He
looked at the Pharisees in their rigid positions, Jesus could discern that they were like wineskins fixed, and without elasticity.
So He insisted that "new wine must be put in new wineskins..."
We can almost hear Him say: "Let me make you anew—and keep
you forever new."

A FUNDAMENTALIST LEADER EVALUATES:

"I have been increasingly concerned for many of my fundamentalist brethren who speak much about the Holy Spirit yet allow Him so little liberty in their ministry. It is true many of these men have known the Spirit's gracious working in their hearts; they have been in the crucible of the Cross where inner spiritual graces have been wrought in their character. Yet it seems they have turned away from the exercise of any spiritual gifts which would allow a full outflow in their ministry. It is no wonder so many have come to an apathy and dissatisfaction in their ministry.

"Yet their fears are not without ground. In observing the extremes of many pentecostals who so magnify experiences and certain gifts, it is little wonder my brethren have been frightened away — assuming that all gift-ministry must be alike. How wrong to make such a generalization, as though the exercise of spiritual gifts were quite unimportant and that the inwrought spiritual graces were really all that mattered.

"On the other hand it has been most encouraging to see how some of my friends have been liberated into a new reality and ministry of life. They have discovered it was not enough to have the Holy Spirit working within, He must be allowed an outflow through the exercise of spiritual gifts. And what a glorious outflow of life is now evident. The hour has come when sane, sensible and spiritually mature men of God must rise to present a proper image of the 'pneumatika' — as God has intended — to the Church."

A PENTECOSTAL LEADER HAS EVALUATED:

"What an awakening! Since I have moved into this LIVING FELLOWSHIP where the stream of life-light-love is flowing out of God I have suddenly realized how warped we pentecostals have been. We have emphasized tongues almost as though it were the only spiritual gift; we have been so zealous in selling this experience when the reality of the experience should have been sufficient to draw and love men into reality. (continued)

"Indeed there are many who exercise spiritual gifts (even as the Corinthians did) who are exceedingly carnal. We have allowed our people to assume that gifts are an evidence of being spiritual, when really they are given to babes that they might become spiritual. Proof of this misunderstanding is evident in our pentecostal churches where fleshly fads and fashions hold sway instead of a Godly simplicity of life; where we can only hold attendance by using soulish entertainment; where people live on a constant diet of glamorous personalities who give unique testimonies of their experiences. Yet all the while our folk manifest so little true hunger or appetite for revealed truth from God's Word.

"Let no one imagine I am critical; I am grieved and yearning that our people shall be awakened to true God-centeredness. As God's watchman I must warn and exhort the people. And though I be misunderstood by my brethren for unveiling our weaknesses I must insist that there is nothing more spiritually dead than a pentecostal church which has sought power without purity, service without sacrifice, exercise of gifts without inwrought spiritual graces and a ministry of life without a 'working of death.'

"It seems I have a constant inner groaning that God may help us as pentecostals to embrace the Cross and all it means. In our quest for spiritual power and glory we have by-passed the Cross and to that extent limited the real effectiveness of Pentecost. This was not so in the beginning of our movement when death was preached as the gateway to spiritual life and power."

HE THAT IS SPIRITUAL
EXPRESSES BOTH GRACES AND GIFTS

FOUR DISTINCT EPISODES in the life of Moses picture whether our ministry is by mere natural energy or from a spiritual source. While it is true we, as believers on this side of Pentecost, have much greater privilege than those of the Old Testament, there is nevertheless a similarity which will help us understand spiritual fruitfulness unto God. In Moses we shall see:

1. The barrenness resulting from natural energy.
2. The limitation when there are graces but no gift.
3. The limitation when there is a gift but no graces.
4. The abounding fruitfulness in both graces and gifts.

First, we see Moses awakened by God for the ministry of delivering Israel from Egyptian bondage. "And when he was full forty years old, it came into his heart to visit his brethren the children of Israel." "And it came to pass in those days, when Moses was grown, that he went out unto his brethren, and looked on their burdens" (Acts 7:23; Ex. 2:11). It seems right to infer that God had been working to place this concern "in his heart." Yet this awakening to their need was but the beginning. Here is the moment of failure in so much service for God. There is many a Moses who sees the need of his brethren and runs to their help without any spiritual preparation or divine sending.

Indeed Moses seems to have reached full natural and physical stature. But in seeing their need, all he had was natural position and natural gift to use for God. And this is the lesson we must emphasize: it is not enough to see need and have abilities to help. The work of the Lord requires more than zeal or an awakened sense of another's need. God's word to Moses—even as to us today—would have been, had he waited to listen: "Moses, it is not by your natural might, nor by your position or prestige as a power in Egypt, but BY MY SPIRIT." We are now only too aware that Moses' attempt to help his brethren was out of God's timing, it was in his own way, and by his own energy. His efforts came to naught and he was forced to flee to the backside of the desert where God enrolled him in His schoolroom for spiritual preparation. Without this preparation, what barrenness! We can only move by natural energy.

In the second episode we see Moses after God has wrought an inward emptying. After forty long years of tending sheep we see a different Moses. God is now about to send him back as the deliverer of His people. Once Moses had seemed to say by his methods: "Lord, I am sure you've picked the right man to deliver—I'm ready for service," but now notice the difference in his response: "Who am I?" There has been an inner emptying of his pride and abilities. The ways of Egypt and the natural man are gone. How often this inward emptiness has caused many to reply exactly as

Moses did: "...they will not believe me, nor hearken unto my voice:" (Ex. 4:1).

So God gives to Moses two signs. First, the rod in his hand turns into a serpent as he casts it to the ground; and second, his hand becomes leprous as snow as he pulls it from his bosom; then is made whole as he pulls it out the next time.

It seems just here God is giving a most graphic picture of the two-fold need in service. As the Scofield Bible footnote suggests: "The heart (' bosom") stands for what we are, the hand for what we do." The heart speaks of inward preparation, the hand speaks of outward preparation. God was placing in the hand of Moses a rod which stood for spiritual authority. What a gift this was for the exercise of his ministry of delivering the people. But in his inner bosom Moses was also to have a new heart and the divine inwrought graces. What limitation there would be in his service if he had only the rod of authority yet no inner preparation. And likewise, what limitation if he had only a bosom free from leprosy yet no rod of authority in his hand. Indeed the hand that holds the rod of God's power should be a cleansed hand swayed by a new heart. Here we see the proper balance in what *we are* and what *we do*.

But there is something all important which happened just before these two signs were given. The angel of the Lord appeared unto Moses in the burning bush. We do not know how much Moses understood of the significance of this burning bush, yet we are sure it was God's way of showing how He would be working within him and out through him. The resources of the I AM who was sending him forth would be unlimited. Did Moses understand? There can be no doubt that God had wrought some very real preparation within Moses during those years of sheep-tending. Yet in spite of those graces wrought within, he is not able to trust God for the gift to speak. "And Moses said unto the Lord, O my Lord, I am not eloquent, neither heretofore, nor since thou hast spoken unto thy servant: but I am slow of speech, and of a slow tongue. And the Lord said unto him, Who hath made man's mouth? or who maketh the dumb, or deaf, or the seeing, or the blind? have not I the Lord? Now therefore go, and I will be with thy mouth, and teach thee what thou shalt say." Surely the Lord had a right to be angry with Moses when he kept insisting that he needed someone to speak for him.

In this we have a picture of that servant whom God has taken through deep preparation and crisis. Yet how strange that such a one, even with the inward reality of standing on holy ground before God, should be afraid to trust God for a supernatural exercise of the gift to speak, or the rod of authority. In my observation it would seem there are many about us who have experienced a very real inward working of the Cross in their lives, yet through prejudice or fear they have not allowed the Holy Spirit to operate by charismatic gift. This is not to discount the Spirit's working in their inner life; it is not that such a one has no ministry. It is merely that the supernatural element is missing unless there is a gift under the anointing of the Spirit. The result is a manifest limitation in ministry as compared with the fruitfulness God would accomplish if there were no quenching of the Spirit. How many are like bottles filled with life yet unable to overflow because the neck opening is so tiny. They have much reality which could be shared, yet no adequate way of sharing.

As we have pictured in the diagram Moses is here like vessel B. God has done some stretching to produce some inward reality within, but unless there is an operation of divine gift through him, God cannot fulfill His highest purpose through him. He will not speak with divine unction nor handle the rod of authority. What is

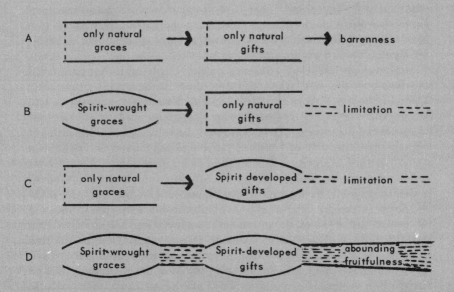

A MINISTRY OF FLOWING LIFE REQUIRES BOTH GRACES AND GIFTS

A   only natural graces → only natural gifts → barrenness

B   Spirit-wrought graces → only natural gifts ---- limitation ----

C   only natural graces → Spirit developed gifts ---- limitation ----

D   Spirit-wrought graces → Spirit-developed gifts → abounding fruitfulness more tragic than to see choice servants of God, men in whom there has been wrought inner graces yet who are without means of expression. These would emphasize the Spirit-filled life and would never think of grieving the Holy Spirit, yet all the while these precious men are quenching the Spirit's flowing through their life in failing to allow expression by some gift of the Spirit.

Oh that God might break up the restrictions and limitations! Instead of merely ministering by natural gift and authority there must come that unhindered flowing of the Spirit through well-developed spiritual gifts.

In the third episode we see the people murmuring against Moses because there was no water to drink (Numbers 20). Here we shall see Moses as one who exercises a spiritual gift yet is so utterly lacking in inward grace. You recall how the people were about to stone him. He cries unto the Lord and God gives him exact directions. Yet Moses is so angry with the people. When he should have spoken to the rock, he smote the rock and spoke to the people. Inwardly Moses is out of tune and falls into the snare of using directions which had worked previously, (Ex. 17) but which were not appropriate for this time.

But the amazing thing is that in spite of the inner heart condition of Moses, the rod of authority is working. Water came out abundantly for the people, but God stood in severe judgment upon Moses for his action. Indeed here is a wonderful gift of God in operation, yet the man who is operating—who had known such inner meekness and grace—stands in shame before God.

We must realize that gifts are called "spiritual" (pneumatika) not because the one who operates them is spiritual but simply because they are from the Holy Spirit. Examples abound in life and in the scriptures of those who exercised gifts, yet so obviously lacked in their inner spiritual development. The prophet Balaam had the gift of prophecy even though he was far from a man of inward integrity. Samson had the gift of strength such that he could perform mighty feats, yet in spiritual understanding or inward purity of life he was of small account before God. How incomplete is the ministry of those who exercise gifts while lacking in inward graces and development. Compromise and selfish lust brought both Balaam and Samson into shame. God could use Samson to fulfill an immediate purpose—no more than that.

We understand that gifts are much like a divine loan given to accomplish a specific purpose; they are never really our possession. But graces are inwrought by the Spirit as the channel through which the life and loveliness of Christ might be manifest. We know many have stumbled and reacted against spiritual gifts because they saw a Balaam or Samson who manifest such glaring inner unreality. They assumed, as so many have, that the presence and operation of gifts was the mark of spirituality. Paul would surely correct this wrong assumption by reminding the Corinthians of their carnality in the midst of much emphasis upon the gifts.

Another look at the diagram will indicate that vessel C is one who operates a gift without inner graces and development. We see how this was true in Moses when he used the rod to get water for the people, while inwardly he was angry and complaining against their murmuring and rebellion. It seems quite amazing that God would allow water to come forth, when he smote the rock instead of speaking to it. Yet the lesson seems to be this: God will not suffer His people to go without just because of the failures and inner lack of the vessel. In His great concern for the people He will give water and often severely judge His servant. We can realize how empty and meaningless a gift can become when it is used without inward reality. Because there is a water flowing forth, it may seem the ministry is effective, yet how limited it is as compared with what God has intended when there is spiritual reality to back it up.

In the fourth episode we shall see Moses in the hour of his greatest effectiveness before God. What a crisis moment it was when God spoke to him in the mount. He unveiled to Moses that people were rebelling again and now building a golden calf. He said to Moses, "Let me alone that I may consume them: and I will make of thee a great nation." But now observe the inward stature of Moses; note the indifference to his own self-interest. Moses totally ignored it. He wasn't even interested. When God said this to him, Moses had not yet seen with his own eyes the enormity of the people's apostasy. But when he had and when he realized that God had spoken no light word in saying He would destroy them, he made up his mind. First he took drastic and fearless steps as God's representative. What authority he manifested that day. No slowness or stammering of speech. He is speaking boldly for God in demanding: "Who is on the Lord's side?" The Levites stepped out and then went throughout the camp to slay three thousand men. They did it "according to the word of Moses . . . " (Ex. 32:28).

Who can doubt that this was the exercise of his gift of speech and rod of authority?

And when Moses came into the presence of the Lord, we have the fullest unveiling of his inward grace: "If Thou wilt forgive their sin—: and if not, blot me, I pray Thee out of Thy book which Thou hast written." Norman Grubb has offered this meaning: "Save them, or damn me with them! If I cannot go to heaven with them, I'll go to hell with them! God can never refuse a holy desperation like that. It changes His mind. Of course it did, because it always was His mind to save them." [28]

Thus we see in Moses that highest effectiveness as he allows the unhindered expression of the Lord through him. What a marked difference where both graces and gifts are operative. It has been God's intention that by inward graces we shall exhibit life, but by gifts we impart that life.

I must confess that for years I was hung up on the conviction that the all important thing in ministering was by *what we are*. The inward graces seemed primary, and *what we do*—or the exercise of gifts—was quite unimportant. But God has His own ways of awakening us when we are about to faint. In fact He can hardly help us until we reach that point of defeat and despair. Then in our moment of fainting He can remind us of Paul's words: "Seeing we have this ministry, as we have received mercy, WE FAINT NOT." Why could Paul say this so confidently? Because his whole life and ministry was built upon this verse in the previous chapter: "Our sufficiency is not of ourselves, but of God." This was his secret.

To exhibit God's graces and reality in the life is wonderful, but not enough. This is why scores and hundreds of choice servants are now fainting in their ministry. Impossible problems plague them on every hand. They can stand as an exhibit of God's working, but they have no supernatural means of imparting reality to others. God has designed that by the operation of gifts there is to be a spiritual impartation.

Recently a friend, whose life has most surely exhibited the working of inward graces, told how a man came into their church fellowship. He was there for weeks, waiting for his wife to recuperate from a serious auto accident. It was evident, and he expressed the same, that he seemed gripped by the reality in the lives of the people, yet he continued on in a stubborn resistance to the Lord. Then one day God moved to give a word of knowledge which both uncovered and answered the deep hidden bitterness of his heart. He was so amazed at the unveiling of his own heart, and the answer which only God could have given, that he fell down before the Lord in submission and repentance. The exhibition of graces had attracted, but the impartation of knowledge to his darkened heart had broken him.

I sat in a meeting of more than two thousand one afternoon where a displaced person from the Ukraine had slipped into the service. Quite unexpectedly one of God's servants on the platform announced that he felt impelled to speak forth a message in another language. Of course no one in the audience knew until this displaced man with weeping explained how his life had been unveiled "by that man on the platform." He could not understand how "that man" knew him and his name. Surely it was God; he fell down before Him, broken by the impartation of light to his darkened heart.

Of course we should not expect God to indulge us with the miraculous or spectacular. Yet in this hour when men skilled in their natural gifts and abilities are fainting, God is awakening many to see how imperative it is to expect the supernatural.

Consider the preacher who is, himself, the example of that message he shares. He not only speaks forth but exhibits. Yet there is restlessness and indifference to his message of truth. Then suddenly the anointing of God comes upon him and he begins to speak forth as though liberated by the Spirit of prophecy. Immediately the hearers are electrified by the words and unction in which he speaks. Instead of mere exhibition, there is now a vital impartation of life, or revelation, or knowledge, or faith or discernment—whatever the need may be. God must have both: the Spirit's *working of graces within* and the Spirit's *working out through well-developed gifts.*

In this final section on spiritual stature we have been emphasizing the importance of the Holy Spirit. In the first chapter we have shown how the Spirit of adoption is leading us unto full sonship. We must rest in the confidence that He is completely adequate for this work. Yet there is our part in cooperation. So in the next chapter we have shown the necessity for the continuous government of the Spirit in our lives. Only then can we experience that stretching of our inner wineskin and the development of graces in our inner stature. In this chapter we have considered how the spiritual man will express both divine graces and gifts in their proper balance. We have been seeking to expose the folly of those who emphasize only gifts or those who emphasize only graces. In closing let me offer the sane advice of Dr. V. Raymond Edman as he pleads for discernment and balance.

"In my understanding of the scriptures there are two extremes to be avoided in understanding the Person and the gifts of the Holy Spirit. One extreme asserts that the gifts were designed only for the apostolic age, to be a confirmation of the message preached by the apostles, and that they ceased to exist with their passing. The other extreme declares dogmatically that unless a believer in Christ has the gift of tongues that he does not possess the Holy Spirit. I understand the plain teaching of the Word to be that the presence of the gifts of the Holy Spirit are to be for the church age until the Lord Jesus Himself returns to take away His own.

"There is always the danger of imbalance between the Word of God and our experience in Christ. There are those whose experience is below the standard and privilege set in the Word, and as a result they can be defeated, discouraged, fruitless Christians, even backsliders. Then there are those who believe that their experience is above the Word and not to be judged by its light. This attitude tends easily toward fanaticism just as the former is inclined to spiritual frigidity and fruitlessness." [29]

> Dear Lord, we loath the barrenness,
>   when serving on our own;
> We yearn for inwrought graces,
>   and the gifts which Thou dost loan;
> That through our open channel,
>   Thy Life might freely flow;
> In our abounding fruitfulness,
>   Great joy Thy heart shall know.

WHAT IS GOD SAYING TODAY? "A striking feature of our time is that so few of the voices have a distinctive message. There is a painful lack of a clear word of authority for the times. While there are many good preachers of the gospel, and while we are not without champions of the vital verities of the Faith, we are sadly in need of the Prophet with his, "Thus saith the Lord," which he has received in a commission born of a peculiarly chastened fellowship with God." (T.A.S.)

THIS IS THE HOUR WHEN LIVING STONES ARE BEING BUILT INTO A CORPORATE EXPRESSION

SOMEONE HAS SAID: "If you would know what is the burning issue or *present truth* which God considers imperative in each generation, just observe where the enemy has concentrated his fire!" Through the past four hundred years since the reformation, many of God's servants have recognized the progressive recovery of certain vital areas of truth. Each new wave of spiritual awakening has not only had in view the immediate renewal of spiritual life in that generation, but also the progressive unfolding of truth for the Church as she moves toward the glorious realization of His ultimate intention and purpose. Even Peter, in his day, seemed to recognize that the young Church needed to be "established in the present truth" (2 Peter 1:12).

For the individual or group who walk with God there is always fresh meat according to their need. There have always been those individuals who saw with God and lived beyond their day; yet there is a most sovereign element in God's working to unfold each new step of present truth.

That which was present truth in the days of Augustine is still truth, but it is not the present truth that God is speaking through His prophetic voice today. That we can be saved simply by faith in the finished work of Christ on the Cross, and not through the forms and ceremonies of the Church, was present truth in the days of Martin Luther, and with this emphasis he shook the world and changed the course of church history. While that is a most essential and foundational truth, it is not the present truth of this hour.

A PILE OF STONES OR A TEMPLE

We can rejoice that in the past hundred years there has been an awakening to Church truth and the importance of unity in the Body of Christ. This concerted thrust of gathering together those living stones in a locality to become a testimony of unity was indeed a present truth for that hour.

But a new hour has come! The truth of gathering together living stones into a pile has now been properly focused and a present truth for this hour has emerged. How foolish it was to assume that a mere "gathering together" according to Church truth was sufficient to build up the stones. Without realizing it, Bible churches, fellowships and independent groups tried to hold individualistic stones merely on the principle of unity or Church truth.   Even those who most boldly championed the cause of Church truth fell into the snare of making Church truth itself as a gathering point.

As we have pictured in the diagram it would seem the present truth of this hour includes this three-fold thrust: There is a (1) "gathering together unto Him" but also a (2) "building up" of living stones in Him through the (3) fivefold ministry given by Him.

THE PRESENT TRUTH FOR THIS HOUR:

A Pile of Stones . . . . .   or . . . . .   A Living Temple

A "gathering together"

"Gathered" but also "built up" in a corporate temple of Living Stones

It is not sufficient to have a pile of stones merely called out of the world or out of a religious system. God must build a spiritual house, often called the temple or body, where there is a functioning together of the living stones.

One look at our present religious system and the almost impossible task of building these living stones into a functioning temple, has caused many to insist: "It can't be done in this age." We are well aware there is a widespread doubt as to whether we are to expect anything in the way of a corporate building up or expressive testimony at the end. Some hold strongly that everything at the end is individual—a conviction that rests for the most part upon the use of the phrase, "If any man . . ." in the message to the Church of Laodicea (Revelation 3:20).

What hinders men from hearing and proclaiming that present truth for this hour? May it not be that many who could be a prophetic voice have become so much involved in a system: a system which puts preachers largely upon a professional basis, the effect of which is to make preaching a matter of demand and supply; of providing for the established religious order and program? We have seen how the old wineskins are usually not stretchable to receive present truth. Little kings who are fearful for their own security or protective for their own little kingdom will not hear nor proclaim that which might destroy their kingdom.

We must be sure to discern two classes of men whose motives are mixed. There are the "loyalists" who fear anything which will shake their little kingdom, so they become over-protective under the guise of being faithful shepherds of God's heritage. Then there are the "opportunists" who are really only ambitious to use any new truth or emphasis in carving out a little kingdom for themselves. They are not primarily concerned with how the present truth will build His Kingdom, but with what it can mean in their own design of opportunism. God must help us who discern the divine course to proclaim the present truth with only one end in view: building His kingdom and not their own.

It would seem there are two things which hinder many from receiving what the Scriptures indicates to be God's way of achieving this glorious purpose. First, they have a wrong conception of the Church. The real failure in grasping God's end-time working is to assume an organized movement, a sect, a society wholly unified is His goal. But in God's sight the Church of the New Testament has never been an organized affiliation of believers and workers. It has always been a purely spiritual thing, spontaneous in life, united only by the Holy Spirit in mutual love and reality. So the Church He is now building and the Church which so many are looking for is indeed quite different. Second, let us see how God designs for the fivefold ministry of Ephesians 4:11 to be a means for

FITTING THE LIVING STONES
INTO A CORPORATE EXPRESSION.

Unfortunately the word "build" as used in Matthew 16:18 is most often rendered as "edify." Now the original does not imply (as does the word *edify*) to improve morally or to benefit spiritually but rather to *build up*. So it is something which happens *to* the stone but really not *for itself*.

Christ has designed that His gifted men—workmen given to the Church after He ascended on high—should perfect each stone "for the work of the ministry." With his tool in hand, the gifted worker begins to shape the stone until it will fit into a certain place — having a gift and ministry to fulfill as a functioning member. Suppose the stone is triangular and the space is rectangular! The stone must be chipped and shaped until it perfectly corresponds to that space allotted by the builder.

What a day when God's gifted ones (those given to the Body at large) awaken to see they are not to minister *instead* of the stones, but rather their one calling is to *develop* the ministry of each living stone to fulfill its own ministry. What a misunderstanding of God's design for individual members to sit in the church week after week waiting to be ministered unto, when God intends for their own ministries to be developed so they fulfill the work of the ministry. How can we expect any full stature in individuals or in the local church when the pastor does all the ministering? It is no wonder the present-day servants are breaking down in despair and depression. They are in the squeeze and caught in a religious system which cannot develop lives who can minister. They must preach, must share, must perform whether they have a special word from the Lord or not. Because they have not discovered God's design in a body-ministry where every member waits for directions from the Head, they are forced to speak whether they have "the burden of the Lord" or not. How sad when men cannot say: "The hand of the Lord was upon me."

What do we mean? The present order and design of services

can never build living stones to fulfill their own ministry. When a man is required to speak at stated times, he *must get* something —he must sermonize—and this necessity means either God must be offered our program and asked to fit into it (which He will not do), or the preacher must *make* something for the constantly recurring occasion.

No wonder servants who face people with desperate spiritual needs each Sunday are going down under the pressure. They are trying to fulfill a place God never intended. It is the individual members of the Body who must be prepared to minister to the others in the Body. God's gifted men (Ephesians 4:11) are given to prepare individuals for their work of ministry. Until we become rightly adjust to the Head we shall hardly understand how every part must be functioning instead of merely being ministered unto.

"For it is from the Head that the whole Body, as a harmonious structure knit together by the joints with which it is provided, grows by proper functioning of individual parts to its full maturity in love" (J.B. Phillips-Eph. 4:16).

Perhaps there is nothing which has so hindered the growth and development of living stones as our wrong conceptions. How often we have met with delightful individuals. Their lives are well-ordered; they are careful about the early morning quiet time and earnest in witness and ministry; they are well edified individuals who call forth the commendation of others. Yet, they remain individualists who cannot be "built." They are precious stones who love to receive and develop their own stature; but they are so precious they cannot be fitted together with common clay or stone. It would seem they are too beautiful to be built up into one building with others, so they remain individualists — lovely for display but no good for building. They are more involved in their own spirituality than in functioning to build others.

All of this is to emphasize: *the full stature which God intends for each living stone cannot be reached apart from a proper relatedness to the corporate stature of the Body of Christ.* How this· wounds our individualistic yearnings! God is not primarily after a lot of separate stones, however polished and beautiful they may be. He wants a complete spiritual house, as one of our Chinese brothers has illustrated so aptly:

"One sister, speaking to me of another said: 'Oh she's such a precious sister, so spiritual!' When I asked more about her, she said: 'Oh she's so humble, so quiet, so gentle; we have never known her to be irritated.' And again she added: 'She's so spiritual!' 'Who is she spiritual with?' I asked. 'Is she an isolated spiritual sister, or has her spirituality related her to others?' 'Oh,' replied the sister, 'singers who strike such high notes as she, find few who can sing with them.'

"Alas, that sister was so spiritual that no one could be her spiritual companion. Such a sister is all right for display purposes, but she is no use for Church building. The kind of sister needed in the Church is one who can have another placed behind her and another in front, another to her left and another to her right, and one below her and one above. And that is the sort of Christian God is seeking today." [30]

Let us be honest. Our real problem in the local gathering is that the "most spiritual" cannot work together. They soon find legitimate "reasons" for their own private kind of individualism. But really they refuse to be "built" into their own place, for they have loved the subtle pre-eminence which comes from their individualism. Behold, the time has come to rejoice and make way for God's own moving! Nothing can hinder His design for accomplishing a spiritual building-up. God has been preparing those who have seen the divine method for building the temple where flowing life and flowing reality can meet every desperate need. Weary pilgrims need no longer endure empty meetings out of the mere sense of loyalty. The strain is gone for those servants who understand they must minister only as He gives utterance and shares his burden. There is a Spirit-wrought ministry of life coming forth to build the stones and pillars into their functioning place.

ALL CREATION AWAITS THE FINAL BUILDING

At the building of Solomon's temple there was one thing which amazed the people of Jerusalem. The stones were brought together without noise of hammer or pounding of chisel and mallet. The timbers from the far away forests of Lebanon fitted into their appointed places until, in silent harmony, the temple arose in all its glory. The noise was in the past. The forests of Lebanon had resounded with the shouts of men and crashing timber, while the quarry walls echoed back the babel of voices and the noise of working men. There had been hours spent in the picking and in the preparation of each stone or each pillar. Now that was all

over. And all Jerusalem wondered as stone was fitted to stone
and timber to timber in that glorious temple built by Solomon for
the glory of the Lord.

What does this temple as a former shadow teach us? Is it not
God's way of unveiling the erection of that Eternal Temple for
His habitation? We see both individual stones and pillars moving
unto full stature as they become a part of that corporate stature.
The Holy Spirit would focus our eye to see those quaries where
the living stones have been under pressure and in preparation.
Almost without noise or commotion—it is so silent—the Spirit is
fitting prepared pillars and stones into their places. Wherever a
few are gathered together and built into a spiritual house—the
Greater Solomon has built a miniature. But we all with abated
breath look for the grand placing: when every miniature house
will be absorbed into that vast Spiritual House. Who has eyes to
see? We can imagine that only those who have learned to dwell
"in Jerusalem" can behold the final gathering and building of
every part into that glorious Temple. Paul must have seen it
when he wrote:

> "...you belong now to the household of God. Firmly beneath
> you is the foundation, Special Messengers and Prophets, the
> actual Foundation-Stone being Jesus Christ Himself. In Him
> each separate piece of building properly fitting into its neigh-
> bor, GROWS TOGETHER INTO A TEMPLE consecrated to God.
> You are all part of this building in which God Himself lives by
> His Spirit" (J.B. Phillips - Eph. 2:20-22).

What a picture of God's ultimate is this! Our individual stature
finds its purpose in full corporate stature. Each stone belongs to
the whole, yet fulfills its own unique place. But we must be careful to realize this is the work of the Greater Solomon, Himself.
There must be no rushing stones out of the quarry before they are
ready. This is wholly His work.

But it would seem the hour of commencement has come! We
have observed in cities across the land how this moment of erection seems to have begun. Local expressions of His life are rising
up. Almost overnight the Lord is bringing together those pillars
who are prepared to give spiritual strength, character and direction. Then how easy to fit the living stones into their place when
the great framework is properly established. Indeed we can rejoice. Things are almost silently slipping into their divinely
ordained place. THIS IS THE GLORY OF HIS ERECTION.

A PASTOR EXPLAINS:

"Suddenly it dawned! This morning in my devotions I realized what glorious fellowship the Father and Son enjoyed in the Eternity before time began. In the days of my being man-centered I always considered how things would benefit me. Now that I've become centered in God and what He receives in us, so many portions of His Word have taken on new meaning. I was reading in Proverbs 8:30 when these words exploded into new meaning. It seems the Eternal Son is saying: "Then I was by him, as one brought up with him: AND I WAS DAILY HIS DELIGHT, rejoicing always before him; ..."

If the Son brought such delight to the Father before the beginning, what delight and pleasure will be His when He beholds that corporate Body of Sons presented to Him: "Every person mature—full grown, fully initiated, complete and perfect—in Christ, the anointed One " (Col. 5:28 A.N.T.).

WHAT IS THE PURPOSE
OF ULTIMATE STATURE?

AS IT WAS BEFORE THE BEGINNING, so it shall be in the glorious consummation when the Father shall receive many sons conformed to the image of His only begotten Son. How often we had been occupied with what full stature would mean to us. But something wonderful has happened! As mature sons together in Christ, we are now concerned for Him. What pleasure and glory! What honor and satisfaction! What delight and rejoicing we can bring to Him!

Indeed "all creation is on tip-toe" waiting breathlessly for that hour when the Father can put on display His family of divinely begotten sons brought to full stature; what a revelation they will be to the vast universe. And when the Son shall have a fully submissive Body for the glorious expression of His authority —what a revelation that shall be! And when the Holy Spirit shall have a living temple of open windows through which to express the attributes of God—what an amazing revelation: that God has then come to fill the whole universe with the glory of Himself.